Belle Starr and Her Times

BELLE STARR
AND HER TIMES

The Literature, The Facts, and The Legends

By
Glenn Shirley

UNIVERSITY OF OKLAHOMA PRESS : NORMAN

By Glenn Shirley

Toughest of Them All (Albuquerque, 1953)

Six-Gun and Silver Star (Albuquerque, 1955)

Law West of Fort Smith: A History of Frontier Justice in the Indian Territory, 1834–1896 (New York, 1957, 1961; Lincoln, 1968)

Pawnee Bill: A Biography of Gordon W. Lillie (Albuquerque, 1958; Lincoln, 1965)

Buckskin and Spurs: A Gallery of Frontier Rogues and Heroes (New York, 1958)

Outlaw Queen: The Fantastic True Story of Belle Starr (Derby, Conn., 1960)

Heck Thomas, Frontier Marshal (Philadelphia, 1962; Norman, 1981)

Born to Kill (Derby, Conn., 1963)

Henry Starr, Last of the Real Badmen (New York, 1965)

Buckskin Joe: The Unique and Vivid Memoirs of Edward Jonathan Hoyt, Hunter-Trapper, Scout, Soldier, Showman, and Friend of the Indians 1840–1918 (Lincoln, 1966)

Shotgun for Hire: The Story of "Deacon" Jim Miller, Killer of Pat Garrett (Norman, 1970)

The Life of Texas Jack: Eight Years a Criminal—41 Years Trusting in God (Quanah, 1973)

Red Yesterdays (Wichita Falls, 1977)

West of Hell's Fringe: Crime, Criminals, and the Federal Peace Officer in Oklahoma Territory, 1889–1907 (Norman, 1978)

Temple Houston: Lawyer with a Gun (Norman, 1980)

Belle Starr and Her Times: The Literature, the Facts, and the Legends (Norman, 1982)

Library of Congress Cataloging-in-Publication Data

Shirley, Glenn.
  Belle Starr and her times.

  Bibliography: p. 300.
  Includes index.
  1. Starr, Belle Shirley, 1848–1889, 2. Frontier and pioneer life—West (U.S.) 3. Outlaws—West (U.S.)—Biography. 4. West (U.S.)—Biography. I. Title.
F594.S8S57   364.1′55′0924 [B]   81-14683
ISBN: 0–8061–2276–5   AACR2

5   6   7   8   9   10   11   12

Contents

Illustrations

Preface

Ninety-some years have elapsed since Belle Starr was assassinated on the bank of the South Canadian River in old Indian Territory and leaped into the national limelight as a "Bandit Queen," "Female Jesse James," and "The Petticoat Terror of the Plains." During this period more than a hundred books and pamphlets, many stage-screen plays, poems, novels, and scores of magazine and newspaper feature articles have extolled her alleged exploits, making her the most maligned and written-about woman in America. For the most part, this mass of Belle Starr literature can be relegated to mythology.

Why another book on Belle? One might say, after nearly a century of tale-telling, that she deserves vindication. My purpose is to provide at least one comparison of contemporary reports and official records with the folklore and legends.

GLENN SHIRLEY

On the Cimarron
Payne County, Oklahoma

Acknowledgments

I should like to express my special thanks to Kenneth W. Hobbs, Jr., director of the Records Management Division, National Archives and Records Service, and Kent Carter, chief, Archives Branch, Federal Archives and Records Center, Fort Worth, Texas, without whose generous and willing aid in helping me dig out relative facts for the Belle Starr story this work might not have been accomplished.

Glenn Shirley

THE LITERATURE

1   From Richard K. Fox
to 20th Century-Fox

On Wednesday, February 6, 1889, the following item appeared on the front page of the *New York Times*, bearing a Fort Smith, Arkansas, February 5 dateline under the heading "A Desperate Woman Killed":

> Word has been received from Eufala [*sic*], Indian Territory, that Belle Starr was killed there Sunday night. Belle was the wife of Cole Younger. . . . Jim Starr, her second husband, was shot down by the side of Belle less than two years ago.
>
> Belle Starr was the most desperate woman that ever figured on the borders. She married Cole Younger directly after the war, but left him and joined a band of outlaws that operated in the Indian Territory. She had been arrested for murder and robbery a score of times, but always managed to escape.

There was no truth in this dispatch except that the woman had been slain. The editor of the *Fort Smith Elevator* sent it to several metropolitan newspapers. Few besides the *Times* picked up the story. In Texas the *Dallas Morning News* used it; here Belle had spent a dozen years of her life. To others the woman's name meant nothing. The *Vinita Chieftain*, in Indian Territory, gave her ambush murder only a paragraph.

Yet, almost overnight, the name of Belle Starr became a household word throughout the nation. She had been elevated to a seat of immortal glory as a sex-crazed hellion with the morals of an alley cat, a harborer and consort of horse and cattle thieves, a petty blackmailer who dabbled in every crime from murder to the dark sin of incest, a female Robin Hood who robbed the rich to feed the poor, an exhibitionistic and clever she-devil on horseback and leader of the most bloodthirsty band of cutthroats in the American West. All this despite the lack of a contemporary account or court record to show that she ever held up a train, bank, or stagecoach or killed anybody; the renegades she supposedly led and kept out of the tangles of the law were only figments of a vivid imagination.

The *Times* item caught the eye of Richard K. Fox, editor-owner of New York's *National Police Gazette* and publisher of dime novels. Fox's empire had grown fat on his sprightly and romantically imaginative presentations of crime and retribution involving the vices of the rich, big-city suicides, counterfeiters, swindlers, baby garroters, opium dens, obscene orgies, labial amusements, and hosannas raised in honor of western sheriffs, cow-town marshals, and assorted desperadoes like Jesse James, Sam Bass, and Billy the Kid. Commanding a circulation that reached mostly into barrooms, gambling houses, billiard halls, tonsorial parlors, livery stables, and brothels, his pen-and-ink illustrated weekly was read by a majority of the male population of the United States—and the female contingent also; it provided a national code of honor and morals, affected our politics, and had a more profound influence on our culture than the works of all other romantic writers of the period. As it pinkly flapped across America, much that was invented for its columns was embellished by word-of-mouth accounts of oldsters from the mountain fastnesses of the Alleghenies, remote bayous, and swamps of the South to the scattered prairie hamlets, lumber and mining camps, jerkwater railroad stops, and desert way stations of the West, and later all this became absorbed into legend.

Many of the western characters were yesterday's news or dead now, and this empty manger spelled trouble for a tabloid that thrived on turning phantom creatures into flesh and blood. Fox was bemoaning the fact that he had been unable to prod his army of writers into coming up with fresh heroes and heroines from the West who could inflame the imagination of his readers. He perceived Belle Starr as a circulation builder and dispatched Alton B. Meyers, bright young freelancer and the *Gazette's* Southwest representative, to Fort Smith.

Another version is that Meyers already was in the notorious border city, nursing a painful hunger with exactly seven cents in his pockets and searching desperately for a story that might bring him a wired advance. He lounged on the wooden sidewalk on Garrison Avenue, wondering how much food seven cents would buy and where he might find lodging for the night. A garrulous old-timer sat nearby, complacently chewing tobacco and perusing the latest issue of the *Fort Smith Elevator*.

"I'll be damned," the old-timer suddenly exclaimed, "they've gone an' kilt Belle Starr!"

Belle Starr! Meyers rolled the name over his tongue. It had a more romantic sound than even Sam Bass, Jesse James, or Billy the Kid.

"Who was Belle Starr?" he asked.

"Oh, hell," the old man spat and snorted, "just a nutty old whore who imagined she was a bandit queen."

Belle Starr! *A bandit queen!* Meyers practically ran to the telegraph office. Within hours he had a cash advance, a hotel room, a full stomach, and a ream of writing paper. Apparently, Belle's son and daughter and her mother, who had arrived from Texas, refused to divulge any family history likely to bring discredit upon themselves, so Meyers had to resort to less-reliable information among her acquaintances. Court records, easily available, were consulted carelessly. Few of the names, dates, or essential facts were correct. Alleged excerpts from Belle's letters and diary—a gag used by most writers of the yellow-journalism school to make their work appear authentic—were pure fabrication.

Meyers' lurid manuscript reached the *Gazette* desk in mid-March, and Fox plunged into the vivid, catchy offering:

Of all the women of the Cleopatra type, since the days of the Egyptian queen herself, the universe has produced none more remarkable than Bella Starr, the Bandit Queen. Her character was a combination of the very worst as well as some of the very best traits of her sex. She was more amorous than Anthony's mistress; more relentless than Pharoah's daughter, and braver than Joan of Arc. Of her it may well be said that Mother Nature was indulging in one of her rarest freaks, when she produced such a novel specimen of womankind. Bella was not only well educated, but gifted with uncommon musical and literary talents, which were almost thrown away through the bias of her nomadic and lawless disposition, which early isolated her from civilized life, except at intervals, when in a strange country, and under an assumed name, she brightened the social circle for a week or a month, and then was, perhaps, lost forever.

Fox did not serialize the biography in the *Gazette*, his usual procedure, but published it that summer as a twenty-five-cent, wire-stitched paperback: *Bella Starr, The Bandit Queen, or The Female Jesse James. A Full and Authentic History of the Dashing Female Highwayman, with Copious Extracts from Her Journal. Handsomely and Profusely Illustrated.*

Thousands of copies were sold, yet today this quaint little volume is practically nonexistent. An original would be difficult to find at any price. An incomplete copy rests in the archives of the Texas State Library; a near-perfect copy in private hands is in the library of Texas' former United States senator, William A. Blakley, who years ago acquired the collection of Ramon F. Adams of Dallas, the well-known bibliophile of western and outlaw books. In 1960 a facsimile edition was printed by the Steck Company of Austin.

Fox's circulation problem was solved, and across the horizon galloped the most beautiful, the most daring, the most exciting female outlaw ever to ride into American folklore. The legend was born, and for almost a century writers for the printed page, radio, stage, and screen have found the Fox opus a virtual treasure chest, using its inventions, scrambling for facts, adding inventions of their own.

The year after *Bella Starr* appeared, Street & Smith of New York published as No. 35 in the Secret Service Series a sensational paperback, *Adventures and Exploits of the Younger Brothers, Missouri's Most Daring Outlaws, and Companions of*

The cover of Richard K. Fox's 1889 paperback Bella Starr, The Bandit Queen, or The Female Jesse James. *Unless otherwise noted, the illustrations in this book are reproduced from pictures in the author's collection.*

SATURDAY, AUGUST 10, 1889.

JUST PUBLISHED.

LIFE AND ADVENTURES

OF

BELLE STARR,

The Noted Bandit Queen of the West.

A Story of Daring Exploits and Adventures.

HANDSOMELY ILLUSTRATED

Mailed to any address on receipt of 25 cents. Agents will find it to their advantage to canvass for this book.

RICHARD K. FOX, Publisher,

FRANKLIN SQUARE, NEW YORK.

First notice of publication of Bella Starr, The Bandit Queen, or The Female Jesse James, *which appeared in the* National Police Gazette, *August 10, 1889.*

the James Boys, in which author Henry Dale alleges that Belle married Cole Younger, that her maiden name was Starr; he makes other a la Fox claims about her that are just as unreliable.

Cesar Lombroso, the Italian physician-criminologist, professor of psychiatry at Pavia in 1862, and later professor of criminal anthropology at Turin, held that a criminal represents a distinct anthropological type with definite physical and mental stigmata and is the product of heredity, atavism, and degeneracy. In 1895 he published, with the noted Italian writer-historian Guglielmo Ferrero as co-author, *The Female Offender,* which was translated into English and reprinted in the Criminology Series of D. Appleton and Company, New York, in 1903. It is not known whether Lombroso relied on the Fox opus for his Belle Starr material. Since he fell for the bogus diary and other *Gazette* fiction, one must assume that he did, or was so careless as to accept it second-hand from Charles Victor Crosnier de Varigny, whom he mentions.

Varigny was the Italian correspondent in New York during the 1890s who furnished the Rome and Milan papers little more than sensational rewrites of American crime news, which he lifted from the *National Police Gazette,* the *Police News,* the *New York Herald,* and Joseph Pulitzer's *World.* In 1893 he published his 322-page *La Femme aux Etats-Unis,* reprinted as *The Women of the United States* by Dodd, Mead of New York in 1895. Here, translated from the Italian (pages 201–203), is his initial estimate of our heroine:

Who will believe the improbable adventures of a Belle Star, the idol of the Western bandits, a living defiance hurled at the law, embodying in herself the audacity, the vices and daring composure of those outlaws who from father to son boasted of dying with their boots on, with their knife or revolver . . . drawn, as she herself did 3 Feb., 1889 at 35 years of age, after the most singular existence imagineable, leaving a daughter and son who follow in her footsteps. . . .

She was born in Carthage, Mo. Her father, the leader of a gang in the South, took an active part in the War of Secession, and from her youth Belle Star had a great liking for fisticuffs, acts of violence, plunder and murder in that bloody period. After the war was over, her father moved to Kansas with the remains of his gang and she accompanied him. A daring Amazon from the age of ten she handled revolvers and lassoes, carbine and Bowie knives. . . .

They hated everything connected with the North. She fell in love with Bob Younger at age 14. She had herself kidnapped by him. Her father refused to consent to her marriage, but she paid no attention to him and got married on horseback surrounded by 20 members of the gang.

In *The Female Offender* (page 174) Lombroso states:

The born criminal is rarely inclined to write much. We know but of three instances among them of memoirs: those of Madame Lafarge, of X., and of Bell-Star, while male criminals are greatly addicted to these egotistic outpourings. Madame Lafarge, the woman X., and Bell-Star, particularly the last, were certainly endowed with superior intelligence.

Under *Synthesis* (pages 187–89), Lombroso observes:

In general the moral physiognomy of the born female criminal approximates strongly to that of the male. The atavistic diminution of secondary sexual characters which is to be observed in the anthropology of the subject, shows itself once again in the psychology of the female criminal, who is excessively erotic, weak in maternal feeling, inclined to dissipation, astute and audacious, and dominates weaker beings sometimes by suggestion, at others by muscular force; while her love of violent exercise, her vices, and even her dress, increase her resemblance to the sterner sex. Added to these virile characteristics are often the worst qualities of woman: namely, an excessive desire for revenge, cunning, cruelty, love of dress, and untruthfulness, forming a combination of evil tendencies which often results in a type of extraordinary wickedness. . . . A typical example of these extraordinary women is presented by Bell-Star, the female brigand, who a few years ago terrorised all Texas.

Lombroso then outfoxes Fox with this absurd summation:

Her education had been of the sort to develop her natural qualities; for, being the daughter of a guerrilla chief who had fought on the side of the South in the war of 1861-65, she had grown up in the midst of fighting, and when only ten years old, already used the lasso, the revolver, the carbine, and the bowie-knife. . . . She was as strong and bold as a man, and loved to ride untamed horses which the boldest of the brigands dared not mount. . . . She was extremely dissolute, and had more than one lover at a time, her admirer *en titre* being always the most intrepid and daring of the band. At the first sign of cowardice he was degraded from his rank. But, however bold he might be, Bell-Star dominated him entirely, while all the time having—as Varigny writes—as many lovers as there were desperadoes in four States. At the age of eighteen she became head of the band, and ruled her associates partly through her superior intelligence, partly through her courage, and to a certain degree through her personal charm as a woman. She organised attacks of the most daring description on populous cities, and fought against government troops, not hesitating the very day after one of these raids to enter some neighbouring town unaccompanied, and dressed—as almost always—in male attire. . . . She wrote her memoirs, recording in them her desire to die in her boots. This wish was granted, for she fell in a battle against the government troops, directing the fire to her latest breath.

Meanwhile, Samuel W. Harman, a Bentonville, Arkansas, hotelman with a bit of newspaper and legal experience, who became acquainted with crime, criminals, and marshals in the Indian Territory as a professional juryman in Judge Isaac C. Parker's federal court, was collecting material to chronicle the epoch. In 1898 the Phoenix Publishing Company (job shop of the *Fort Smith Elevator*) published his 720-page volume *Hell on the Border; He Hanged Eighty-Eight Men*, which sold for two dollars a copy. The title page lists Harman as author and C. P. Sterns, who assembled most of the transcripts from court records and biographical sketches of major court personalities, as compiler. But it was J. Warren Reed, a well-known Fort Smith attorney who argued so many cases before Judge Parker, who commissioned the work, tabulated the court actions, wrote the land grants and statutory information on the court's beginnings and jurisdiction, and paid the printing bill. Reed's florid style and unabashed praise of his courtroom performances are apparent, yet his name does not appear as co-author. The episodes on deputy marshals, the Indian Territory outlaws tried and condemned in the court, and the classic

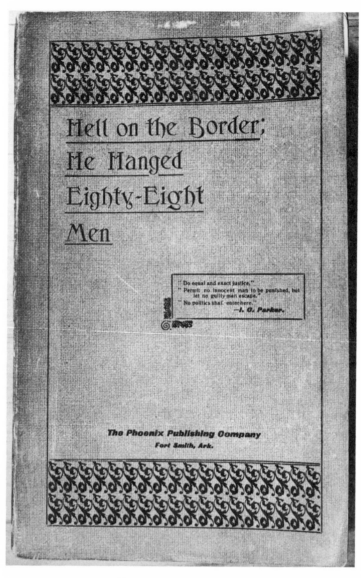

Hell on the Border;

He Hanged

Eighty-Eight

Men

> "Do equal and exact justice."
> "Permit no innocent man to be punished, but
> let no guilty man escape."
> "No politics shall enter here."
> —J. G. Parker.

The Phoenix Publishing Company
Fort Smith, Ark.

Cover of the original 1898 edition of Hell on the Border. *This book became the basis for many a Belle Starr legend.*

moralizing and teaching by example which dominates the work are Harman's; reliability is questionable, especially his 62-page chapter "Belle Starr, the Female Desperado."

Because of the reputation of Judge Parker's court, the first printing of *Hell on the Border* was exhausted quickly. Only a few copies reached libraries. It is one of the most sought-after books and the chief source of practically every book and feature story on the subject. In 1930, eight years after lawyer Reed's death, J. W. Rice, an early Indian Territory printer, published an abridged edition of one thousand copies set on a Linotype in the printing department at Kendall College, Tulsa, Oklahoma. This edition, reduced to 320 pages by eliminating most of Reed's land grants and statutory material and cutting what Rice deemed "overlong accounts of cases" and "useless description," sold for $2.50. Either edition, the first in stiff green wrappers and the second in stiff yellow wrappers, now commands a fancy price. A third printing (a reprint of Rice's abridged edition), consisting of 303 pages in stiff brown wrappers, was issued in 1953 by Frank L. Van Eaton, World War II veteran and self-styled "dyed-in-the-wool promoter," who "developed the idea" while confined to a bed in the Veterans Tuberculosis Hospital at Livermore, California. Finally, a fourth "Indian Heritage Edition" of one thousand hardbound copies autographed by its editors, Jack Gregory and Rennard Strickland, was issued by the Hoffman Printing Company of Muskogee, Oklahoma, in 1971 to "make this frontier classic available to a wider reading audience." This 214-page version "concentrates" on twenty-four "major figures and incidents" from the rare first edition, "edited and regrouped in an effort to supply continuity and eliminate repetition." In 1954 the Frontier Press of Texas at Houston issued a separate printing, in stiff blue wrappers, of the Belle Starr chapter from the original *Hell on the Border,* with photographs from the Rose Collection of Old Time Photos, then owned by Ed Bartholomew.

Much of Harman's *Belle Starr, the Female Desperado* is founded upon the wildly fictitious Fox tale and is full of the same errors. Here, in part, is his introduction of our heroine:

Of all the noted women ever mentioned by word or pen, none in history have been more brilliantlly [sic] daring nor more effective in their chosen roles than the dashing Belle Starr, champion and leader of robbers; herself a sure shot and a murderess, who never forgot an injury nor forgave a foe; who was a terror alike to those she hated and to false friends. . . .

Her ideas of outlawry seemed to have been more for the wild pleasure of the chase than for any desire to take human life, and it is claimed that it was only when angered beyond control by some act of betrayal or when driven to a corner, that she committed the crime of murder. Love of money, horses and books was with her a ruling passion, and she would go to almost any ends to procure the former; it was on that account that she confined the greater part of her efforts, while on scout. . . . Her mature life was a strange mixture of the sentimental, the terrible and the grotesque; her childhood was as sweet and innocent as the new blown flower; her end was tragic.

In 1903 the press of the Henneberry Company, Chicago, printed *The Story of Cole Younger, By Himself: Being an Autobiography of the Missouri Guerrilla Captain and Outlaw, his capture and prison life, and the only authentic account of the Northfield raid ever published.* Cole says he felt called upon to rehearse the story of his life because, on the eve of sixty, he had come out of prison "to find a hundred or more books, of greater or less pretensions, purporting to be a history of 'The Lives of the Younger Brothers,' but are all nothing more than a lot of sensational recitals" in which "there could not be found six pages of truth." This 123-page, fifty-cent paperback is important in that Cole categorically denies the allegations of Dale, Harman, and others that Belle's daughter was his illegitimate child. He states (pages 72–73):

These fairy tales have told how the "Cherokee maiden fell in love with the dashing captain." As a matter of fact, Belle Starr was not a Cherokee. Her father was John Shirley, who during the war had a hotel at Carthage, Mo. In the spring of 1864, while I was in Texas, I visited her father, who had a farm near Syene [sic], in Dallas county.

Belle Shirley was then 14, and there were two or three brothers smaller.

The next time I saw Belle Shirley was in 1868, in Bates county, Mo. She was then the wife of Jim Reed, who had been in my company during the war, and she was at the home of his mother. This was about three months before the birth of her eldest child, Pearl Reed, afterward known as Pearl Starr, after Belle's second husband . . . Sam Starr.

But the die had been cast. D. C. Gideon's long section on Indian Territory outlaws, in his 1901 *Indian Territory, Descriptive, Biographical and Genealogical, Including the Landed Estates, County Seats etc., with a General History of the Territory*, repeats the early Belle Starr fiction; and a 1907 paperback, *Oklahoma, Past and Present: Brief Sketches of Men and Events in Oklahoma History—from Coronado to the Present*, perpetuates the tale of how Belle refused to identify her dead husband, Jim Reed, so that the deputy sheriff who had killed him could not collect the reward.

Her legend so flourished in this decade that Frederick S. Barde, one of Oklahoma's ablest newspapermen, made an on-the-scene search in 1910 for facts on her life and death in Indian Territory. In a dispatch from Porum, Oklahoma, to the *St. Louis Republic* on August 20, Barde wrote:

> The ghost of Belle Starr still rides the Indian Territory. . . . remembrance of her among the people does not grow dim, and they talk of her now almost as frequently as they did when she was alive. . . . Strangers that come here never fail to ask about her and to inquire if this or that story is true. . . . Time has thrown about her life a tinge of romance, yet those who knew her well see no glamour in what she did—she was merely a dissolute woman, unfortunate in her early life, and in her later years merely a companion of thieves and outlaws. It is doubtful if she herself ever did more than steal horses. . . . Much of her subsistence came from money and plunder given to her by the disreputable characters to whom she gave refuge.

Barde's final evaluation, "The Story of Belle Starr," appeared in *Sturm's Oklahoma Magazine* of September 1910:

> With an education superior to her surroundings and with a natural

sagacity that enabled her quickly to separate the spectacular from the commonplace and use it to best advantage, [Belle] acquired a reputation for daring outlawry that has survived the passing of many years, however threadbare and paltry were the facts upon which this reputation was based. She had the love of admiration common to women, and her being a woman undoubtedly gave prestige to her career. A sentimentalism common in the South prior to the Civil War, joined to more than ordinary vanity, led Belle Starr to affect and imitate the ways of cheap melodrama.

There is no proof that she ever helped rob a train or a traveler, ever fired a shot in a personal encounter—she was not a good shot—or ever stained her hands with blood.

John F. Weaver, a *Fort Smith New Era* compositor who became manager of the *Southwest Independent* in 1880 and, later, editor of other papers, including the weekly *Elevator*, wrote Barde on November 26:

I read your Belle Starr story with much interest, and am satisfied it was the only true history of that notorious woman that ever appeared in print. I have lived in Fort Smith practically all my life, and was here all the time she was in her heyday so to speak. . . . was one of the editors of the *Elevator* and at one time published a brief sketch—I think a column or two of her life—written by herself. Unfortunately the file of the paper with her story has disappeared, as also has the manuscript of the story which I preserved.

William J. Weaver, John's father, an early emigrant to Arkansas Territory, was a writer for the *Fort Smith Independent* and a valued correspondent of several big eastern dailies. He was past eighty when *Hell on the Border* was published, and he wrote a series of copyrighted reminiscences on early Fort Smith and its court for the *Elevator* as late as September 1906, acknowledging that "much of what has appeared in print concerning Belle Starr is rot." However, Barde predicted that "fifty years from now tradition will have lifted her exploits into that shadowy region where posterity no longer will look upon them as crimes, but as deeds of daring to be celebrated in verse and prose, as have been those of clan leaders of Scotland." He could not have prognosticated better.

In a rare little 1914 book, *Flying Sparks, as told by a Pull-*

man conductor, Marion Ebenezer Munsell relates his experiences with some of Oklahoma's outlaws. His Belle Starr chapter is identical with Harman's in *Hell on the Border*, except for the paragraphing, and contains the same errors.

Also in 1914, Lockard Publishing Company of Memphis, Tennessee, published *Under the Black Flag* by Captain Kit Dalton, *A Confederate Soldier. A Guerrilla Captain under the fearless leader Quantrell [sic], and a Border Outlaw for seventeen years following the surrender of the Confederacy. Associated with the most noted band of free booters the world has ever known.* Dalton makes wild claims about his friendship with Quantrill and his participation in many of the James boys' robberies. Either he was suffering from hallucinations or, in his dotage, desired to share their notoriety. Alongside his assessment of "Belle Star, The Fearless Indian Outlaw" (pages 143-46, 156), the Fox writer, Dale, Varigny, Lombroso, and Harman were pikers:

The history of Arkansas would be as incomplete without the name of Belle Star as it would without that of Jeff Davis of sacred memory.

There was a time within the memory of men now living when this dread name struck terror to the hearts of the timid and caused brave men to buckle an extra holster about their loins before setting out through the territory of her operations.

History may have slammed its doors in the face of this maroon Amazon, but the criminal records of the Great State of Arkansas have not neglected her.

Belle Star was the unfortunate combination of a Cherokee squaw and a *pale face* lady of the upper tendum—a savage of the bloodiest type; a lady of tender emotions; a finished graduate of Carlisle University and a typical daughter of the plains. In her sentimental moods she was a worshipper of Verdi, Gottschaulk, Rubenstein and Wagner. In her thoughtful moments, a devotee of Pliny, and the naturalists; Socrates and the philosophers; Voltaire and the satirists; Homer and the epics; Moore and the lyrics.

When her savage nature predominated, her ideals underwent a sudden change, amounting to a complete somersault, and she paid homage to King Philip, Tecumseh, Powhatan, Sitting Bull, Rain-in-the-Face and Geronnymo.

A more accomplished musician never coaxed dumb ivory into

melody; a more daring bandit never hit the trail nor cut a throat for the love of vengeful lust. A more winning smile never illumined the face of a Madonna; a more cruel human never walked the deck of a pirate ship. She dispensed charities with the lavish hand of true philanthropy and robbed with the strong arm of a Captain Kid. No human ever risked life and liberty in more perilous ways for friendship's sake than did this phenomenally beautiful half savage, nor was the gate to a city of refuge ever opened wider for the distressed than were the doors of her humble mountain home. . . .

To sum up her character in one trite paragraph, I will simply state that Belle was a maroon Diana in the chase, a Venus in beauty, a Minerva in wisdom, a thief, a robber, a murderer and a generous friend.

Equally absurd is Charles Kingston's chapter on Belle in *Remarkable Rogues: The Careers of Some Notable Criminals of Europe and America* (1921). He says she was the only child of a "Texas bushranger" named Star, a "powerfully built man, with rugged features and gorrilla-like arms" who, with "a half dozen tried and trusted comrades" after the war, became "the terror of Texas." The mother died shortly after Belle was born; at five "she could handle a pistol," and at ten "she was an expert in the use of the lasso, carbine and bowie knife." At age fifteen she killed her first man, a camp robber, by choking him to death "with her small white hands," and when "Star was slain in a running gun fight," Belle "succeeded to the vacant leadership" of the gang. Disguised as an old lady, Belle robbed a bank at Galveston, Texas, and horsewhipped a judge "in a populous town near Austin" for insulting her. Hundreds of farmers paid her weekly tribute to avoid being raided by her bandits; she disposed of a young spy in her employ whom she suspected of having betrayed one of her plans by putting a bullet in his brain, robbed a post office, and killed two soldiers who tried to arrest her. "At least four pitched battles" were fought between her gang and government troops before "one last desperate attempt" was made to break through and Belle fell "riddled with bullets . . . the death she had always desired.

Zoe A. Tilghman condensed Harman for her account of

Belle in *Outlaw Days: A True History of Early-Day Oklahoma Characters* (1926), which has been used extensively as source material by later writers. Also in 1926, the Norton Printing Company of Pine Bluff, Arkansas, published *The Only True History of the Life of Frank James, Written by Himself*, which deals with our heroine (pages 117–20) in a style as pathetic as the information:

> Bell Star was a native of Kansas. Her maiden name was Shirley. . . . At age of sixteen years, her brother Captain Shirley sent her to the camp of Federals, a distance of twenty-five miles, to learn their movements. She soon learned . . . that her brother's camp would be attacked. . . . When the soldiers found out that Bell was Capt. Shirley's sister they had her arrested and put under guard, with orders that she not be turned loose until after the raiders who had been sent out to visit her brother's camp had been gone one half hour.
>
> When the half hour had expired Bell was turned loose. When she gained her liberty she mounted her pony and was off like the wind, through fields and pastures, jumping fences, on and on, until she was hid from view among the low hills of the Kansas prairies. When the detachment of soldiers arrived at Shirley's camp he was gone. Bell had got there first. This famous ride gave Bell the name of bronco rider.
>
> When the civil war was over Bell married Jim Reed, a noted highwayman, who had served under Quantrel. . . . A short time after Jim Reed died Bell married Henry Starr. Henry Starr was killed in a pistol duel with a United States marshal. After Henry Starr was killed Bell married John Starr. He also went the pistol route. She afterwards married Sam Starr, a son of Tom Starr. Bell had a girl by Cole Younger, named Pearl Starr. Her name should have been Pearl Younger, after her father, Cole Younger, according to nurse papers handed out to the world.

This book obviously was ghosted despite the claim that it was written by James "at odd times, during his latter years." The real Frank James died in Missouri on February 18, 1915. He was a literate man who could quote classic poetry and Shakespeare, and it is unlikely that he would have allowed such nonsense.

Duncan Aikman's chapter on Belle in *Calamity Jane and the Lady Wildcats* (1927) is a mixture of fact and fiction. He admits in his foreword to having drawn "liberally" on Harman's *Hell on the Border*. However, Aikman pens a much more readable story than his predecessors. It reappears, with some alteration, as "Belle Starr, the Prairie Amazon" in *Roundup Time: A Collection of Southwestern Writing,* edited by George Sessions Perry (1943).

Hands Up! Stories of the Six-Gun Fighters of the Old Wild West, as told by Fred E. Sutton and written down by A. B. MacDonald (1927), has an "Outlaw Queen" chapter. Sutton, a bystander when the Old West pageant went by, makes it appear that he had personal contact and friendship with such worthies as Billy the Kid, Pat Garrett, Wild Bill Hickok, Bat Masterson, Jesse James, Judge Isaac C. Parker, Cherokee Bill, Bill Doolin, the Dalton and Jennings brothers, Black-Faced Charley Bryant, Arkansas Tom, and Henry and Belle Starr. He relies heavily on *Hell on the Border* and claims to have witnessed the alleged Belle Starr–Blue Duck exploit at Fort Dodge, Kansas. Sutton was a gun collector, and in 1926 he acquired from Pearl Starr's daughter a rifle carried by her grandmother.

Cameron Rogers, in the "Belle Starr" section of his anthology *Gallant Ladies* (1928), observes that Belle, "impeached and not softly" in scores of journals as a Bandit Queen, Lady Desperado, and Petticoat Terror of the Plains, belonged "less in a Western Newgate Calendar than in a more considerable chronicle of Homeric and super rogues." He repeats most of the widely circulated legends and says she learned to handle a rifle and the heavy pistols of the 1860s like a veteran gunfighter and became "so indisputable a force" in Indian Territory that she had to be brought down from behind.

In *Wild Men of the Wild West* (1929), Edwin L. Sabin devotes a chapter to "Wild Women," including Belle, but does little more than recap Fox and the *Hell on the Border* legends.

Owen P. White, for years an editor with *Collier's* magazine, was an El Paso, Texas, native with a passion for sin, and he, too, made a stab at Belle in *Lead and Likker* (1932). Most of his chapters on western outlaws, especially the one on Belle, are fictional and unreliable.

About the time White's book appeared, a woman in search of her "roots," who had been "reared by German gentlefolk north of the Mason-Dixon line . . . unaware of her Southern heritage" and with a family of her own, suddenly learned she was Pearl Starr's daughter and that Belle was her grandmother. Under the byline "Flossie" (she preferred not to sign her full name for personal reasons), she published a two-part feature in the *Dallas Morning News* of April 30 and May 7, 1933; it was titled "The Story of My Grandmother, Belle Starr" and "The Story of Flossie, Belle Starr's Granddaughter." Unfortunately, "Flossie" merely paraphrased what Harman and others had written on the life of her grandmother. The value of her strange quest is the disclosure of how her mother came by the name Pearl Younger.

The Belle Starr legend lay dormant the next several years, except for a historically worthless chapter in Roscoe Logue's paperback *Tumbleweeds and Barb Wire Fences* (1936) and a couple of equally unreliable rehashes in Anthony Gish's *American Bandits* and C. B. Glasscock's *Then Came Oil: The Story of the Last Frontier* (1938). Belle also was revived that year in a stage drama, *Cheat and Swing,* written and directed, under the auspices of the national play policy board of the Works Progress Administration, by John Woodworth, a thirty-one-year-old junior high school teacher at Roosevelt, Oklahoma. And New York City's Broadway Theatre was the scene of an experimental but not very successful comedy, *Missouri Legend,* based on incidents from the life of Jesse James, in which no less an actress than Elizabeth Beall Ginty played Aunt Belle.

J. H. Plenn, *Saddle in the Sky: The Lone Star State* (1940), devoted a few pages to Belle, repeating the fiction about her refusing to identify her dead husband (to keep his killer from getting the reward) and including the tale about how she

Advertisement for the 1941 movie Belle Starr *produced by 20th Century-Fox starring Gene Tierney as Belle and Randolph Scott as Sam Starr.*

"turned on her charm" to "captivate" a banker but actually abducted him and collected "a nice fat ransom." Plenn claims she "was shot at the head of a band robbing a bank."

In the spring of 1941, 20th Century-Fox produced *Belle Starr,* with Gene Tierney in the title role and Randolph Scott playing Sam Starr. Some of the scenes were filmed in southwest Missouri. *Belle Starr* did not become too popular. In December the United States entered World War II, and thereafter little attention was given to the movie. An "Encore Hit!" was rereleased by 20th Century-Fox in 1948.

The 1941 movie touched off three decades of revisionist writing. Random House of New York published Burton Rascoe's *Belle Starr, "The Bandit Queen"* in time to meet the release date of the motion picture. Here, a la *Police Gazette,* are the book's subtitles: *The True Story of the Romantic and Ex-*

citing *Career Of the Daring and Glamorous Lady, Famed in Legend and Story throughout the West As the Beautiful Girl Who Would never have Went Wrong if Things Hadn't Gone Wrong— The True Facts about the Dastardly Deeds and the Come-Uppence Of Such Dick Turpins, Robin Hoods and Rini Rinaldos As The Youngers, the Jameses, the Daltons, the Starrs, the Doolins and the Jenningses—The Real Story With Court Records and Contemporary Newspaper Accounts And Testimony of Old Nesters, here and there, in the Southwest—A Veritable Exposee of Badmen and Marshals and Why Crime Does Not Pay!* As the subtitles indicate, much of Rascoe's book deals with other bandits. His history of Belle Starr remains the most complete work to date, but vague. He offers good criticism of writers in the field before him, pointing out weaknesses in the logic and exactness of their accounts, but does not reach many conclusions that can be regarded as facts. Consultation of court records and contemporary reports, despite the subtitle claim, is sadly lacking. He propounds the legend of Pearl Starr as the illegitimate offspring of Belle and Cole Younger and improvises thirteen pages of scene and dialogue in attempting to prove it.

Enter Vance Randolph. Between the mid-1920s and the mid-1940s, this noted Ozark folklorist and folklore collector wrote scores of booklets and co-authored or edited ten others under a dozen pseudonyms for Emmanuel Haldeman-Julius, publisher of the popular Little Blue Books, at Girard, Kansas. Two of Randolph's works deal with our heroine: *Belle Starr, The Bandit Queen* by William Yancey Shackleford (1943) and *Wildcats in Petticoats* by Anton S. Booker (1945). Randolph is a revisionist in the sense that, as a boy in Kansas during the early 1890s, he heard many firsthand accounts of Belle's exploits from his father and grandfather (who knew her personally) and attempts to separate fact from fiction. For outside information, he relies more on Barde's interpretations than on Harman, Rascoe, and others. In the Booker opus, he recaps the highlights of Belle's career very well, but some dates, places, and ages of participants are incorrect.

Fred Harvey Harrington's chapter "Belle Starr, Horse Thief" in *Hanging Judge* (1951) deals with her 1882–83 arrest and trial in U.S. District Court at Fort Smith, Arkansas. Harrington errs in stating that Belle "was neither Union nor Confederate" and accepts the claim that she "was the mistress of Cole Younger for a while."

The analysis of "Belle Starr, the Outlaw Queen" in B. A. Botkin's "Law and Order, Ltd." section of *A Treasury of Western Folklore* (1951) is as accurate as his sources: Aikman and Rascoe.

In his "Sam Bass & Belle Starr" chapter of *The Lusty Texans of Dallas* (1951), John William Rogers relies largely on Rascoe for a summary of Belle's life in that Texas city but considers it "a mixture of little fact and much legend." He doesn't quite swallow the illegitimacy of Pearl Starr.

Homer Croy, in "The Jail; and the Prison Wagon" and "Belle Starr; and the Rufus Buck Gang" chapters of *He Hanged Them High: An authentic account of the fanatical judge who hanged eighty-eight men* (1952), gives humorous accounts of Belle's arrest by deputy marshals and her antics in Fort Smith. He states, inadvertently perhaps, that "one item in her attire was a holster which she wore becomingly at her waist. It contained *two* revolvers." In *Last of the Great Outlaws: The Story of Cole Younger* (1956), Croy follows the Fox-Harman versions of Belle's early life and, like Rascoe, improvises a half-dozen pages of scene and dialogue to support the claim, despite Cole Younger's denial that Cole was Pearl's father. He also is "inclined to believe" the Belle Starr–Blue Duck Episode at Fort Dodge.

James D. Horan, *Desperate Women* (1952), describes Belle as "A Woman Who Has Seen Much of Life." Although it debunks some of the legends, his chapter follows Rascoe and Croy. The James and Younger brothers rob the Clay County Savings Bank at Liberty, Missouri, on "St. Valentine's Day, 1866," and go into hiding at Belle's home in Texas, where the gang "drank her father's corn and Cole wooed Belle in the moonlight. Before the gang rode off she was pregnant." Horan also falls for the Fort Dodge episode and the alleged Belle-Jim Reed horse-back wedding officiated by the outlaw John Fischer. However, in his "Notorious Belle Starr" section of *Pictorial History of the Wild West* with Paul Sann (1954), Horan doubts the Belle-Cole Younger relationship, stating "there is not positive evidence" that Cole "fathered her first-born, a daughter named Pearl."

My own effort, "Lady Desperado" in *Law West of Fort Smith: A History of Frontier Justice in the Indian Territory, 1834-1896* (1957), follows Harman, Aikman, White, and Rascoe for the most part and repeats the same errors.

J. Gladstone Emery continues the pattern in *Court of the Damned: Being a Factual Story of the Court of Judge Isaac C. Parker and the Life and Times of the Indian Territory and Old Fort Smith* (1959). Belle Starr is "an expert markswoman," always with "shooting irons at her side"; "the most desperate criminals were puppets in her hand"; she claimed "nearly a thousand trackless acres" in the bend of the Canadian and named it after the Younger brothers, "one of whom had been Belle's second husband who had died years previously 'with his boots on' in blazing gunfire." Emery also states that a valuable pistol known to have been buried with Belle "was once the property of Cole Younger, her first husband's brother."

For Belle Starr material, Paul I. Wellman, *A Dynasty of Western Outlaws* (1961), follows Harman at times but largely Rascoe, whom he praises for demolishing "the dime-novel extravagances concerning her" and making "a good case for his theories . . . even when he falls back on conjecture." Wellman calls Belle "A Brushwood Courtesan," who was "well fitted to perpetuate and disperse the infection of outlawry, of which she seemed to be a 'carrier,' like Typhoid Mary." He defends Sutton's *Hands Up!,* thinks Anthony Gish's *American Bandits* "surprisingly accurate," believes the alleged Frank James autobiography, and attempts to relate Belle to the James brothers by common-law marriage. He makes several other assumptions based on tales created by the Fox writer and Harman.

A "Belle Starr" chapter in *Jesse James and the Lost Cause* by Jesse Lee James III (1961) is brief but so ridiculous it is hardly worth mentioning.

Harry Sinclair Drago, *Red River Valley: The Mainstream of Frontier History From the Louisiana Bayous to the Texas Panhandle* (1962), devotes a few paragraphs to our "bony, flat-chested" heroine with "a mean mouth and a vicious tongue." Some dates are incorrect. He says the only phase of her legend that stands up under examination is that she loved and owned several fast horses, which she "raced on the Fort Smith and Texas tracks." He is somewhat more accurate than preceding writers in *Outlaws on Horseback: The History of the Organized Bands of Bank and Train Robbers Who Terrorized the Prairie Towns of Missouri, Kansas, Indian Territory, and Oklahoma for Half a Century* (1964). Here Drago points to "many horrific errors" of the "always caustic" Rascoe and the "honest mistakes of fact and opinion" of Wellman. However, he believes beyond reasonable doubt that Cole Younger was Pearl Starr's father, accepts the "famous horseback marriage . . . with John Fischer functioning as preacher," and forms several questionable opinions of his own. Dealing with "Pearl Starr, Daughter of the Bandit Queen" in his *Notorious Ladies of the Frontier* (1969), Drago states that Pearl "was born out of wedlock and fathered by the famous outlaw Cole Younger" and that the only remaining point of controversy about Belle is "the identity of the man who killed her," but he accepts Croy's verdict that the assassin was Edgar Watson. He maintains both positions in his *Road Agents and Train Robbers: Half A Century of Western Banditry* (1973).

In *Belle Starr and Her Pearl* (1963), Edwin P. Hicks contends that Jim Middleton, brother of John Middleton, murdered Belle to avenge John's death. His history of Belle contains the errors in his sources: Harman, Rascoe, Croy, Harrington, and Horan. His contribution to outlaw history is the story of Belle's daughter, Pearl.

Belle Starr in Velvet by Kenneth D. Scott as told by Jennette S. Scott, Belle's granddaughter (1963), is, according to the author, the "family version" of Belle's life and times "compiled from articles in Belle's own scrapbook, and handed down and added to by her daughter Pearl . . . then handed down to Pearl's daughter, Jennette." The first book in three-quarters of a century to treat Belle kindly, it contains many erroneous statements and is generally unreliable.

This Is Three Forks Country by Phil Harris, based on his "Round-Up" columns in the *Sunday Muskogee Daily Phoenix and Times-Democrat* (1965), contains a brief chapter titled "Belle Starr, 'Queen of the Outlaws.'" Harris describes our heroine as "cruel and heartless and given to terrible rages . . . a deadly shot with revolvers, who delighted in making men fear her." He acknowledges that persons still living in the area who saw or remember Belle, and their children and grandchildren, "have heard and retold many stories about her, and in the retelling the fanciful tales far outnumber the factual and become hard to separate." He errs in stating that Cole Younger was "a former husband" and that her husband Sam Starr was "one of the sons of old Sam Starr."

Gunman's Territory by Elmer LeRoy Baker (1969) is a compilation of episodes based on the diaries, letters, and statements of James Robert (Bob) Hutchins. Hutchins, who died in 1951, had begun his career fifty years before as the youngest deputy marshal in Indian Territory. Later he was an Ardmore police chief and an inspector and guard on the Mexican border for railroad companies and the government. Hutchins deals with our heroine in two episodes: "Belle Starr—Friend of Friend and Foe" and "Belle Starr's Avenger." His alleged investigation of Belle's death is fiction. So is his contention that her last husband, Jim July Starr, was her murderer.

The Bandit Belle by Carl W. Breihan and Charles A. Rosamond (1970) has a section on "Bella Starr, Oklahoma Whirlwind." The authors take "great pains" in checking the actual date and place of Belle's birth with the promise to "strip away . . . legend and rumor" but accept most of the tales of preceding writers.

Grace Ernestine Ray's "The Bandits' Beloved Belle Starr"

in *Wily Women of the West* (1972), Gary Bradner's contribution "Belle Starr: The Bandit Queen" in *Outlaws of the West*, Charles Anderson, compiler and editor (1973), and Web Maddox's "Belle Starr" section in *Black Sheep* (1975) add nothing new, following the pattern of Harman, Rascoe, and others.

Colonel Charles W. Mooney's *Doctor in Belle Starr Country* (1975) is billed as a "partial . . . 'Fictionalized Biography' . . . based on fact with nothing embellished or added" of his father, Dr. Jesse Mooney, Jr., who "became Belle's personal physician." The author "reveals" and "divulges" for the first time "without doubt or contradiction, who the killer of Belle Starr was"; the "authentic details about how Belle was seduced by Cole Younger" in the "almost sordid description by Pearl" seven years after Belle was in her grave; and a number of other "facts" which we shall consider.

More than fifty other books and pamphlets published between 1941 and 1969 mention Belle. These will be dealt with where applicable.

Belle Starr's memory has been perpetuated in both verse and song. She was first "Immortalized in Rhyme" in Fox's *Bella Starr* (1889). Oklahoma poet George Riley Hall wrote "The Last Ride of the Bandit Queen," published in the *Muskogee Phoenix*, January 13, 1898; Stanley Vestal (Walter S. Campbell) included "Belle Starr" in his little book of ballads, *Fandango* (1927); "Belle Starr Rides Again" appeared in *A Collection of Cash Stevens' Poems* in 1948; two other moralizing epics handed down through the years and of unknown origin are "Belle Starr, Queen of the Desperadoes" and "A Two-Gun Woman."

Several novels purport to portray our heroine and her times, among them George C. Appell's *Belle's Castle* (1959), my *Outlaw Queen* (1960), *Belle Starr* by Speer Morgan (1979), and a 1979 Carlyle Book, *The Legend of Belle Starr* by Stoney Hardcastle. They are of no importance to this study.

THE FACTS AND THE LEGENDS

2   The Shirleys of Missouri

Belle's biographers are not certain of the date or place of her birth. The Fox [1] opus states: "Bella, or Myra, for such was her baptismal name, was the daughter of J. R. Sherley [sic] of Carthage, Missouri, where she was born in 1850; her father in those days was wealthy and connected with some of the leading families of the State." Harman[2] says she was born "Myra Belle Shirley . . . in Carthage, Missouri, February 3, 1856 . . . the *only* daughter of Judge John and Eliza Shirley, wealthy people of Southern antecedents"; she was "just past fifteen years old when the first gun fired upon Fort Sumpter [sic] . . . had a twin brother, Ed, known as Captain Shirley, to whom she was devoted." Aikman[3] and Cameron Rogers[4] accept Harman. Granddaughter "Flossie"[5] thinks "the twins, Edward and Myra, were born February 3, 1848, and were about 10 years old when the family moved from Medoc to Carthage." Rascoe[6] elects to believe that Belle was born "in a log cabin in the Missouri wilderness . . . in Washington County, perhaps even in the present town of Shirley . . . on February 5, 1848" before her parents moved to Jasper County in June. Shackleford[7]-Booker[8] writes: "Nobody knows exactly when or where Belle Starr was born. . . . The newspapers of my boyhood have it . . . near Georgia City [Jasper County], Mo., Feb. 3, 1846, on the old Shirley farm on Spring River. . . . Her exact age is not known but she was apparently about 15 years old in 1860." Horan[9] accepts Rascoe; sometime before 1848 the Shirleys settled in Washington County, where a town was named for the clan and "Belle was born." Croy[10] places the event "on a farm twelve miles northwest of Carthage . . . February 3, 1848; her father did not move [to Carthage] until she was six or seven years old." Wellman[11] says she was "fifteen years old, ripening into maidenhood" in 1863. Drago[12] settles for February 3, 1848, "either in or near Carthage, in Jasper County." Mooney[13] claims "Feb. 3, 1846, in Washington County . . . moved to Carthage June 1848" and says "Ed was a twin brother." Scott[14] states: "On February 3, 1846, the twins were born, a boy named Edward Dell, and a girl named Myra Belle Shirley." Breihan and Rosamond[15] are more specific: "She was born at a point called Medoc . . . ten miles [from Carthage] . . . on February 5, 1848"; christened Myra Maybelle Shirley and later "changed her middle name to Bella on a whim of her own"; Edwin Benton (not Edward Dell) was "fourteen months younger" than Myra, so they were not twins; her father was a farmer and hotel proprietor, "judge" being an honorary title only.

Here is the Shirley family chronology:

Belle's grandfather, Samuel Shirley, was a native of Virginia, where son John was born in 1794. His wife died soon afterward, and Samuel went with his former brother-in-law to Blountville, Tennessee, where he met and married Phoebe Cook, a New York girl. They moved to Caldwell County, Kentucky. Samuel died in 1842. He and Phoebe had three sons: Samuel Perry, Elijah Steven, and Danial.

Samuel Perry Shirley, born in 1824, was a member of the Blackwell-Shirley tobacco company of Louisville in the 1860s. His first wife, Clarissa, bore him eight children; his second wife, Martha Ann Stephens of Crittenden County, Kentucky, one-half Cherokee, bore him ten children, one of whom was Samuel Mack Shirley. Samuel Mack resided in Kentucky until 1875, then settled in Jack County, Texas, later moving near Duncan in the old Chickasaw Nation, Indian Territory, where he died in 1901.

Elijah Steven Shirley, born in 1828 and orphaned at fourteen, received medical training in Kentucky; practiced in Alabama, Kansas, and Illinois; and died at Xenia, Illinois, in 1901. His first wife was Martha Casey; his second, Mary Graves. Neither bore him children.

Daniel Shirley left no known descendants. He died in Ken-

Eliza Shirley, wife of John Shirley and mother of Belle Starr.

tucky at age 104.

John Shirley was considered the black sheep of the family and had little contact with his half-brothers. By the time Samuel Perry was born, John had gone to Clark County, Indiana, where he married a Nancy Fowler, April 6, 1818. They moved to Floyd County, where Nancy bore him two children: Preston Raymond, in 1826, and Charlotte Amanda, in 1828. John divorced Nancy shortly afterward, and on May 15, 1829, married a Fannie Munnick in Floyd County—no children from this union. Finally, he divorced Fannie and married (date and place unknown) teen-aged Elizabeth ("Eliza") Hatfield, related to the feuding Hatfields of West Virginia–Kentucky. In 1839, John Shirley took his family to the rolling slopes of the Ozarks in southwestern Missouri, which the Osage Indians had claimed as their hunting ground before being driven back into Kansas and Indian Territory by Governor Lilburn W. Boggs's militia in the Sarcoxie War of 1837.

White settlers were numerous in southwest Missouri, coming mostly from Tennessee and North Carolina, but some were from Illinois, Iowa, and Kentucky. Generally they located along the clear and sparkling Spring River and Center Creek, flowing parallel the length of Jasper County and joining near the Kansas border. These streams, fed by the North Fork of Spring River, Coon Creek, Dry Fork, Buck Branch, Turkey Creek, and others, abounded in fish, and their fall was sufficient to water-power flour mills. The prairie and timber sustained various game, especially deer, wild turkey, quail, and prairie chicken. The soil was adaptable to general farming, fruit growing, and stock raising.[16]

John Shirley filed patent on eight hundred acres of land about four miles southeast of Medoc near a small settlement, later called Georgia City, on the North Fork of Spring River. He raised wheat, corn, hogs, and fine-blooded horses, and prospered. Here Eliza bore him three more children: John Allison M., nicknamed "Bud," in 1842; Myra Maybelle, whom the family called "May," February 5, 1848 (the date inscribed on her tombstone); and Edwin Benton in 1849.[17] On May 6, 1847, Preston married Mary Avilla Chelson, an Iowa girl, and left home but remained in Jasper County.[18]

The 1850 Federal Population Census was the first to list the name, age, sex, color, and birthplace of the head of the family, his wife, children, hired help, and any other persons living at his address. It also showed the profession, occupation, or trade of each male person over fifteen years of age. The census of

Jasper County, enumerated on October 17, 1850, gave the following information on the Shirley household:

Name	Age	Sex	Occupation	Birthplace
John Shirley	54	M	Farmer	Va.
Eliza	34	F		Va.
Charlotte A.	12	F		Ia.
John A. M.	8	M		Mo.
Myra	2	F		Mo.
Benton	9/12	M		Mo.

John Shirley's real-estate holdings were appraised by the census taker at six hundred dollars.[19]

The settlers of Jasper County raised their own meat, fruit, and vegetables and ground their corn and wheat at mills along Center Creek and Spring River. Old-fashioned wood fireplaces supplied heat for their stone houses and log cabins and usually were their means of cooking. They made most of their clothing and subsisted mostly through the exchange of commodities among neighbors. By these standards, the Shirleys were considered wealthy.

The 1850 head count included Preston's family:

Name	Age	Sex	Occupation	Birthplace
Preston Shirley	24	M	Farmer	Ia.
Mary A.	20	F		Ia.
Christian T.	2	M		Mo.
John F.	9/12	M		Mo.

Preston's real-estate holdings were valued at only fifty dollars.

The books of Jasper County's recorder of deeds list the granting of a U.S. government patent on the 800 acres southeast of Medoc to John Shirley on June 30, 1848. By this time he had lived on the land as a homesteader and had improved it enough to establish his right to title. He began selling off his holdings in 1850. On March 16 he sold 160 acres to David Martin for $700; in June, 1851, he bought from John and Melinda Richardson two quarter-acre lots in the town of Carthage.

By act of the Missouri Legislature, approved January 29, 1841, Jasper County was organized from the northern part of Newton County; Carthage had been established as the county seat and was developing in a substantial way. In 1856, John Shirley sold most of his remaining acres to George W. Broome. When Broome, in turn, offered the land for sale in the *Carthage Southwest News* on March 29, 1861, it was described as "600 acres of Spring River bottoms . . . situate in Jasper County . . . 100 acres in cultivation, has on it a small apple orchard, dwelling house, kitchen, stable & c., has a good well. The larger portion of it is heavily timbered; stone coal is abundant in the vicinity, and a more desirable stock farm could not be found in the Southwest." After the sale, John Shirley moved his family into Carthage and constructed a hotel-tavern on the lots he purchased from the Richardsons.

John continued to prosper during the next four years. According to the Federal Population Census enumerated on June 28, 1860, Eliza had borne him two more sons, he owned two slaves, and he had established himself as an innkeeper:

Name	Age	Sex	Occupation	Birthplace
John Shirley	66	M	Hotel keeper	Va.
Eliza	45	F		Va.
Allison	18	M		Mo.
Myra	12	F		Mo.
Edwin	11	M		Mo.
Mansfield	8	M		Mo.
Cravens	2	M		Mo.

The census taker estimated his real-estate holdings at four thousand dollars and his personal estate at six thousand dollars.[20] His wayside inn, including a livery stable and blacksmith shop, occupied most of the block on the north side of the public square.[21] The *Southwest News* of March 29, 1861, carried this advertisement:

CARTHAGE HOTEL
North Side Public Square,
John Shirley, Proprietor.
Horses and Hacks for Hire.
A good stable attached.[22]

In 1860, Carthage had five hundred residents, a two-story brick courthouse, a brick jail, and a number of brick business houses and residences. *The Star of the West and Southwest News,* first newspaper in the county, began publication at Carthage in 1859. It had a good circulation, exerted considerable influence in molding public opinion, and advocated slavery. During the campaign of 1860, it endorsed all candidates except the great champion of the antislavery movement, Abraham Lincoln.[23]

Sarcoxie, in southeastern Jasper County, was the second-largest town, with a population of four hundred, but it had the best gristmills and was the strongest proslavery settlement. Other towns, such as Avilla, Medoc, Preston, Minersville, and Fidelity (just south of Carthage), were little more than villages with no organized municipal governments, all strictly agricultural except Minersville (present Oronogo). A mining operation had begun on Turkey Creek, called Leadville (the present site of Joplin), and a lead smelter and general store two miles farther west on Center Creek were known as French Point. Old Sherwood, in southwestern Jasper County, founded in 1847, was an important trading center. Here Judge Andrew McKee, Tennessee native and agent for five Indian tribes, stocked a complete line of merchandise in his large brick store. During the winter he bought great quantities of hogs and similar produce, which he shipped south in the spring on flatboats down Center Creek and Spring River, thence by way of the Grand and Arkansas rivers, to Fort Smith and Little Rock, Arkansas.[24]

In 1852, Captain Randolph B. Marcy, seeking a new route to Santa Fe, had mapped a shorter, almost direct trail from Fort Smith through central Indian Territory, and gold seekers coming up the Missouri River by boat to Independence turned south through Carthage to Fort Smith to take the Marcy route instead of the old Santa Fe and Oregon trails to California. So Carthage was an excellent location for John Shirley's wayside inn. Besides this transient patronage, scores of pioneer planters, preachers, and lawyers riding circuit from other county seats, along with Ozark hill people, enjoyed the services and hospitality of the Carthage Hotel. The varied fare and somewhat civilized cooking whetted appetites accustomed to corn pone and sowbelly, and the fragrantly mixed liquors suggested drinking pleasures other than those obtained from getting plastered on red-eye and squirrel whiskey. Farm wives and women from wagons on the trail learned tricks of ladylike coquetry, used by southern gentlewomen, that Eliza Shirley affected. In the hotel parlor her worn but highly polished piano stood as the ultimate symbol of refined achievement.

No less an attraction was John Shirley's fine library of novels, histories, biographies, and works on philosophy and moral improvement. Lawyers and preachers considered him their intellectual equal, political leaders consulted him in important Democratic matters and proslavery patronage, and his influence was felt in 1855 when Jasper County citizens began to plan larger educational opportunities for their daughters and the Carthage Female Academy was organized and chartered.

Teaching at the academy were Principal Samuel M. Knealand, a Mr. Hurley, and Miss Alice Walker. The school was patronized by the best families in the county and had begun to flourish when the war brought an end to it.

Myra Shirley was one of the first to master its curriculum of reading, spelling, grammar, arithmetic, deportment, Greek, Latin, Hebrew, and music, and she learned to play the piano. She also attended a private school conducted by William Cravens in a second-floor room of Masonic Hall on the northwest corner of the public square. Mrs. James Brummett, one of Myra's schoolmates, recalled in a *Carthage Press* interview on September 7, 1922, that

at this time she was about ten years of age . . . small and dark, bright, intelligent . . . but of a fierce nature and would fight anyone, boy or girl, that she quarreled with. Except for this trait, she seemed a nice little girl. . . .

In fact, the entire Shirley family were nice people.

Mrs. Brummett recalled that Myra was inclined to flaunt her prominence as the little rich girl of Carthage. She grew up a hotel child, always with an audience. Many flattered her accomplishments beyond their worth, others encouraged her with small gifts and requests for recitals on the piano, and teasing strangers sparked the last bit of fire in her volcanic temperament one minute and spoiled her the next, just to pass the time. Two interests obsessed her: horses and the outdoors. A competent horsewoman, she spent much of her time roaming the hills with brother Bud. Throughout his teens, Bud was wild and daring, an excellent rider, and handy with firearms.

In the rough-and-ready times which preceded Secession, Bud taught Myra how to handle a rifle and pistol.[25] The chaotic events of the period soon afforded an opportunity to put her abilities to use.

The Kansas-Nebraska Act, passed by Congress in 1854, was the last of three compromises between the slavery expansionists of the South and their antislavery opponents in the North; it incited the radical abolition sentiment of the North to aggressive action. Such militants as lanky, ne'er-do-well John Brown of Torrington, Connecticut, who was twice married and let his children starve while his brain burned with organizing and agitating the abolition of slavery, added fuel to the hostilities, and an undeclared civil war erupted between Missouri and her neighbor Kansas long before the War Between the States began. Kansas retained bitter memories of the Border Ruffian raids of the 1850s, and Missourians harbored an intense hatred of the horse-stealing Kansas Abolitionists.

In December, 1860, South Carolina withdrew from the Union, and Mississippi, Florida, Alabama, Louisiana, Georgia, and Texas quickly followed. Governor Claiborne F. Jackson, himself secretly a Secessionist, believed that Missouri should be with the Confederate States of America, but in a special message to the legislature in January, 1861, he suggested a course of armed neutrality. In a state convention called at Jefferson City on February 28 to decide Missouri's position,

the ninety-nine delegates divided into three parties: Secessionists, Conditional Union, and Unconditional Union. The Secessionists favored joining the Confederacy at once; the Conditional Union men, led by Sterling Price, and the Unconditional
delegates, headed by Frank P. Blair of St. Louis, stood with
Governor Jackson. Missouri should not secede unless the federal government tried to force the Southern States back into
the Union. This sentiment prevailed, and the vote was almost
unanimous.

Excitement subsided somewhat until the fall of Fort Sumter.
President Lincoln called for seventy-five thousand volunteers,
and the secretary of war telegraphed Governor Jackson to
enlist four regiments (Missouri's quota) for federal service.
Jackson refused, called for fifty thousand volunteers to defend
the state, and appointed brigadier generals to command the
several brigades to be organized. Senator James S. Rains of
the Jasper County district was one of the generals. He recruited
a company of eighty men at Sarcoxie and raised the first Confederate flag in Missouri. Elsewhere in Jasper County, Southern sympathizers organized minutemen companies, called
Border Rangers and Border Guards, and began drilling nightly
at Medoc, Carthage, Minersville, and Sherwood in preparation
for the struggle they sensed was coming. A number of Union
men in the county left immediately for Kansas, enlisting in
the Sixth Kansas Cavalry, mustered into federal service at
Fort Scott.

On May 10 a considerable portion of the Missouri State
Guards, in camp near the St. Louis arsenal for drill but suspected by Union men of being there to seize its forty thousand
stands of arms, was captured by federal volunteers under Captain Nathaniel Lyon. Although Captain Lyon soon freed his
prisoners, the Conditional Union men considered their capture an act of war, and Sterling Price, president of the convention which had voted against secession, offered his sword to
Governor Jackson. Price was appointed major general commanding the Missouri State Guards.

Price met with General William S. Harney, commanding the Division of Missouri at St. Louis. The two agreed to bend their best efforts toward keeping the war out of the state. However, Harney was relieved of his command by President Lincoln and replaced by Lyon, now a brigadier general. Price and Governor Jackson conferred with Lyon, offering to disband the Missouri State Guards if Lyon would disband the Missouri (Union) Volunteers; Lyon refused. Jackson returned to Jefferson City, ordered his generals in the several military districts to assemble their commands for active service, and issued a call for the legislature to meet in special session at Neosho, Newton County. Price departed for Arkansas to persuade General Benjamin McCulloch of the Confederate army to furnish troops for Jackson's relief and assist in mobilizing the state army at some point in southwest Missouri near the temporary capital.

Jackson abandoned Jefferson City and started for Neosho with his fugitive government, gathering troops as he went. At Boonville on June 17, seven hundred of his hastily assembled State Guards under General John B. Clark were attacked and scattered by General Lyon. Brigadier General Thomas W. Sweeney sent troops to Springfield to hold that section of the state for the Union and prevent Jackson's escape to the south, but escape Jackson did. He was joined at Lamar by General Rains with eighteen hundred men of the Second and Eighth divisions and by Captain Jo Shelby's horse-trained, rifle- and bowie-knife-toting Rangers. General Sweeney ordered Colonel Franz Sigel, an experienced German soldier commanding a brigade of eleven hundred well-armed and disciplined U.S. volunteers, to the area to prevent the juncture of Jackson's and Price's armies.

Jackson's force now consisted of about five thousand followers, including state officers, legislators, and a long and elaborate wagon train loaded with furniture, official records, pots, pans, and feather beds. The troops were commanded by Brigadier General Monroe M. Parsons. General Price, joined by hundreds of eager boys on his southern march, was encamped on Cowskin Prairie near the junction of the Arkansas-Missouri-Indian Territory borders. Sigel learned that other columns, under the command of Lieutenant Governor Thomas C. Reynolds and former U.S. Senator David Rice Atchison, were coming. These forces quadrupled Sweeney's army; should McCulloch cross from Arkansas, the enemy's superiority would be overwhelming.

The old German commander was accustomed to hazards. He swung his army into Neosho, leaving a company of men to hold the town against invaders from the south, sent a courier pounding off to Springfield to apprise Sweeney of the situation, then marched north. On the evening of July 4, 1861, he arrived at Carter Springs on the east edge of Carthage, where Union sympathizers informed him that Jackson's army was camped eighteen miles to the north. General Parsons received word of Sigel's presence shortly after sundown; early next morning the state forces moved south as a unit.

The two armies met in battle at Coon Creek, twelve miles from Carthage, and the fight lasted all day. Although they held the advantage in numbers, Jackson's troops were not well disciplined and withdrew gradually until General Rains sought to flank Sigel and get behind him. Sigel, hoping to destroy or scatter the state army with the help of General Lyon (erroneously thought to be following Jackson closely), now retreated. The battle continued to the outskirts of Carthage, where Sigel suddenly withdrew eastward on the road to Sarcoxie. It was none too soon. General Price and General McCulloch, with some three thousand well-equipped men neatly uniformed in Confederate gray, marched into Carthage the next morning. The company of men Siegel left at Neosho were their prisoners.

General Price led the army into McDonald County to begin drilling and organizing. The minutemen companies formed in western Jasper County were mustered into service and became the nucleus for a regiment known as the Eleventh Missouri State Guard; they joined Price's army. Governor Jackson established his mobile state capital at Neosho, which he soon was forced to abandon. Carthage was fortified by a small garrison of U.S. troops, but by this time all civil government in Jasper County had been suspended and its official records and treasury removed to various points of safety.

Because of the Union military movement from Springfield, General McCulloch suggested that Price destroy all forage on Spring River below Carthage to keep it out of Federal hands. Price replied that it would be inhumane to lay waste to the country and burn its mills, leaving women and children, most of whom were in sympathy with the South, to starve. The proposed devastation was not carried out.

Hatred between sympathizers of the two armies passing and repassing through Jasper County grew intense, and it became the site of almost constant irregular fighting in which the rules of civilized warfare were disregarded. The western two-thirds of the county was not under military control of either army, and the eastern part, including Sarcoxie, had only token protection from detachments of federal troops from Springfield. All inhabitants were forced to join one side or the other. Old friendships were broken; neighbors and frequently whole families became bitter enemies. On August 23 a group of Confederate sympathizers organized to go south and some Union men en route to Fort Scott to enlist in the Federal army clashed at Medoc in the first skirmish between armed bands after the Battle of Carthage. The same month, a group of marauders, supposedly Kansans, swept down on George W. Broome's trading post on the farm he had obtained from John Shirley, murdered Broome, looted and burned his house, and drove off forty head of horses.[26]

Thomas R. Livingston, former merchant and lead miner at French Point, organized and led a company of guerrillas responsible for much of the incendiarism and destruction in the region. The guerrillas took some Carthage Union men prisoner; to secure the prisoner's safety, the Federals took Judge John Onstott and several others to Fort Scott as hostages. The judge eventually was released. During his absence, Colonel N. F.

Ritchie's command of Federal Indians looted his house, stealing two hundred dollars in currency.[27] Ritchie's Indians, officially the Second Indian Home Guard, composed of Cherokees, Osages, Quapaws, and some Negroes, was one of several such Union army organizations which made expeditions into Jasper and adjoining counties to obtain supplies and break up bands of Southern sympathizers. The Indians became a terror to the country as they robbed and plundered friend and foe alike.[28] Many Union sympathizers received anonymous warnings and moved to Kansas or to states farther north, and a number of ardent Jasper County Secessionists went to Texas and settled there permanently. Among the latter was Preston Shirley.

Those who remained found themselves at the mercy of brigands and guerrillas who raided first one commonwealth and then the other. Governor Charles Robinson of Kansas regarded the gathering of Confederate forces in southwest Missouri as tantamount to a declaration of war and ordered hundreds of armed Kansans to the border to repel invasion. Other Kansans declared that the best policy was to keep the Missourians from their doors by giving them something to do at home. Foremost among this group were the Jayhawkers and Red Legs of guerrilla chiefs James Montgomery, Charles R. Jennison, and James H. Lane, who laid waste to Missouri towns and settlements. Missouri retaliated; bushwhackers under George Todd, William ("Bloody Bill") Anderson, and the indomitable, sharp-faced William Clarke Quantrill desolated the Kansas countryside with fire and sword.

Quantrill, born in Canal Dover, Ohio, was a schoolteacher who abandoned pedagogy for horse stealing and other outlawry. He stole slaves and returned them for the reward and did some quiet murder during the Border Ruffians raids of the 1850s. Then he moved to Missouri, passed himself off as a firm believer in slavery, double-crossed sundry of his friends, and got together a group of eight men in Clay and Jackson counties as a nucleus of his Confederate marauders. Within a year he built his small group into an army of hard-riding, well-disciplined raiders whose exploits attracted the later cream of frontier badmen: Frank and Jesse James and Cole Younger, who took to the brush after Federal militiamen led by Captain James Walley murdered Cole's father. But many members of Quantrill's band were some of the finest men in the state, and John Shirley, like hundreds of other Missourians, looked upon Quantrill as the dashing hero of their cause. A hot-blooded Southerner, Shirley rejoiced in the firing upon Fort Sumter, took comfort in the news of the Federal defeat at Bull Run in Virginia, and enthusiastically abetted his son Bud's involvement with a band of bushwhackers.[29]

Bud Shirley, listed as "John A. M." in the 1850 Federal Population Census and as "Allison" in 1860, was six years older than Myra and twenty-one at the time of his death in 1864. This is corroborated by Schrantz,[30] quoting the personal narrative of George Walker, an old Confederate soldier who was sworn into service at Carthage under Captain James Petty. Walker mentions:

> Bud Shirley, one of our men who lived in Carthage . . . was medium sized, dark complexioned and weighed probably 160 pounds. Bud was as good a companion and as brave a man as you could find anywhere. His age was about 22.

Myra Maybelle watched her beloved brother ride away with the little band of Jasper County sympathizers, cheered on by the strains of *Maryland! My Maryland!* and allegedly vowed to harass the Yankees on her own in every way possible. Information was needed about the location of Union detachments, what they were planning, their strength, and the mobilization of equipment and supplies for the armies of the North.

3   Myra's "Daring Ride" and the Death of Bud Shirley

The Confederate guerrilla forces, free from restraints of army discipline, sometimes committed deeds that disgraced the cause they served, but Sterling Price and most of the other generals thought men like Quantrill and Anderson no worse than their Union counterparts and used such organizations at every opportunity. Livingston's guerrillas and Colonel S. D. Jackman's Scouts continually furnished useful information, frequently served with the regular forces, and were excellent guides. Their most valuable service was forcing the Union army to keep in the country large numbers of troops which otherwise would have been adding weight to the decisive campaigns of the war. This was the role Bud Shirley and his Rebel companions played. George Walker[1] recalls that the company consisted of about forty men whose purpose was to join Jo Shelby. Unable to do so for some time, they operated in various parts of the country.

Such activities caused Lieutenant Colonel Powell Clayton of the Kansas Cavalry to move on Carthage in March, 1862, capturing nearly a score of the most prominent rebels in the community. Neither Bud Shirley nor his companions were among them. In July, Major Benjamin S. Henning, the post commander at Fort Scott, sent another force into Jasper County to protect Union men from a new wave of guerrilla warfare designed to regain control of the region. However, the bands had moved north into western Missouri, cutting railways and winning at least three fair-sized victories, the most notable at Lone Jack, near Kansas City. On August 11, Major J. M. Hubbard of the First Missouri (Union) Cavalry, stationed at Newtonia in east-central Newton County, had a skirmish with some Shelby men who moved through Jasper into Barton

County, and on August 26, General James G. Blunt of the Kansas Cavalry reported that his soldiers had followed a group of Confederate recruits south to Carthage so closely that their route was marked by hats and caps dropped from the heads of riders sleeping in the saddle and by bodies of horses that had died of exhaustion.

Toward the end of September, Brigadier General Frederick Salomon, commanding four thousand five hundred Union troops at Sarcoxie, clashed near Newtonia with four thousand Confederates and three regiments of Cherokee, Choctaw, and Chickasaw Indians under Colonel Douglas H. Cooper. The battle, which lasted four days, proved a reversal for the Federals, who were dribbled into the fight against superior forces. Union troops hurried to Sarcoxie from every direction. Finally, on October 4, General J. M. Schofield, in command of them all, moved on Newtonia. Reluctant to engage these combined forces, Colonel Cooper withdrew, and Schofield's troops entered the town practically unopposed. Bud Shirley and two bushwhacker companions were spying on the Union maneuvers, and Bud almost got his everlasting. Mrs. C. C. Warner, who lived south of Carthage, recalls:

In the woods near our farm . . . Berry Bedford [who resided] a half mile from us . . . Bud Shirley and James Moorehouse, of Carthage [were] met by a band of federal men. Bedford was captured but the other two men got away by running through a field. Bedford was brought down to the road in front of our tenant house close by to wait for the men who were in pursuit of the other two.

Meanwhile, some of the men came to our house thinking the fugitives [Moorehouse and Shirley] had come there for refuge. The fleeing men had not come near the house, however, and after search had been allowed the visitors were satisfied [stating] that they had caught Bedford. . . . Bedford's daughter was visiting us girls at the time. . . . The men said that if a single person left our house he would be forthwith shot down. But even while they were saying this, we were flying down the road. . . . We found Mr. Bedford in custody . . . his daughter threw her arms around his neck and begged that he be spared. The rest of us girls comforted her and also joined in her plea. The men treated us nicely as if everything would be all right and eventually persuaded us to go back to the house.

Soon after we got back, however, we heard a volley of shots and some of the men came by the house and told us we could have our man now. As expected, we found him shot to death.[2]

After occupying Newtonia, the Union army went in pursuit of Cooper's Confederates, and quartermaster wagons from Fort Scott passing through Jasper County to troops in the field became the objective of the guerrilla bands. On the night of November 5, Quantrill attacked the Union garrison at Lamar in Barton County, burned a portion of the town, and moved south through Jasper, causing great alarm. Major G. W. Kelley, commanding the Fourth Missouri Militia, was sent into Jasper County to assist Captain Theodore Conkey's company of Third Wisconsin Cavalry in protecting the wagon trains. On November 27, Kelley's troops dispersed Colonel Jackman's Scouts in a short but desperate engagement near Carthage, killing two and taking six prisoners, their horses, and a quantity of arms. Captain Conkey's cavalry and Captain C. F. Coleman's Ninth Kansas, encamped near Carthage, clashed with Livingston's guerrillas on Cow Creek, pursued and intercepted them near Sherwood, killing five and taking four prisoners.

Quantrill with one thousand men came within ten miles of Newtonia, intending to attack the Federal garrison there. Upon hearing of Jackman's and Livingston's defeat and that Union troops were being thrown into the section in great numbers, he moved on into McDonald County and thence to Fort Smith, where his band was attached to the command of Jo Shelby.

The Federal situation in Jasper and Newton counties improved during the next few weeks. On December 31, Major Edwin B. Eno, commanding a company of Eighth Missouri Cavalry at Newtonia, reported that the valleys of Center, Jones, and Shoal creeks were swarming with guerrillas; he had killed eight of them, and if horseflesh and ammunition did not fail him, he would root out the rest, stem and branch. One man at the top of his bushwhacker list was Bud Shirley.

At this time Myra Maybelle reportedly was spying on Eno's troops for her brother. Harman provides this adventure:

On her sixteenth birthday, February 3, 1862, as Belle, returning from a scout, was riding through the village of Newtonia . . . thirty-five miles, as the crow flies, from her home town . . . she was intercepted by a Major Enos [sic] who . . . was stationed in the village and who had his headquarters at the home of Judge M. H. Ritchery [Matthew H. Richey].

It is a quaint old place; the house, a long structure, of red brick, with broad verandas and an L, located at some little distance back from the highway, the centerpiece of beautiful grounds dotted here and there with fine old shade trees. The house is still standing, and is the home of Professor and Mrs. S. C. Graves, the latter being a daughter of Judge Ritchery. The place is a romantic one; scattered here and there are seven solid shot dropped on the grounds during the cannonading incident to several likely skirmishes. The cornice of the house, in several places, still shows where portions of the architecture were carried away by shells. . . . Across the road from the grounds still stands a large, but considerably dilapidated, stone building, first built for a mill and afterwards successively used for a hospital, first by the Confederate and then by Federal troops.

On the day of Belle Shirley's capture . . . Major Enos had sent a detachment of cavalry to Carthage for the purpose of capturing her brother, Captain Shirley, who was known to be on a visit to his home. Belle, or Myra, as she was then called, had ridden into that section of the country for the purpose of obtaining information that might be of value to her people, and having discovered that men had been sent to capture her brother, was on the point of hastening to warn him. . . . She had been in the habit of riding recklessly where she pleased, and as scarce any Union soldier would think of molesting a woman, especially . . . a beautiful and buxom girl, her plans had not, hitherto, been disarranged. It happened that Major Enos, who had resided in Carthage, was acquainted with both her and her brother, as children, and this was why he had ordered her arrest; he rightly surmising that she was about to go to her brother's assistance. The girl was taken to the chamber of the Ritchery home and guarded by the major himself, who laughed at her annoyance. This served to anger her and she would sit at the piano and rattle off some wild selection in full keeping with her fury; the next instant she would spring to her feet, stamp the floor and berate the major and his acts with all the ability and profanity of an experienced trooper, while tears of mortification rolled down her cheeks, her terrible passion only increased by the laughter and taunts of her captor. At last, believing his men to have had plenty of time to reach Carthage ahead of her, Major Enos said:

"Well, Myra, you can go now. My men will have your brother under arrest before you can reach him."

With eagerness, trembling in every lineament, she sprang to the door, rushed down the stairway and out to a clump of cherry bushes, where she cut several long sprouts for use as riding whips. The judge's daughter, now Mrs. Graves, accompanied her.

"I'll beat them yet," said the girl, as with tearful eyes she swallowed a great lump in her throat. Her horse stood just where her captors had left it; vaulting into the saddle, she sped away, plying the cherry sprouts with vigor. A short distance from the house she deserted the traveled road and, leaping fences and ditches without ceremony, struck a bee line in the direction of Carthage. She was a beautiful sight as she rode away through the fields; her lithe figure clad in a closely fitting jacket, erect as an arrow, her hair unconfined by her broad-brimmed, feather-decked sombrero, falling free and flung to the breeze, and her right hand plying the whip at almost every leap of her fiery steed. The Major seized a field glass and ascending to the chamber watched her course across the great stretch of level country.

"Well, I'll be d — —," he ejaculated, admiringly, "she's a born guer-rilla. If she doesn't reach Carthage ahead of my troopers, I'm a fool."

The Major was right; when his detachment of cavalry galloped leisurely into Carthage that evening they were greeted by a slip of a girl mounted on a freshly groomed horse. She dropped a courtesy and asked:

"Looking for Capt. Shirley? He isn't here — left half an hour ago — had business up Spring River. 'Spect he's in Lawrence county by this time."[3]

Harman's version, including incorrect date and name spellings, is recapped with much embroidery by most later writers.[4] Major Eno and his troops did not occupy Newtonia until the winter of 1862-63, nearly a year after the date of this alleged incident. Eno made voluminous reports on his daily operations, his assessment of the disposition of enemy forces, everything that happened to him, and does not mention arresting or questioning Myra Shirley.

Croy[5] tells what he thinks is the "true" story, handed down in the Richey family and told by Mrs. Mildred Graves Sanders, Richey's daughter-in-law, to Mrs. Louise Brock Murphy of Neosho, who with her husband Ralph bought the old mansion and were restoring it when Croy visited them. A girl of about fifteen rode up to the mansion one evening in February 1863 (not 1862), introduced herself as Myra Belle Shirley of Carthage, stated that she had "got lost" while visiting friends, and asked to stay overnight. The "unsuspecting" Mr. Richey took her in; she ate supper and visited with the family. The Richeys knew the Shirley family in Carthage, but "did not like them." Richey was a Union man and in the habit of sheltering Federal soldiers and sympathizers. His house guests at the moment were Major Eno and his officers; the enlisted men were using the stone barn and mill as barracks; some were encamped in the town. "Interesting things" for Myra to know. After supper the family and guests retired to the parlor, where there was a rosewood grand piano, and Myra "obligingly sat down and played." After breakfast next morning she thanked the Richeys for their hospitality. Her horse was "saddled and brought." She had to get home as fast as possible, so that her parents would not worry, and wanted some switches for her horse. Richey's daughter accompanied her to a clump of cherry bushes; she cut "two or three," then got into her sidesaddle and sped off in the direction of Carthage. The cutting of the switches was a signal to Confederate lookouts, and after she had gone two or three miles, "hell struck the Richey house." A fusillade so damaged the mansion that Major Eno no longer could use it for headquarters. Later, in a desperate battle at Newtonia, the mansion was used as a hospital, and two or three Union soldiers died in the room where Myra had slept. "Quite a little victory for Belle," Croy concludes.[6]

Fox's writer did not use the story but claims this sidelight:

Beneath the roof of the old Sherley house in Carthage the James, Younger, Quantrell families were constant guests. [Myra] returned from school a beautiful girl of sixteen . . . on first beholding her, Quantrell was deeply smitten with the lively young lass . . . would have sacrificed gain and glory to possess her, but his suit was set aside when the junior lieutenant of the guerillas . . . Jim Read, a reckless, dashing young fellow . . . put in his claim.[7]

It is true that Myra was the sweetheart of young James C. Reed. Jim was the fourth son of Solomon Reed, a well-to-do farmer who lived southwest of Rich Hill in north-central Vernon County near the Bates County line. The 1860 Federal Population Census for Vernon County lists the family members as follows:

Name	Age	Sex
Solomon Reed	45	M
Susan Reed	42	F
F. M. Reed	21	M
William Reed	19	M
S. B. Reed	18	M
James Reed	14	M
Sarah Reed	12	F
Jasper Reed	10	M
Solomon Reed	8	M
Amanda Reed	5	F
Richard Reed	3	M
George Reed	10/12	M

Solomon Reed's real-estate holdings were appraised at $6,900 and his personal property valued at $2,395.[8]

Jim's older brothers—F(rancis) M(arion), William (Scott), and S. B. Reed—were Southern sympathizers, but family sympathies were not such to cause them to take part in the war. When the Jayhawkers made things hot around Rich Hill in 1861, the family moved to Carthage, where Jim and Myra became acquainted when Myra was thirteen. Jim was a quiet, religious boy, the most helpful and kindly disposed of Mrs. Reed's several sons, but events connected with border warfare stirred in his veins the blood of some adventurous ancestor and he took to the hills to duplicate the feats of Cole Younger and Frank James.[9] He joined Quantrill at age seventeen, was never a lieutenant but a tall, hawk-faced, sandy-haired tough who was handy with fists and guns and whom the older heads among the guerrillas respected.

It is perhaps through this Fox sidelight and Myra's association with young Reed that Harman and other biographers have Myra riding with Quantrill's marauders disguised as a man, taking part in many battles, burning homes of Yankee sympathizers, and killing four men before she was eighteen years old.[10] The record shows only two women ever rode with Quantrill: Anna Walker and Kate Clarke. Anna was the former wife of Riley Slaughter, a respectable Blue Springs merchant and physician who divorced her for her infidelity; afterward she had a number of lovers, among them Quantrill and George Todd. In April, 1862, she married Joe Vaughn and lived with him somewhere north of the Missouri River until the end of the war, when her father died. With the proceeds from her inherited part of her father's land, she set up a bawdyhouse at Baxter Springs.[11] Kate, a young girl from Jackson County (her real name not known), was practically kidnapped by Quantrill, lived in the brush with him as his mistress until he headed for Kentucky in 1864, and later opened a fancy house in St. Louis with money given her by the guerrilla leader.[12]

There is no evidence that Myra Shirley ever met Quantrill or was ever closer to him than she was when he passed through Jasper County with his men in November, 1862, en route to the Confederate lines in Arkansas. Harman also is wrong in stating that Myra's daring ride "availed Capt. Shirley but little . . . except an opportunity to give up his life in battle a few days later during an engagement in the brush with Federal cavalry."[13] Bud Shirley would carry on his bushwhacking activities for several months to come.

By February, 1863, some thirteen thousand Union militiamen had been organized to repel guerrilla raids into Missouri and relieve volunteer units for service on more active fronts. The general tactics were to garrison certain towns and defend them while the remainder of the troops struck hard at guerrilla bands wherever they could be found. Although the units in Jasper County did effective work, they were supplemented in emergencies by Major Eno's Eighth Missouri at Newtonia and by Company C, Seventh Enrolled Militia Cavalry, commanded by Captain Green C. Stotts, which occupied Cave Springs and Bower Mills on the Jasper-Lawrence county line.

On February 19, two weeks after Myra Maybelle's exploit and in connection with the dispersal of Jackman's Scouts and Livingston's raiders in November, Eno led his troops on a scouting trip down Center Creek, thence up Spring River to Carthage. The militia from Bower Mills overtook Livingston on Dry Fork, fought him briefly, and came charging back through Carthage, swearing because they could not catch him. With Captain Moore's Wisconsin volunteers in the vicinity of Lamar, Eno doubted that Livingston had fled north, so he marched back to Jones and Jenkins creeks west of Sarcoxie, where he engaged part of the guerrilla band near Fidelity, wounding one man and capturing three.

Livingston fled south. On the night of March 3, the guerrilla chief and one hundred men dashed into Granby, Newton County, where twenty-five of the major's men were stationed, captured his patrol guard, killed two other soldiers, and rode northwest without attacking the squad at the stockade. A few days later, Captain David Mefford of the Sixth Kansas Cavalry clashed with Livingston near Sherwood, wounding several horses. Major Eno turned his course to Neosho, reaching that place at sundown.

Livingston fled into Indian Territory. There he rested in the Creek Nation until May, then returned to Jasper County. On May 14, Eno attempted to surround and destroy him at a loghouse retreat near the Center Creek mines east of French Point. The three-pronged attack lasted fifteen minutes. Many of the guerrillas were dressed in Federal uniform, and before they discovered their mistake, the men in one of Eno's detachments suffered a galling fire, allowing Livingston to escape toward Spring River. Eno pursued him over the prairie until the trail divided and finally diverged in every direction. For the next ten days his troops searched the region five miles down Spring River, across again on Center Creek, almost continually sighting their quarry, flushing scattered squads of four to ten men and chasing and firing on them until they disappeared into the brush and pursuit became impossible. Four of Eno's troopers were killed and two wounded. Total loss to the enemy was an estimated fifteen killed and twenty wounded in the skirmishes at various points in crossing and recrossing the creek.

Livingston moved north out of Jasper County. On the afternoon of July 11, he surprised and attacked the militia at Stockton in Cedar County, but Lieutenant W. A. McMinn, commanding the Seventy-Sixth Enrolled detachment garrisoning the town, with headquarters in the courthouse, was prepared for any emergency. Livingston and three of his men died on the field of battle, and fifteen wounded were left by the enemy at Whitehair, ten miles southwest of Stockton. The remaining guerrillas made their way back to the Confederate lines near Maysville, Arkansas, and only scattered bands of bushwhackers remained in Jasper County.

In the latter part of July, Captain James Petty's band of sympathizers, including Bud Shirley, moved on Carthage from the west. According to George Walker, they were unaware that a Union militia unit had occupied the county seat a few days earlier:

We camped on Oak street road . . . near where the Moniter school now stands. By this time there were about forty men in our company. The camping place was only a short distance south of my home and since I had not been there for some time, I obtained permission to go over to the house. A little while prior to this Bud Shirley . . . had ridden toward town to see his family. . . .

I had gone only a short distance toward home when I heard Captain Petty call me to return and I did so. Bud Shirley was with him, just having ridden up . . . and I knew something was up or Bud would never have returned so soon.

"I want you to go to Carthage with me," said Petty. "Bud has learned that there are six militiamen in a house there and we are going to get them. . . ."

He chose eight others besides Shirley and myself and the eleven of us rode into town. The house . . . was several hundred feet southwest of the southwest corner of the square and we reached it without seeing any signs of federals. We dashed up to the house with drawn pistols, Petty in the lead with Shirley on one side of him and me on the other.

A militiaman stepped out of the door as we galloped up, snatched a rifle from beside the door and fired. The bullet struck Captain Petty squarely in the head and he slid from his horse, instantly killed. Both Shirley and I snapped our pistols at his slayer and either of us could have gotten him except that the caps failed to explode. We always had difficulty getting good pistol caps and the bunch we now had were wretched ones. . . .

The militia, aroused by the noise, were now coming out of every door and window. Instead of six there seemed at least thirty-five. . . . There was a lively fusillade for a moment, they firing and we firing and snapping. The shooting was pretty wild . . . the militia being surprised by our sudden attack and we being surprised by their unexpected number. I noticed one soldier by the fence who had just reloaded his rifle and who was trying to put a cap on the nipple. I picked him for mine and pulled the trigger at close range, my revolver again snapping instead of exploding. The soldier . . . slid the cap on the nipple and I whirled my horse, becoming aware for the first time that my comrades were already gone. My enemy fired about this time and hit me in the right arm, the ball passing clear through. As I raced down the road a considerable number of other soldiers blazed away at me but never touched me, and I safely regained camp. Captain Petty was the only man that they had killed and I was the only one wounded. . . . One of the lieutenants took command of our company and when Shelby came through on his raid in October we joined him.[14]

In early August, Companies L and M, Eighth Missouri Cavalry, commanded by Captain Milton J. Burch, took post at Carthage and prepared the courthouse and two other brick buildings for defense. Mount Vernon, Lawrence County, also was garrisoned, and Neosho more strongly fortified because of its proximity to Confederate forces on the Arkansas-Indian Territory border. The stirring event mentioned by Walker began on September 22.

Starting from his base at Arkadelphia, Jo Shelby broke through the Union lines into Missouri. He was joined at Pineville by Colonel J. T. Coffee with four hundred men, including the remnants of Livingston's guerrillas, and the following day captured Neosho and its garrison of three hundred men. Halting only long enough to distribute arms and ammunition, Shelby pushed rapidly northeastward to Jones Creek, where he rested and fed his command. On October 4 he passed through blackened and desolated Sarcoxie, then went on to Bower Mills, which he reported as a "notorious pest spot for the militia . . . sacked and swept from the face of the earth to pollute it no more forever."

Meanwhile, Captain Burch had left Carthage with a detachment of Eighth Cavalry for Turkey Creek, where Union families had reported the presence of about forty guerrillas (probably the remains of Petty's outfit). Burch struck trail at the creek crossing, surprised the guerrillas at a point fifteen miles southwest of Neosho, and chased them four miles, killing ten and capturing two and taking twenty-five horses. Bud Shirley was not among the slain or captured.

Burch started back to Carthage by way of Neosho, but upon being informed by his scout that the place was crawling with Confederates, he abandoned both horses and prisoners, reaching the Jasper County seat the morning of October 5. Major A. A. King with four companies of Sixth Missouri Cavalry had been forced back toward Carthage from a point between Newtonia and Pineville by Shelby's advance. King started toward Newtonia to learn what was going on in that direction and ordered Burch to move his baggage to Mount Vernon and follow the trail taken by the enemy. Within hours after Burch and his troops left Carthage, a column of about five hundred heavily armed and splendidly mounted men passed twelve miles to the west. They were variously clad in uniforms and civilian dress, writes Schrantz, but most wore a peculiar kind of overblouse "cut low in front, the slit narrowing to a point above the belt and ending in a ruffle bunch or rosette"— the article of apparel known as the guerrilla shirt—for "the riders comprised the band of W. C. Quantrill . . . and with him were Bill Anderson, Cole Younger, Frank James, W. H. Gregg, Dave Pool, George Todd, John Jarrette and others" on their

way south and carrying between them "about $2,200 in gold
and silver . . . looted in Lawrence."[15] The band rode quietly
out of Jasper County and on October 6 attacked the fort at
Baxter Springs. They were beaten off, but they surprised and
routed a column of one hundred Third Wisconsin and Four-
teenth Kansas Cavalry escorting General Blunt and a supply
train to the fort. Blunt barely escaped; his adjutant was slain,
and the guerrillas butchered nearly eighty fleeing soldiers.

Quantrill rested in Indian Territory. The Baxter Springs
Massacre and dissension over the Lawrence raid virtually
ended his leadership; his men soon divided into small groups.
Some joined the regular Confederate army, Gregg rising to the
rank of captain in Shelby's brigade. In the latter part of October, Bill Anderson's band made a foray into Jasper County
and burned the Carthage courthouse and two brick buildings
which Burch and his militia had used as a fort and had abandoned temporarily. George Todd obtained command of Quantrill's original raiders, and although Quantrill accompanied
him north in April, 1864, nominally in authority, he accomplished nothing. Quantrill led a few of his followers into Kentucky, where he was wounded, captured and died two days
later.

From Bower Mills, Shelby swept north to the Missouri River,
battling Union militia concentrated at many points to oppose
and pursue him. In heavy action at Marshall, Saline County,
he was cut in two. Part of his force turned off at right angles
and galloped south to save itself from destruction; Shelby
continued west to Waverly, dumped his supply train in the
river to prevent its capture, and fled south. At Carthage on
October 18 he clashed with General Thomas Ewing's Eleventh
Kansas Volunteer Regiment, moved east and then south again
before reaching Sarcoxie, and finally reached the Confederate
lines in Arkansas.

The surrender of Vicksburg in July, 1863, so important to
the war in the West, and the defeat of General Robert E.
Lee's 76,000-man, 190-gun army the same month at Gettys-

burg convinced the outside world that the cause of the South was lost. Nor did the situation hold many bright aspects for Southern sympathizers in Jasper County. Their only hope was that General Sterling Price in Arkansas would regain the state and redeem the Confederacy's fortunes. Most of the guerrillas in western Missouri had gone south with Shelby; Bud Shirley and a few rebel companions were still lurking southeast of Carthage.

The early months of 1864 in Jasper County were relatively quiet. Carthage was occupied by Captain William J. Walker's company of the Seventh Enrolled Militia Regiment; Company C of the same regiment, commanded by Captain Stotts, remained at Cave Springs. Each company was reduced to fifty men. By spring, with the brush in leaf again, the guerrillas began returning from Arkansas and Indian Territory. On the night of April 24, Colonel Jackman and 125 men passed near Carthage, avoiding roads and traveling fast. They committed no hostile act, their purpose being to get to the ground they had chosen for summer operations. However, local bushwhackers began to give the militia trouble. On June 16 a detachment of Third Wisconsin Cavalry from Fort Scott, bringing cattle out of Jasper County for use in the government trains, was attacked by a small force of rebels at Big Fork near Preston. A private was killed, three enemy were wounded, and the cattle were scattered so badly through the timber that they could not be rounded up without great sacrifice.

It is not known whether Bud Shirley participated in this ambush, but he had become one of the most sought-after bushwhackers in the region. Toward the end of June, some troopers from Company C at Cave Springs learned that he and a Sarcoxie youth, Milt Norris, were taking meals in Sarcoxie at the home of a Mrs. Stewart. Mrs. Sarah Musgrave tells what happened:

> While the two men were in Mrs. Stewart's house getting fed, the militia surrounded the house. Both men broke and ran. Shirley was shot as he leaped over the fence and fell dead on the other side.

Norris got a rifle ball . . . as he went over the fence, but was not much hurt and escaped in the brush. . . . Mrs. Stewart's residence [was] not far from my home. I went over and helped take care of the dead body of Shirley. . . .

Norris came to Carthage post haste and told the Shirley family of Bud's death. Next day Shirley's mother and Myra Shirley, the 16-year-old sister of Shirley, appeared at Sarcoxie, the latter with a belt around her waist, from which swung two big revolvers, one on each side. She was not timid in making it known among those she saw that she meant to get revenge for her brother's death. . . .

Next morning the militia returned and burned Mrs. Stewart's home for harboring bushwhackers, and also burned Mrs. Walton's home, nearby, as she had also assisted in entertaining [them].[16]

The popular version among Missouri old-timers has Mrs. Shirley prostrated by the news of Bud's death and Myra accompanying her father to Sarcoxie to claim the body. While curious citizens waited and a squad of soldiers supervising the proceedings glared stonily, John Shirley carried the body from the house and placed it in the wagon. Mrs. Stewart brought out Bud's cap and ball revolver in a belt holster and laid it on the seat beside Myra. John Shirley went to the shed, led out Bud's horse, and hitched it to the tailgate. Myra was fondling the holster and revolver.

"Put down the gun, May!" he said.

"You damned blue-bellies will pay for this!" Myra cried, and snatched the big gun from its scabbard.

The onlookers scattered in panic. John Shirley sprang to the front of the wagon, but before he could reach her, she had the revolver leveled at the troopers, thumbing the hammer rapidly.

The weapon clicked. They had taken the precaution of having the caps removed. Myra sat helplessly in tears, and the soldiers laughed as the wagon rolled off on the road to Carthage.

Some of Belle's biographers accept this version.[17] True or not, the star of the Confederacy was waning. The war in Jasper County turned into nothing more than a succession of bloody reprisals.

On July 21, sixty guerrillas commanded by a former Livingston aide surprised a detachment of Enrolled Militia grazing their horses on the outskirts of Carthage, killed Lieutenant Brice Henry and six men, and took eleven prisoners. Colonel J. D. Allen at Mount Vernon replied in kind. He sent Captain Thomas B. Sutherland, Company D, Seventh Provisional Regiment, with thirty men to reinforce Carthage and sent twenty men to Cave Springs to scout the country. During the last week of July they killed four bushwhackers. On August 2, Captain Ozias Rurark of the Eighth Missouri Cavalry killed the notorious guerrilla Lieutenant J. R. Goode as he and his southern Jasper County and northern Newton County rebels lay in wait for a Federal forage train on Diamond Grove Prairie. Before the summer ended, nearly a score of Jasper County sympathizers had been slain and their homes and barns burned, allegedly by the troops of Captain Sutherland.

On September 19, General Sterling Price and twelve thousand Confederate cavalrymen entered southeast Missouri near Doniphan on his long-heralded but abortive expedition to regain the state. In the confusion and excitement of concentrating Federal forces to drive him back, Carthage again was abandoned; three days later it was sacked and burned by two hundred northbound Rebels who had camped on Jones Creek. McGregor writes: "All that remained of Carthage was less than a dozen dwellings of the poorer sort, all else . . . jail, academy, business houses and dwellings, were destroyed, and the town was a heap of rubbish, exposing to view open cellars, standing chimneys and occasionally part of the brick walls of what had been some of the more pretentious buildings."[18] The fort Captains Walker and Sutherland had reconstructed from the ruins of the courthouse (burned in 1863) was demolished. "All inhabitants . . . who lived to tell the tale of their privations and sufferings [were] compelled to leave the county and seek safety elsewhere," McGregor writes.

John Shirley wasn't around to see his hotel, blacksmith shop, and livery stable reduced to ashes. During the summer, sick at heart over Bud's death and his business ruined by the theft and destruction, he disposed of his property, loaded his family and household goods into two Conestoga wagons, and set out for Texas, where his son Preston and a number of other Missourians had settled and much land was still available. Shirley's destination was Scyene, a small settlement ten miles southeast of Dallas. Myra, a dutiful daughter, drove one of the wagons.

4   Texas

There is no record of the Shirley family's journey to Texas. Rascoe[1] suggests, because the Civil War was still raging in Indian Territory and white intruders were forbidden, that they followed a route through the Ozarks to present DeQueen, Arkansas, then turned west to Dallas and Scyene. Had John Shirley dared to head his ox-drawn wagons west from Fort Smith, Rascoe speculates, he would have followed the Marcy route and crossed the South Canadian River on the Briartown-Eufaula Trail near Whitefield and the cabin of Myra's future father-in-law, Tom Starr, six miles above the ferry. From there he would have turned southeast to Edwards' Trading Post on Little River near present Holdenville, Oklahoma, on the Texas Trail (Road) before heading for the Red River crossing at Preston, where he would have gone almost due south to Dallas. Horan[2] accepts the DeQueen route. Croy[3] prefers having the Shirleys pass "the crookneck in the South Canadian River that Belle made famous as Younger's Bend." Drago[4] thinks they would have gone as far as the South Canadian down the old trail from Sedalia, the railroad terminus for wagon-train trade from southwest Missouri, Kansas, Indian Territory, and Texas, which, despite many Confederate raids, had increased steadily throughout the war.

These writers were considering conditions in Indian Territory a year before the Shirleys left Carthage. When the Shirleys arrived at Fort Smith in the summer of 1864, the resources of the Territory and the energies of its people had been exhausted. Their spirits were as tattered as their clothing and as hungry as their stomachs, and the war had become more of an attempt to control supply depots than land. With Indian refugees already returning to their homes and hundreds of hard-handed settlers with their determined women hauling every possession down the Texas Road toward the Land of Canaan, as Texas was called, it seems more logical that John Shirley struck southwest from Fort Smith along the old Butterfield Overland Mail route, covering 192 miles and a dozen stage stations through the Choctaw and Chickasaw nations, to Geary's on the Texas Road, thence to Boggy Depot, thence south to Nail's Crossing on Blue River, thence to Carriage Point, and on across Red River at Colbert's Ferry near the vice-ridden settlement and trading post of Preston Bend. Here the family was able to replenish supplies and relax, and John Shirley bought his first legal drink since leaving Arkansas.

Introducing whiskey in Indian Territory was a federal offense, but almost nothing was prohibited in Texas. For half a century a sturdy, courageous, yet reckless people had found plenty of space in which to kick up their heels, and to kill a man for refusing a sociable drink was justifiable homicide. Since 1850 the state had become so notorious a refuge for desperate characters and frontier flotsam and jetsam that Gone to Texas was a national byword and the servers of process in other states and territories, unable to find those for whom they held warrants and subpoenas, were wont to initial their returns "G. T. T."

When the Shirleys rolled through it, Dallas had fewer than two thousand residents. Its streets were rivers of mud when it rained and ankle deep in dust during dry spells. With the war boom of the 1860s, it rivaled Austin and San Antonio for wildness and bustling confusion and vied with its sister city Fort Worth as the entertainment capital for cattlemen and *caballeros* who rode in from the plains spoiling for action. Stores, restaurants, saloons, and gambling halls lined Main Street; the southwest part of town was built up mostly with dance halls and brothels. The most pretentious buildings boasted two-story false fronts; wooden sidewalks were roofed over to form galleries, and customers hitched their teams and saddle horses to iron rings on the supporting posts. Myra

Maybelle must have viewed Dallas with interest. She would know the town intimately in years to come.

About a mile east of Scyene above South Mesquite Creek, John Shirley took a fertile piece of land suitable for agricultural crops and stock raising. The family lived in a dugout at first,[5] finally constructing a four-roomed clapboard house, which was something of a mansion in that part of Texas at the time. Other families living in the vicinity and east toward north Mesquite Creek were the Bradfields, the Johnsons, the Whites, the Millers, the Pooles, and the McCommases. Amon McCommas, who preached in the Christian or Campbellite church, had fathered nine children.

Apparently the Shirleys got off to a bad start over their use of the communal water well. Both branches of Mesquite Creek often were dry, and the long haul from the Trinity River made the water problem no trivial matter. In later years two elderly residents told how the Shirleys showed a lack of consideration for their neighbors by dragging their barrels on ground sleds to the well and drawing water until not enough was left for the next fellow. It took some time for the well to fill up again. The informants also considered the family clannish, but this taciturnity might have been attributed to the end of the war because Reconstruction held Texas tight in a carpetbag. There was desperation and fear everywhere, an ambitious program for the Negro, economic instability, and political animosities. With vivid memories of Missouri, the Shirleys kept their mouths shut, which most hearty, back-slapping Texans probably thought unsociable.

Although most of the emigrants, who were from the South, found the flat, black soil excellent for raising cotton, John Shirley used his Texas prairie as he had used the rolling, timbered slopes of the Ozarks: he raised corn for corn pone, roasting ears, and hominy and to feed his oxen and milk cows. He raised hogs for meat, supplementing the family larder with wild game from the creek bottoms. Sorghum cane was grown for sugar and molasses. What cash he needed he got by raising and trading horses and keeping a blooded stud to stand for a fee. As time dragged on, he paid twelve hundred dollars for some lots in Scyene and announced his intention of opening a hotel similar to the one he had operated in Carthage. The plan never materialized.

Meanwhile, Myra attended the one-room community school conducted by Mrs. Poole but came rather irregularly. She was older than most of the pupils. Having mastered the curriculum of a female academy, she looked down on them and, with her scathing tongue and quick temper, was considered wild. At home she did chores and hoed in the garden with sixteen-year-old Edwin Benton, washed dishes, made beds, and helped care for her smaller brothers, Mansfield, now thirteen, and seven-year-old Cravens, whose name the family had changed to John Allison out of respect for the memory of the dead son, Bud. For entertainment Myra visited her cousins (Preston's two children), made frequent rides along Mesquite Creek, and collected news from Missouri.

Dallas newspapers continuously registered vigorous protests against carpetbagger rule and the civil-rights program which had disfranchised not only those who had served in the Confederate forces but also those who could be accused, falsely or otherwise, of having given aid and comfort to the Rebels. The general amnesty proclaimed for all pillagers, arsonists, and murderers among the Federal guerrillas did not apply to Confederate guerrillas. They were subject to arrest for crimes they were accused of committing during the war. Unable to return to peaceful pursuits, many took to stealing cattle and horses, which was fairly easy in Texas and increased with the development of the cattle industry.

There came from Missouri the news that Frank and Jesse James, the Younger brothers, and other former followers of Quantrill and Bill Anderson were riding as a robber band. On the raw, cold morning of February 13, 1866 (not Valentine's Day, as Rascoe[6] and preceding James biographers[7] have it), a dozen armed men rode into Liberty, Missouri, looted the Clay County Savings Association of $15,000 in gold coin, silver, greenbacks, and $45,000 in U.S. bonds, and killed seventeen-year-old George Wymore, a student at William Jewell College, during their indiscriminate firing and wild dash out of town. Several days later, the Wymore family received a note, supposedly from Jesse and Frank James, expressing regret at their son's death and the hope that they would "believe it an accident." The note was never authenticated; however, most Clay County residents were convinced that the James boys and perhaps Cole Younger were among the robbers or had instigated the affair.[8] In any event, it was the first in a long line of bank and train holdups attributed to the Jameses and the Youngers and was a basis for the part of the Belle Starr story so hotly contested by writers.

The robbers divided only the silver and greenbacks; the U.S. bonds, which were not negotiable, were thrown away. The gold, says Rascoe,[9] was incriminating evidence against the possessor (few people used gold for money), and so six of the gang rode three hundred miles to San Antonio, Texas, where a Mexican broker named Gonzales accepted it for currency at 40 percent discount, no questions asked. On their return north in July, 1866, the gang (Rascoe names five of them as Cole, Jim, John, and Bob Younger and Jesse James) stopped at Scyene for a night's lodging with the Shirleys, whom Cole had known in Missouri.

Rascoe[10] finds "no way of verifying how long the Youngers stayed at Scyene or what they actually did there" but valiantly provides in fictional detail a love affair between Cole and Myra Maybelle; two months after Cole rode on, Myra confided to her shocked parents that she was carrying a child "born into the world bearing the name Pearl Younger." Rascoe[11] offers as evidence (1) the insistence of "old-timers of Haskell, Mac-Intosh [sic], Muskogee and Latimer Counties," Oklahoma, that Belle's first child was Cole's daughter and Cole her first "husband," and (2) the "only authenticated interview" she ever gave, published in the Fort Smith Elevator of April 30, 1886, in which "Belle said that the first man she ever fell in love with and the first man she married was 'a noted guerrilla,' but she didn't give his name." Here is the *Elevator* reference:

> When less than 15 years of age she fell in love with one of the dashing guerrillas, whose name she said it was not necessary for her to give.

The "dashing guerrilla" was Jim Reed, which even the Fox writer and Harman acknowledge.

However, Rascoe[12] persists, citing other fabrications, such as Belle's secretly supplying funds for Cole's legal defense when he was captured after the disastrous bank robbery attempt at Northfield, Minnesota, on September 7, 1876; her "unremitting efforts" to secure his pardon after his incarceration at Stillwater Prison; and her "sentimental memory of Cole Younger all her life." Rascoe[13] claims as a "clue to the enigma" the "equivocal statement" of Cole Younger in prison when a St. Paul reporter brought him word of Belle's death and newspaper allegations that she once was married to him: "I have never been married, so it can't be true. I knew the lady slightly some years ago, but it has been many years since I have seen her." Cole being "a religious and extremely conventional man," Rascoe[14] concludes, he would not have disclosed any intimacy with any woman, especially one "just murdered who had two living children." Finally, Rascoe[15] admits that his "Myra Belle Shirley's first sweetheart" contribution is "pure conjecture, but which may, in time, become part of the folk legends about 'The Bandit Queen.'" He predicted well.

Horan[16] decides that "Belle never had a chance" with the handsome, personable Cole. He wooed her in the moonlight and left her pregnant.

Croy[17] outstrips Rascoe with an absurd depiction of the gang arriving at the Shirley farm, staying two days, and Cole returning to woo Belle; of their rides together; of Cole's "mysterious trips . . . up No'th" for more money to "fling around" Dallas gambling houses; and of the birth in the Shirley home in 1869 of a child named Pearl Younger. Cole comes to live with the

Shirleys; they try to break up the romance, and he goes to Dallas, where he wounds a man in a gunfight and leaves the country after arranging for Belle and the child to stay in a Texas town until he can send for them. Belle's father tricks her into returning home through the faked illness of her mother, confines her to an upstairs room, and threatens to take the child if she tries to escape to Missouri with money Cole has given her. To free herself from this semi-imprisonment," she agrees to go to school in an adjoining county; here Cole rescues her "before the staring, incredulous students," and they go "flying away" to a "carefree life" with the most deadly band of outlaws in the United States. This story would have delighted a *Police Gazette* editor.

Wellman[18] thinks the seduction "not very difficult, for Cole was good to look upon," and says Pearl was born in 1867 when Myra "had passed her nineteenth birthday."

Hicks's[19] account of "Belle Starr and Her First Love" surpasses Rascoe and Croy in absurdity and ludicrousness. Belle and Cole ride in and out of Dallas and dash about the Shirley farm, Cole unable to beat or even equal her equestrian skill. Belle learns to "knock over a prairie dog" and other targets at a reasonable distance with one of Cole's .45s, which pleases him so much "he made her a present of a fine six-shooter." They rehash the war, the killing of her brother *Ed*, joke about the Liberty robbery, and lounge in mesquite groves. Cole reads to her from a Bible dug from his saddlebag and the next moment, imbued with her "dash and go," makes love. One morning Belle disappears from the farm with Cole and the gang that had come to Scyene. Months pass before John Shirley receives a letter; Belle appears "none too happy." John tricks her into returning home with the lie about her mother's illness. Belle shows no resentment; she has broken with Cole because he began treating her like a prostitute and didn't want a pregnant woman following him. Finally, "one day in 1867, Belle's child was born . . . to whom she gave the name, Pearl Younger.

These concoctions apparently led Robert Elman[20] to assume that Myra "in 1866 . . . had a brief love affair with Cole, resulting in an illegitimate daughter," which "scandalized the family," and they were the source for Peter Lyon's[21] outburst: "When Cole Younger . . . hid out in Texas . . . who should he find down there . . . but li'l ole Myra Belle Shirley! . . . before long she was the mother of his bastard, a girl she named Pearl Younger."

Mooney[22] offers this "new revelation": Pearl acknowledged (at the funeral of her brother, of all places) that her mother told her Cole was her "real Pa" and gave a sordid, blow-by-blow description of the week-long orgy and the trysting place where she was conceived.

These writers ignore Cole Younger's autobiography,[23] in which he denies the romance. Cole's mention of Myra's having "two or three brothers smaller" at the time he visited the Shirleys near Scyene in 1864 (not 1866) lends credence to his knowledge of the family, for the federal census records confirm two younger children not mentioned elsewhere. Cole also is correct about Myra's marriage to Jim Reed and that she was at the home of Reed's mother in Bates County, Missouri, when he next saw her in 1868, six months pregnant.

The questions to be settled at this point are when and where Myra and Jim were married and whether Reed fathered her first child. The Fox opus places the marriage

in a bend at East Fork [later designation of North Mesquite Creek] one Sunday morning in July, 1867. It was a runaway match and the bride and bridegroom were on horseback while the ceremony was performed, John Fischer, the desperado, holding both horses. Scarce three weeks had elapsed when Jim Read was declared an outlaw by the State of Texas and a large reward was offered for his arrest, so he flew to his native State and remained in concealment for some time. Myra returned to her father's house, and, yielding to the advice of her parents, consented to go to school close to Weatherford . . . where cousins of her own name resided.[24]

Fox's writer was aware that, during the preceding winter, Preston Shirley had moved his family west into the broad valleys of Parker County on the Clear Fork of the Trinity.

It was not long, the Fox opus[25] continues, before Reed returned to Texas and went into hiding "a few minutes walk from the schoolhouse." Fearing that she was being watched and her husband's retreat would be discovered, Myra did not join him but instead

sent a letter stating that she would be ready to elope any night he fixed upon. . . . Read arrived beneath her window with an extra horse in readiness, which she soon mounted, having climbed through a window . . . without disturbing the family. The pair travelled . . . to Carthage, Missouri, on horseback. It was upon reaching the old State that our heroine first formed the acquaintance of the Younger brothers, Cole, Bob, and their cousin Bruce. . . . The Youngers, especially Bruce, were much smitten with her. Her horsemanship was perfect, and not one of the gang could excell her with the pistol. Of the two years campaign in her native State, Bella has little to say in her journal of May 30, 1870. Early in the month she had given birth to a daughter, now known to the press by the name of Pearl Younger.

Harman's[26] version is that Reed served in the Confederate army, in Company B of Sidney G. Jackson's famed Sixteenth Cavalry, after Quantrill's forces broke up and that Reed, with some of his former comrades, visited their old sympathizer friend John Shirley in 1866:

It was a pleasant reunion and Belle assisted her father in supplying their guests with every luxury. When they departed they were accompanied by Belle. Jim Reed had failed to gain the consent of Judge Shirley to the request for his daughter's hand . . . and the pair were married on horseback, in the presence of twenty of his companions. The horse upon which the girl sat was of high mettle and was held, while the ceremony was performed by John Fisher, afterwards a noted outlaw. Soon after this Reed found it necessary to leave the country . . . and Judge Shirley sent his daughter to school in Parker County [where] the young husband again stole his bride and bore her away to his father's home in Missouri. . . . In September, 1869, Belle became the mother of a beautiful baby girl. Belle idolized her and named her "Pearl," though the baby's grand parents and uncles always insisted on calling her "Rosie."

As has been noted, the Reeds were well-known, prosperous

people. Toward the end of the war, they returned to their home southwest of Rich Hill. Solomon Reed died in 1865, and his widow, Susan, with sons Jim, F. M., Scott, and all the younger children, went to Texas, near McKinney, where a couple of relatives were living. On December 3, 1866, Enoch Yeates, administrator of the estate, swore an affidavit that the

names and places of residence of the heirs of Sol. Reed, decd., are respectively as follows: Susan Reed, widow of said, descendants Francis M. Reed, Wm. Scott Reed, Talitha L. Huse, Sarah F. Reed, Jasper Columbus Reed, Solomon L. Reed, Amanda J. Reed, Geo. R. Reed, James C. Reed, Richard Reed, Minerva A. Reed who reside in the County of Colin [Collin] in the State of Texas and Margaret Ann Brock who resides in the State of Tennessee.[27]

In Texas the Reeds and Shirleys renewed old friendships, especially Jim and Myra. Jim was no wanted man, only a disfranchised former Confederate guerrilla, which was considered an honor in Southern-dominated Dallas County. If John and Eliza Shirley had any objections to their daughter's choice for a husband, there is no record of it. Myra was eighteen and Jim was twenty when they were married by the Reverend S. M. Wilkins in Collin County on November 1, 1866.[28]

After embarking upon the sea of matrimony, Jim Reed moved into the Shirley ménage, helping with the hog raising and stud farm. For a time in 1867 he was a salesman for a saddle and bridle maker in Dallas and expressed his intention to acquire a piece of land near Scyene and raise horses and cattle. It is possible that his father-in-law agreed to raise the needed money; the following advertisement appeared in the September 21, 1867, *Dallas Weekly Herald:* "Six yoke of first class oxen and a No. 1 wagon may be had on reasonable terms by applying to John Shirley, Scyene."

The land deal did not materialize. By the end of the year, Susan Reed and her brood were back in Missouri and Jim was farming with his brothers. Myra accompanied her husband to the parental roof in Bates County at Rich Hill, and when John Shirley next heard from his daughter, he was about to become

James C. ("Jim") Reed, Belle's first husband, slain by Deputy Sheriff John T. Morris northwest of Paris, Texas, on August 6, 1874.

a grandfather. Early in September, 1868, Myra gave birth to Rosie Lee.[29] She idolized the child and referred to her as her pearl; thus Rosie Lee became known by her nickname, as history relates.

Myra Maybelle Shirley, the future Belle Starr, about the time of her marriage to James C. Reed in 1866.

Soon after Rosie Lee's birth, Myra's brother, Edwin Benton, was slain by Texas officers. The Fox opus says "summer of 1867" and attributes the "unfortunate tragedy" to Edwin's "natural recklessness":

Marriage license issued to Myra Maybelle Shirley and James C. Reed in
Collin County, Texas, November 1, 1866.

Thrown as he was among the members of the old Missourian
families . . . he partook of the turbulent spirit of his associates. To
ride at random through the country, visit the frontier towns and dis-
charge pistols in public was part of the programme. . . . A writ was
soon issued for his arrest and that of his associates [and placed in
the hands of] Joe Lynn, a deputy marshal. . . . Determined to resist
its service, they barricaded themselves in an old log hut close to the
highway on the banks of Spring Creek.[30]

Fox's writer then quotes "Bella's journal";

The boys had been three days in the cabin . . . their provisions
were exhausted . . . I carried them a quantity of bread and meat.
. . . Before twenty minutes had passed we heard the tramp of horses
and saw four armed men approaching; it was Lynn and his posse.

They rode around to the rear of the old house where there was a
frameless window, and called to the boys to come out. My brother
put his head to the window and said, "Never, by G—; I will die
right here!"

. . . One of the posse jerked his pistol and fired into the room,
the ball whistling close to my face and striking one of the boys in
the shoulder. Ed grasped his gun and discharged a random shot
through the window. He was standing right in the line of fire. . . .
Seeing his danger I threw my arms around his body with hope of
drawing him aside. It was too late. A ball struck him in the temple,
and the blood spattered me in the eyes and all over the face. I fell,
sinking with the burden of a dead brother in my arms. Oh! God! the
anguish of that hour, the scalding tears, and the first terrible thirst
for revenge! Without further opposition the cabin was taken by the
posse. Lynn would not enter. He stood at the door, and grew deadly
pallid when he saw me rise to my knees and heard me swear an oath
of vengeance over the body of my murdered brother.

Later in the opus,[31] Myra's oath of vengeance against Lynn
is carried out. Rascoe[32] and Hicks[33] say the cause of Shirley's
death is unknown; Drago[34] and Mooney[35] say he was "killed
in, or after, a quarrel with a man named Lynn"; they accept
the year 1867 and name Preston, not Edwin, as the victim.

Lynn is a fictional character. The *Dallas News* states: "Ed
Shirley, a noted horsethief, was shot off his horse near Dallas
in 1868."[36] This is consistent with the census records of 1870;
on October 8, the census taker enumerated only John and Eliza
Shirley and two children: Mansfield, age seventeen, and John
A. (Cravens), age 12,[37] whom the family called "Sugar" or
"Shug."

Myra was still in Missouri, but it is probable she returned
to Texas for a brief interval to see Edwin laid to rest in a now
unmarked grave in the old Scyene cemetery. It was John and
Eliza Shirley's first opportunity to become acquainted with
their new granddaughter.

The next several months (when most Belle Starr biographers
have her roistering in gambling houses, playing a piano in
dance halls, and dashing about Dallas on a fiery black steed)
Myra spent in Bates County, Missouri, with Mother Reed.
An aged resident, Mrs. Gertrude Higgins—a young girl at the

Tom Starr, Belle Starr's second father-in-law.

time—recalled attending Bethel Baptist Church with Myra; it was near Reed's Creek at Rich Hill. Myra always came on horseback, riding sidesaddle, with her child in her arms. Impressing Mrs. Higgins most was Myra's devotion to her daughter and the fine clothes she provided for her. Even during the sermon Myra would look at her little girl instead of the preacher.

Jim Reed was seldom at home; farming had never appealed to him. He raced horses on the tracks at Fort Smith, Arkansas, gambled some, and spent a great deal of time at Tom Starr's stronghold in Indian Territory seventy-some miles west of Fort Smith. Reed had become acquainted with this patriarch of the Starr clan of Cherokees while Cole Younger and Frank James were making his place a retreat after the breakup of Quantrill's forces.

Tom Starr was fifty-five years old. He stood six feet, five inches tall, straight, with great muscular strength to match, and wore size 13 boots. His eyes, generally with lashes plucked, were steel gray, showing mixed blood, and could pierce the darkness of night. His shoulder-length black hair was combed straight back from a broad forehead beneath a weatherbeaten felt hat that he wore almost constantly with the brim turned up from the face. Sometimes he donned a red fur cap with a tail hanging down the back. His favorite item of attire was a long homespun hunting jacket woven in stripes of red, gray, and black with red fur trim, made for him by his wife, Catherine. Usually he wore rough clothes, enhanced by a rawhide necklace studded with the dried earlobes of men he had killed, and he had a habit of smiling when engaged in some particularly murderous activity. His robberies, butchery, and house burnings were a source of embarrassment to the proud Cherokee Nation,[38] and "people in towns and around [said they] had rather meet the devil himself than Tom Starr."[39] Let us mark him well, for he and one of his sons, Sam Starr, were to figure prominently in Myra Maybelle's future role as Bandit Queen.

5   Tom Starr and Youngers' Bend

The Starrs were in one of the early bands of Eastern Cherokees who emigrated west on their own resources in 1836 and
1837 to join their Western or Old Settler brethren in Indian
Territory rather than be driven there forcibly by U.S. troops
over the Trail of Tears. The family located in the Flint District
of the Cherokee Nation west of Evansville Arkansas. James
Starr, Tom's father, was a political figure and statesman of the
Old Nation in Tennessee and Georgia and was one of the
signers of the Removal Treaty of 1835 along with such Indian
leaders as Major Ridge, his son John Ridge, Elias Boudinot,
and his brother Stand Watie.[1]

Although these men believed it best for their people to sub-
mit to the wishes of the federal government and prevent a
war of extermination in the States, they had neither council
authority nor the blessing of a tribal majority and knew that
they were running a dreadful risk of the death penalty de-
creed by Cherokee law for any member of the tribe agreeing
to a land-cession treaty.[2] When the main body of Eastern
Cherokees under Chief John Ross arrived in the territory in
1838, the tribe divided into two hostile camps: those who had
favored removal, called the Treaty or Ridge party, and those
who opposed it, led by Ross. There were also two governments,
which Ross determined to meld into one with himself in control.[3] The Ridge party people allied themselves with the Western chiefs and Old Settlers, who did not consider the treaty
signers criminals, and the dispute erupted in bitter, tragic civil
strife.[4]

Fulfilling of the old blood law was long overdue. On June
22, 1839, Major Ridge, his son John, and Elias Boudinot were
assassinated by secret posses made up of Ross henchmen.[5]

James Starr and Stand Watie were marked for death on the same day but received warnings in time to escape. James Starr and a number of prominent Ridge party members took temporary refuge at Fort Gibson. Watie, heedless of danger, took to the field with sixty warriors to search in vain for the assassins. Some time later he fought and killed James Foreman, a Ross favorite, who had boasted of bushwhacking Major Ridge.[6]

The Ross Council reacted by collecting eight hundred men, patently to do scout duty and preserve the peace but actually bent on putting down resistance wherever they could find it. Watie had disbanded his warriors; alarmed by such a large group abroad, he reassembled them at old Fort Wayne and laid in a store of provisions in event of an all-out attack. There was no attack, but there were several outbreaks and skirmishes along the Arkansas border in which eleven men were killed and eighteen wounded. In other action, Lewis Rogers, son of a former chief of the Old Settlers, was slain as he was leaving their council at Fort Gibson, and another treaty signer, John Fields, was killed at Cowskin Prairie, Delaware District, by Ross culprits.[7] It was only a matter of time and place until others would be murdered.

James Starr sought safety at Fort Gibson on many occasions. The attempts on his life aroused the slumbering fire in the hearts of relatives and friends, particularly his sons, Tom, Washington, Ellis, and Bean Starr, and a cousin, Suel Rider, who decided to take the offensive. On September 15, 1843, after killing a Ross spy named Kelly, Tom, Ellis, and Bean Starr and Arch Sanders murdered Benjamin Vore (a Ross man and licensed trader), his wife, and a stranger who was stopping for the night at their house on the Military Road thirty miles from Fort Gibson. After looting the residence, the gang set fire to the premises and bodies of the victims.[8] R. P. Vann, a prominent Cherokee settler, related in an interview with Grant Foreman that he had once talked to Tom Starr about the Vore tragedy. Vann said Starr told him that while the house was burning "a little boy about five years old came running out and begged him not to kill him, and Tom . . . just picked him up and threw him in the fire. He said he didn't think God would ever forgive him for that and I said I didn't think He would either."[9]

The Ross Council authorized a reward of one thousand dollars each for the apprehension of the "Starr boys"; the gang escaped into Arkansas. A few weeks later, while making their way to the Texas border with ten horses and mules stolen from Ross sympathizers, they were overtaken by a company of police twenty-five miles above Fort Washita. A fight ensued; Bean Starr was slain, and the stolen animals were recovered.[10] Charles Smith, a member of the gang, later stabbed to death John M. Brown, a lieutenant in the police company, who had killed his friend Bean. Charles was the son of Archillah Smith, a treaty signer executed by the Ross government on January 1, 1841. Young Smith was hunted down and slain by a party of "fifteen or twenty" officers who claimed he seized a gun and resisted when they undertook to arrest him.[11]

On November 2, 1845, the home of Ross's son-in-law, Return Jonathan Meigs, near Park Hill, was plundered and burned by a party of disguised bandits. Two Indians who witnessed the deed were found murdered in the neighborhood two days later. Meigs identified the bandits as Tom Starr, Washington Starr, Ellis Starr, Suel Rider, and Ellis West.[12]

The Ross Council decided that "James Starr was, or must be, cognizant of the alleged acts of his sons . . . obviously designed to exhibit their contempt for the Ross government." On November 9, thirty-two Ross adherents, armed and in war paint, descended upon Starr's house in the Flint District. This time James Starr had no warning. He was on the front porch, washing his face for breakfast, when the party "riddled his body with bullets." His crippled fourteen-year-old son Buck, who was standing nearby, made a valiant effort to flee and was gunned down by the assassins. Three smaller sons, the eldest eleven, were about the place. The raiders shouted, "We are going to kill all the male members of this house!" They attempted to shoot the three boys, but the mother wrapped her skirts around the two youngest, while the grandmother hugged the eldest tightly to her bosom. When it became apparent they would have to kill the women in order to kill the boys, the raiders mounted their horses and dashed away. They then proceeded a half-mile to the home of Suel Rider and shot him down in his yard. As he lay on the ground mortally wounded, an Indian named Stan jumped from his horse and plunged a knife into his heart. A short distance farther they encountered Washington Starr on the road and opened fire on him. Washington was desperately wounded but managed to escape.[13]

Tom Starr lived within two miles of his father's house. Creek Starr, one of the younger boys, ran through the woods to convey the news of their father's death. Only the women of the family dared attend the funeral. About a month later, Buck died of his wounds and Tom Starr vowed to his wife: "I will get every man who killed Buck and pa. I will not stop killing until I do, and I will never be taken alive." The Indian, Stan, soon was rounded up by the Starr boys and stabbed to death in the same manner in which he had slain Suel Rider. One authority estimates that Tom and his followers took the lives of "no less than twenty persons" during this period of retaliatory bloodletting.[14] William H. Balentine, a neighbor who knew Tom well and visited with him often in later years, wrote historian Grant Foreman from Tahlequah on September 25, 1933: "Once when I was talking to him he said, 'You know there was thirty-two men that slipped up and killed my daddy, well I got most of them except a few that got sick and died in bed before I could get to them.'—that was his idea of justice."[15]

In 1846 a truce was called between the Cherokee factions. Stand Watie did not ally his force with the Starr gang but stood his ground at Fort Wayne as protector of the Old Settlers and leader of the Ridge party until compelled to leave by federal troops; then he departed for Washington to join a delegation of his partisans.

President James K. Polk suggested that since the Cherokees could not settle their difficulties it might be best to divide their nation into three separate territories and governments, so such a bill was introduced in the House of Representatives by a member of the House Committee on Indian Affairs. Chief Ross was dismayed and urged all possible opposition against it. President Polk gave him an ultimatum, and Ross made sufficient concessions to effect a peace agreement with the Ridge party and the Old Settlers. On August 14 the three delegations met in the office of the Commissioner of Indian Affairs and officially approved the treaty ratified by the Senate. The validity of the Removal Treaty of 1835 finally, and for the first time, was recognized and the Cherokee Nation was reunited, with John Ross as principal chief. Ross and Stand Watie shook hands in the presence of President Polk—"a concession on the part of both"—and assured the president that all the old animosities were "forgotten and forgiven."[16]

Under the peace document, no further party distinctions were to be countenanced except as necessary for its execution. The laws of the Cherokee Nation were to provide the right to assemble and petition; jury trials were to be guaranteed; all military organizations, including the Ross police, were to be disbanded and only civil authority was to enforce the law and furnish equal protection to all. A special clause provided that "all offences and crimes committed by a citizen of the Cherokee Nation . . . are hereby pardoned." This provision, reported the *Cherokee Advocate* of February 4, 1847, was "aimed at the pardon of the Starrs, particularly Tom Starr," and historians agree.[17] H. F. and E. S. O'Beirne note: "Rarely has a government or a nation been forced to the extremity of entering into a treaty of peace with one of its own subjects."[18]

Tom Starr moved to the far-southwestern Canadian District west of the Arkansas River near present Briartown in Musko-

gee County. Despite the amnesty, he still considered Ross
Cherokees legitimate prey on all occasions. When the Civil
War began, he went with the Confederacy, serving as a scout
for General Watie's Indian Brigade in carrying the fight against
the devilish Pin Indians,[19] who followed John Ross, and the
Federal forces that overran the Cherokee Nation in 1862. Tom
had showed Quantrill, who was his guest several times, a trick
or two.

After the war, Tom conducted a lively business in whiskey,
cattle, and horse thievery. He became firmly entrenched in a
wild, remote domain on the South Canadian, surrounded by
his eight sons, Sam, Ellis, Cooper, Molsie, Tulsie, William,
Jack, and Washington; his two daughters; and all their in-laws
and cousins, the Toneys, Phillipses, McClures, Mabrys, and
Wests, who were his bodyguards and intelligence service. Former Quantrill guerrillas and new outlaws of the Reconstruction disorder found his place a haven. Cole Younger used
Tom's ranch so often during the war and on trips to and from
Texas with his brothers afterward that old Tom named the
great crookneck in the river Youngers' Bend in their honor,
long before the country heard of Belle Starr.[20]

Jim Reed undoubtedly participated in some of the Starr
gang's looting excursions during 1868 and early 1869, in which
stolen cattle and horses were driven south through the rugged
San Bois country of the Choctaw Nation to Texas markets
below Red River or sold to white fences around Tom's former
stomping grounds at Evansville, Arkansas. Belle Starr biographers have Jim meeting Myra in secluded places outside
Rich Hill, away from the prying eyes of neighbors and local
officials, where she counted the loot he brought each trip and
thrilled to his tales of Tom Starr's escapades.

Rascoe[21] concludes from the "many connecting threads of
the James–Younger–Belle Starr narratives" that Reed was "James
White," who rode with the James-Younger outlaws during this
period. On October 30, 1866, the gang robbed the banking
house of Alexander Mitchell and Company at Lexington, Mis-

souri, of two thousand dollars and on March 2, 1867, took the banking office of Judge William McClain, the financial stronghold of Savannah. At Richmond on May 23, 1867, they took four thousand dollars from the Hughes and Mason bank, then rode over into Kentucky, where they entered the Southern Bank of the quiet little Logan County community of Russellville on March 20, 1868, and galloped off with fourteen thousand dollars.

James-Younger biographers consistently have James White participating in these robberies and include White's brother, John, in the Richmond affair. Warrants were issued for both, but a Missouri justice of the peace acquitted them for lack of evidence. James White was a different man entirely. On October 30, 1866, the date of the Lexington robbery, Jim Reed was obtaining his marriage license in Collin County, Texas. Reed may have been invited to join in the Russellville raid of 1868. William H. Balentine stated in an interview with Carolyn Thomas Foreman:

> Right after the Civil War, Jesse and Frank James came in the Younger's Bend country . . . after a while Cole Younger and his brothers joined them and they stayed around the Starr home. . . . When they planned to rob the bank at Northfield, Minnesota, they came to get Jim Reed to go with them. He was married to Belle then . . . and she wouldn't let him go. . . . they didn't know the people or the country.[22]

Balentine probably meant Russellville, which coincides with the time mentioned. The Northfield fiasco occurred nearly eight years later.

6   Flight to California

Whatever connection Reed had with the Starr and James-Younger gangs, he did not become a fugitive until 1869. A year after Pearl's birth, according to Harman, he

killed the slayer of his brother . . . the outcome of the attempt by three brothers named Shannon to murder a man named Fisher, at a point in Indian Territory only a few miles from Fort Smith. By chance Scott Reed passed where the brothers were in ambush and was mistaken by them for Fisher.[1]

After avenging Scott's death, Jim returned to Missouri for Myra and little Pearl, "accompanied by a young man whom Belle had never seen." The young man, legend has it, was Tom Starr's son, Sam, then about twelve years old. "Not daring to remain in Missouri," Harman continues, Reed "at once left, taking wife and child with him and in the course of time landed in Los Angeles."[2]

"Flossie" says:

It was customary for the boys in a neighborhood to train a horse and take it to the county fairs. James Reed and some Shannon boys took a horse to the races in Fort Smith. A dispute arose with the Fisher boys as to which horse really won . . . in the quarrel that followed . . . Scott Reed was shot by mistake. James Reed took the law into his own hands and killed Scott's slayer.[3]

She does not say whether Jim killed a Shannon or a Fisher but adds:

The quarrel almost assumed the proportion of a neighborhood feud. His friends slipped James Reed away to Tom Starr's place . . . feeling insecure even in Indian Territory, he fled to California and settled in Los Angeles. James went across country on horseback and Myra and her baby made the trip by stage coach.

Rascoe[4] identifies the Shannon boys' feudist enemy as "John Fischer," who "married" Jim and Belle on horseback, claims that Harman borrowed his "pretty story" from Fox's writer, and points to the "hiatus" in the following newspaper interview that Francis M. Reed of Metz, Missouri, gave reporters who were seeking information about Belle after her death:

In 1868, brother Scott was assassinated by some Shannon boys, between whom and a family of Fischers there had previously been some killing done. Brother Jim went immediately to this scene of Scott's murder and allied himself with the Fischers and participated in the killing of two of the Shannons in retaliation. After this, the Arkansas officials hunted him until he moved to California.

Rascoe has Jim Reed fleeing to California with a price on his head after chalking up two murders instead of one.[5]

U.S. District Court records show that during his trips with the Starrs to Evansville, Arkansas, Reed became associated with an outlaw band led by John K. Fisher. The gang consisted of Fisher, Calvin Carter, Charles Bush, and James Black—"Black" being an alias, along with "Jones" and "Miller," which Reed used later—and engaged in bootlegging and stock thievery in Indian Territory, apparently in competition with the Shannon brothers. On February 12, 1869, Finnis M. Shannon swore a writ against Fisher, Carter, Bush, and Black for introducing spirituous liquors into the Indian country,[6] a crime for which Shannon had been arrested many times by Fort Smith federal marshals. In response to this capias, Deputy Marshal B. F. Little "proceeded to the Indian Nation" with a posse of four men and "was gone in constant and active search for thirty-six days" without finding his quarry.[7]

Two letters giving somewhat conflicting details of later developments between the factions were published by the *Fort Smith Weekly Herald*. The first, under the pseudonym of an Evansville citizen, appeared on June 12:

Editors *Herald*
I see an account of the murder of Fitzwater and Stout of this

place . . . calculated to leave a false impression in the minds of the
public, in regard to that affair [the slaying of Scott Reed and the
killing, on June 2, of two men named Fitzwater and Stout].

I would not have you suppose, for a moment that I would desire
to exonerate the Fishers from blame in this matter, but desperate
men as they are, it is but justice that they should be truly represented. The facts are these: The Fisher and Shannon parties were in
the habit of gambling with each other. On one occasion, Maj. Fisher
won a horse of one of the Shannon's, and afterward learned that the
horse was not, nor never had been the property of Shannon. They
subsequently met in a drinking saloon and an altercation ensued.
Pending the altercation and while Fisher was leaning on the counter,
Finnis Shannon, a brother to the one engaged in the quarrel, stepped
in the door, and without exchanging a word with Fisher, shot him.
A few days afterward some of the Fisher party were going up the
street and the Shannon party fired upon them from an old stable,
killing a young man by the name of Reed. Shortly after this the
Fisher boys killed Dr. McKinney, after which they left the country.
During their absence the Shannons have been driving peaceable citizens out of town by threatening their lives, on account of their supposed friendship with the Fishers and by their insults and threats
they compelled the Misses Fisher to leave Evansville and seek a home
in the Cherokee Nation; and, when the young ladies visited town to
make purchases, they were insulted by the Shannons; Fitzwater one
of the party, taking a particular interest in this amusement.

A short time since the Fishers returned on a visit, to their sisters,
and I have been credibly informed, to take them out of the country
—they heard of the treatment the young ladies had received and
determined to have revenge. They came to Evansville, on the 2nd
inst., and learned that the Shannon party were armed, and stationed
at a house in the suburbs; that they knew of their return and that
Fitzwater and Stout were in town, acting as pickets to carry the information of their arrival, that the Shannons might attack and kill
them. They also learned that Shannon had offered five hundred dollars cash and five hundred dollars worth of personal property to any
one that would kill them. In a short time they saw Fitzwater and
Stout coming down the street and peeping into the house where they
were visiting, and they fired upon them killing Fitzwater and in-
flicting wounds on Stout of which he died the following day.

It is truly a deplorable state of affairs; and instead of the indica-
tions for any improvement being flattering, it is very probably that
while the two parties live, we will be in a state of excitement and

trouble. I know I speak the feelings of a majority of the citizens of this portion of the country when I say we would be glad if the Shannons would leave our midst, as we consider the Fishers the better of the two parties.

I am, gentlemen, yours truly
ADON WERT

The *Herald* of June 26 carried Finnis M. Shannon's rebuttal:

Editors, Fort Smith *Herald*

Dear Sirs: I see a communication from Evansville in your paper of the 12th instant headed "The Evansville Murders," signed "Adonwert," in which communication I feel myself and friends aggrieved and slandered. . . . The account of difficulty referred to in that communication is, I assert, wholly a misinterpretation and a falsehood.

It will be remembered that on the 26th of December last, I killed J. M. Fisher, for which deed the law justified me. Then on the 21st of January, John K. Fisher, without cause or provocation, wilfully murdered Dr. McKinney, my father-in-law; the same evening, fired into a posse of citizens who was endeavoring to arrest them [the Fisher gang], wounding Samuel Alberty, an aged citizen, killing a horse, and again the same evening, fired upon myself and John Finley, while in George Washington's dwelling, wounding Finley in the head—fired some 30 or 40 shots into the house; Washington and family were all present at the time—they being concealed in fence corners and behind trees. Then again on the 3d of February they came into Evansville, five in number, viz: John Fisher, Calvin Carter, C. Bush, W. S. Reed, and Charlie Roberts, late from the Van Buren jail, swearing to hold Evansville at all hazards, and bidding defiance to all process of law or justice either civil or military, when Sheriff Little, together with a posse of citizens, came upon them, and some 150 shots were fired by the two parties and W. S. Reed was killed, in openly aiding and defending an outlaw and a murderer. Fisher and his colleague then abandoned the country until recently.

The circumstances of the late murder is as follows: Fisher and colleague came in and concealed themselves in an old crib during the night-time, and on the morning of the 2d inst., N. C. Fitzwater and Stout were passing down the street on the opposite side, when Fisher and party fired upon them, killing Fitzwater dead and wounding Stout, who died on the 4th inst. Fitzwater was struck in twenty-one places, and Stout in six different places, with shot and balls. The murderers then hastened across the Cherokee line, whooping and swearing after crossing the line that they were at home. No person in the village seems to have known anything of their presence whatever, until their dark deed was committed. All the above facts will be sworn to by every respectable citizen in Evansville.

Furthermore, I proposed to pay a reward of $500 in money and $500 in good horse property for the arrest of John K. Fisher, Calvin Carter and C. Bush, and I still offer the same, dead or alive.

Respectfully,
F. M. SHANNON

Although these letters leave many questions unanswered, Jim Reed obviously did not kill two Shannon brothers. Neither is he linked to the January slaying of Shannon's father-in-law, nor listed present during the February street battle in which Scott was slain, nor included among the Fisher gang members for whom Shannon offered a reward. However, it appears that Shannon soon learned he was one of the assassins of Fitzwater and Stout (the "two Shannon boys" referred to by Francis M. Reed), and this, coupled with the federal writ for introducing whiskey into Indian Territory, caused Jim to seek less-hazardous climes, taking with him Myra and Pearl.

How Reed earned a living on the Pacific Coast is conjecture. Author Scott[8] says he was soon "working steady" in a Los Angeles gambling house; nobody was interested in where he and Myra came from or "in looking up their family tree." Rascoe[9] feels "safe to guess"—and Hicks[10] agrees—that Reed was operating with Frank and Jesse James and the Younger brothers, Cole, Jim, and Bob, "named as participants in a stage robbery near San Diego." On the contrary, Jesse and Frank completed their visit to their uncle Drury Woodson James' Hot Sulphur Springs spa at Paso Robles—where they spent the summer of 1869 allegedly recuperating from old wounds received during the war—and were returning on horseback to Missouri about the time the Reeds arrived in Los Angeles.[11] That the Youngers were with the James boys in California in 1869 is emphatically denied in Cole's autobiography:

In the fall of 1868 Jim and Bob went with me to Texas. Mother's health had failed perceptibly, the result in a large measure of her exposure at the time the militia forced her to burn her house, and we sought to make her home in a milder climate in the southwest. The next two or three years we spent there gathering and driving cattle, my sister joining us and keeping house for us at Syene [sic] . . . where we made our headquarters. . . . In 1870 and 1871 Jim was deputy sheriff of Dallas County. Jim and Bob sang in the church choir there . . . Bob was only seventeen, and in love with one of the local belles.[12]

The immunity enjoyed by the Youngers in Dallas County may be explained by the fact that most of the peace officers were either former Confederate army men from Missouri or members of the guerrilla bands. Colonel Charles H. Nichols, acting sheriff of Dallas, entered the army at age seventeen and served out his enlistment with the Missouri State Guard. He then organized and commanded an independent company, rising to the rank of major, subsequently was elected lieutenant colonel of Jackman's Regiment attached to Shelby's Division, and later commanded this regiment until the end of the war. In his autobiography Cole adds this pertinent item:

John, my brother [then nineteen] . . . accompanied me to Texas. Clerking in a store in Dallas, he became associated with some young fellows of reckless habits and drank somewhat. One day, while they were all in a gay mood, John shot the pipe out of the mouth of a fellow named Russell. Russell jumped up and ran out of the room. "Don't kill him," shouted the crowd in ridicule, and John fired several random shots to keep up the scare. Russell swore out a warrant for John's arrest.[13]

With some reluctance, Sheriff Nichols rode out to Scyene. An account of what transpired, headed "Obituary," appeared in the *Dallas Herald* of February 4, 1871:

Colonel Charles H. Nichols is dead! He . . . went out to Scyene on Monday morning [January 16] to arrest . . . John Younger, who had been guilty of some offense against the good order of society. Col. Nichols saw Mr. Younger and informed him he had a writ for him in Dallas. Younger readily consented, but asked permission to eat his breakfast first, to which Col. Nichols consented. Having known Younger in Missouri and confiding in his honor, he neither disarmed nor guarded him, but sent some men to watch the stable where were the horses of Younger and a friend of his, recently from Missouri, named Porter. On going toward the stable for their horses, and seeing it was guarded, they hurried to the store where were Col. Nichols and a gentleman he had summoned to aid in the arrest of Younger. They entered the house and commenced shooting at Col. Nichols and his friend. The latter was instantly killed, and the former mortally wounded, but not until he had wounded Younger in the arm.

Younger then mounted on the horse of Col. Nichols and hastened to escape—his friend with him.

Col. Nichols lingered until Friday, the 20th ult., when at 7:30 A.M., he fell quietly asleep, aged 28 years. He was buried in Dallas the next day with Masonic honors, followed to his last earthly resting place by his weeping wife and a long train of sympathizing mourners.

Some three years later, on the occasion of John Younger's death in Missouri at the hands of Pinkerton detectives, the *Dallas Daily Commercial* recapped Nichols' assassination as follows:

Col. Nichols arrested him; Younger asked for parole until he could get his breakfast. Nichols granted the request, and sat down in a store to await Younger's return. In a few moments Younger stepped to the door and fired at Nichols with a shotgun, the load taking effect in the colonel's neck, from . . . which he died in a short time. Younger mounted Nichol's horse and fled. . . . He was pursued to the Indian country, when his trail was lost. The governor of Texas offered $500 for the arrest of John Younger.[14]

Cole's autobiography coincides with the *Herald* and *Commercial* accounts, except he gives the date "Jan. 17," identifies Nichols' assistant as "John McMahon," Porter as "Thompson McDaniels," and claims "McDaniels shot Nichols, and in the melee McMahon was shot . . . by my brother."[15]

The foregoing details of Nichols' assassination and John Younger's involvement are important here because the Fox[16] writer and Aikman,[17] as do several latter-day journalists, not only say the warrant was issued for Jim Reed but locate the event on the streets of Dallas and attribute the killing to "Bella."[18] The Reeds were still on the Pacific Coast and Myra was pregnant again. On February 22, 1871, little more than a month after the murder of Sheriff Nichols, she gave birth to her second child, a boy, named James Edwin for his father and Myra's slain brother and nicknamed "Eddie."[19]

The Reeds remained in California until late March, when Jim was accused by federal authorities of passing counterfeit currency. Whether Jim intentionally committed the act or the money was picked up in a poker game is not known. During their investigation, the authorities learned he was wanted for murder in Arkansas. By the time they set out to arrest him, according to "Flossie,"[20] he had fled the state at night on horseback and Myra and the children were on their way to Texas. "Flossie" thinks Myra and the children "made the trip by boat, around Cape Horn." Harman indicates they traveled by stagecoach:

Belle . . . in some way discovered that she was watched by officers with a view to following her and thus apprehending her husband and securing the reward. Officers in various parts of the country were notified to look out for "a woman with a little girl and a baby." Belle dressed Pearl as a boy and thus eluded the sleuths. At one place where it was necessary for them to stop at a hotel for a night the proprietor was greatly attached to Pearl, whose golden hair hung in beautiful curls, and calling her to him, said:

"Oh, what a pretty little curly headed boy!"

Pearl replied: "No thir! I ain't a boy; I'm my papa's little turly headed dirl," whereupon Belle, controlling her emotions, explained that on account of the little boy's pretty hair her husband called him his little curly headed girl.[21]

7   The Grayson Gold Robbery

Some biographers have the Reeds returning to Texas in 1872, others in 1874. Contemporary reports show that Cole Younger's chronology is correct:

In 1871, while I was herding cattle in Texas, Jim Reed and his wife, with their two children, came back to her people. Reed had run afoul of the Federal authorities for passing counterfeit money at Los Angeles and had skipped between two days. Belle told her people she was tired of roaming the country over and wanted to settle down at Syene [sic]. Mrs. Shirley wanted to give them part of the farm, and knowing my influence with the father, asked me to intercede in behalf of the young folks. I did, and he set them up on a farm, and I cut a lot of the calves from one of my two herds and left with them.[1]

Cole never saw Myra Reed again. He drove his herds north through Indian Territory to Woodson County, Kansas, and returned to Missouri early in May. The slaying of Sheriff Nichols had made the Youngers unpopular around Scyene and Dallas, even with Confederate sympathizers. Their ailing mother returned to the residence·of Lycurgus A. Jones, Cole's brother-in-law, in Cass County, where she died of consumption and attendant complications. Jim and Bob hastened home for the burial. The reward on John Younger's head precluded his return, except by stealth, and made many an old friend a bounty hunter and an enemy. The Youngers soon rejoined their guerrilla cronies, Frank and Jesse James, and during the next two years their sins accumulated so swiftly and were multiplied and magnified so much by prejudice and the public press that Missouri was forced to hang its head to the ignominy of its nickname, "The Robber State."

On June 3, 1871, the Obocock Brothers Bank at Corydon,

Iowa, was robbed by seven heavily armed men believed to be Jesse and Frank James, three of the Youngers, Clell Miller, and James White. On April 29, 1872, five men (the descriptions indicate they were Jesse and Frank James and Cole, Jim, and Bob Younger) robbed the Deposit Bank at Columbia in south-central Kentucky. Here, Cashier R. A. C. Martin boldly refused to give up the keys to the safe and reached for a gun in a drawer nearby; the maddened, quick-blinking Jesse blew out his brains. At the Kansas City Fair on September 26, 1872, three men on horseback swept down on the gates after the receipts had been counted and carried off an estimated ten thousand dollars. It was determined later that two of the bandits were Frank and Jesse. And on May 27, 1873, Jesse James, Cole and Bob Younger, Bill Chadwell (alias Bill Stiles), and Clell Miller took four thousand dollars from the Savings Association Bank in the dreamy little paradise of Ste. Genevieve on the Mississippi River.

Greatly encouraged by the success of these operations, the James-Younger fraternity turned to the new and more reckless adventure of train robbery. On July 21, 1873, six masked brigands removed the spikes from a rail on the Chicago, Rock Island & Pacific road just west of the whistle-stop community of Adair, Iowa. The engine went through the break and toppled on its side, injuring the fireman and crushing Engineer John Raffety to death. The bandits rifled the express car but found less than three thousand dollars. To soothe their disappointment, they went through the coaches, relieving the excited, demoralized passengers of money and valuables.

News of this outrage aroused such public indignation that the gang split up and went into hiding. Although the banks had done little to curb the outlaws' activities, the railroads were dead serious: they posted rewards of several thousand dollars and engaged the Pinkerton National Detective Agency to assist in an all-out effort to kill the James-Younger bandits or put them behind bars.

During this period, according to many article writers and

some Belle Starr biographers, Myra and Jim Reed were riding with the Jameses and Youngers through Iowa, Kentucky, and Missouri, taking refuge between exploits in Indian Territory at the secluded domicile of Tom Starr. Rascoe[2] says other hideouts were Cole's old Rest Ranch in Collin County, Texas, and John Shirley's stock farm near Scyene and that a warrant was issued for Shirley for harboring criminals, but he concedes "there is no record of [his] having been arrested or convicted."

The Fox[3] opus has Myra "taking up resident with the Elam family of Scyene . . . while her husband was ranging the country, [and] making a pretty display in the infant streets [of Dallas] in a handsome team and buggy," securing a passport to some of the best homes through her "remarkable conversational powers, full of sparkle and repartee." Aikman[4] thinks she found hiding places for Jim Reed "in the residences of the best Dallas families [or] innocent-appearing jobs on nearby ranches" and used "her livery stable" (allegedly acquired with loot from her robberies) as a vantage point while accumulating "range ponies for which no authentic bills of sale were in evidence." Rascoe[5] has her entertaining in a Dallas dance hall; "dealing poker and faro as a professional gambler"; dressing "spectacularly" in a high-collared bodice jacket and flowing skirts; riding a one-hundred-dollar sidesaddle; and "cussing out" Cole Younger, who returned to Dallas with the "notion of doing right" by asking her to become a "kitchen slavey" to his "outfit of punks."[6]

Harman thinks Reed purchased a home nine miles from Dallas near the Shirley ranch, where Myra lived in safety, but he was able to be with her for only brief periods:

The greed of gold, since the reward was offered, made him fear every man . . . when he came home at all it was by stealth. A good portion of his time was spent in Indian Territory at the home of Tom Starr . . . sending word to Belle, who would leave her children with "Grandma Shirley" and go to him for a visit. . . . During [these visits] they attended dances together, often riding twenty to thirty miles . . . and it was not unusual that Sam Starr . . . several years

Belle's junior . . . rode behind, on Belle's horse, the three attending the homey fetes together.[7]

Actually, after returning from California, Myra and Jim and their children lived on the farm John Shirley (at Cole Younger's persuasion) had "set up" for them, not nine miles from Dallas but on Coon Creek in Bosque County, Texas, as verified by the *Dallas Commercial:*

Reed at an early age entered the gang of the notorious Quantrill, and from those associations and that school he graduated it would seem, with high honors.

Soon after the war he married a Miss Shirley, a highly educated and accomplished lady, but no influence seemed sufficient to check his viciousness. We first hear of him in California, in 1870-71, when . . . he left the State and came to Texas, buying . . . a farm on Coon Creek, Bosque County, where, for a while, his generous manners won the esteem of his neighbors. Soon, however, ugly rumors floated through the neighborhood, the stock disappeared . . . and he drew around him . . . horse thieves and desperadoes from all sections.

In February, 1873, Dick Cravey, living sixteen miles from Meridian [the county seat], was called from his bed and murdered. Four men were engaged in this cold blooded killing for robbery alone. It has since been learned that Jim and Sol Reed, his brother, were two of the four murderers.

In August of the same year these two brothers murdered a man named Wheeler, who had been a confederate of theirs, but had become alarmed at the attitude assumed toward the Reed gang by the citizens, and had disclosed some things, and for this, and to prevent further disclosures, his life was taken and his tongue cut out. For this they were run from the county by a posse of citizens. Jim Reed then moved to Scyene, and bought property, settling the same on his wife. . . .

Rewards of $500 each [were] offered by the Governor for the apprehension of the two Reeds for the murder of Wheeler, in Bosque County.[8]

Sol Reed returned to Missouri and was never arrested. Jim, wanted for murder in both Texas and Arkansas with a fifteen-hundred-dollar bounty on his head, again sought refuge in Indian Territory; Myra left the children with her parents at Scyene and accompanied him. On November 19, 1873, she allegedly participated in the gold robbery of Watt Grayson.

It was no secret that old man Grayson was wealthy. He had served as a judge of the Creek Supreme Court in 1868-69 and later was chief justice of the Supreme Court of the Muskogee (Creek) Nation. Before the Civil War he was one of the few slave owners in the North Fork, or Old Town, area of Indian Territory. North Fork Town was about three miles east of Eufaula at the point where the road from Fort Smith crossed the Texas Road near the confluence of the North and South Canadian rivers and where the Creek and Choctaw nations touched the southwest tip of the Cherokee Nation. North Fork was a thriving village until 1872, when the Missouri, Kansas and Texas (Katy) Railroad built through Eufaula and merchants and travelers began to bypass it for the more lively town to the west. Grayson lived on a cattle ranch a few miles south, below the South Canadian, in the Choctaw Nation.

The Fox opus dates the robbery incorrectly "in November, 1874":

Our heroine and her husband . . . having arrived in Eufaula met with an old member of the Quantrell band, who was at this time known by the name of Tom Roberts. . . . He told them that he had recently located a bonanza in the shape of Watt Grayson . . . on whose premises were buried or hidden . . . $30,000.

They talked over the matter . . . Roberts suggested that operations be carried on from the "Younger Bend" which was not far distance. . . . [They] finally rode into the country . . . and for the first time Bella saw that beautiful spot she afterwards adopted as her home.

Fox's writer then quotes the "Bandit Queen's diary":

We found the old Younger cabin in possession of a man named Roach, and a Cherokee boy, both of whom had been residing with Roberts for several months. . . . On the evening after our arrival— it was November 28—we made preparations and set out for the Grayson ranch, four in number [including Roach], and ready to accomplish anything.

When we reached the Grayson house it was decided that I should tap at the door, and when the old man came to it that the others should enter by force. . . . The door was thrown open, however, and there was no difficulty in securing the proprietor. . . . The old lady screamed with terror, but I placed the cold muzzle of my pistol against her brow, and that silenced her . . . old Grayson was secured, but he deliberately refused to divulge the whereabouts of his treasure. A rope was then produced and one end of it placed around his neck, the other thrown across a rafter. I was chosen as hangman, and bore down on the old Creek until he gasped for breath. Grayson was grit from away back and stood it like a stoic until he had to cave in. At last . . . he walked over to a table, which he removed from . . . a wolf-skin rug. This he raised, and behold!—a trap door. Raising the trap, he descended, Roberts following him with a lantern. They returned from the cellar with two oyster cans full of gold pieces. The second trip developed a rusty kettle full of gold coin, which took the efforts of all hands to raise from the cellar. The third and last trip resulted in three large bundles of notes, which added greatly to the spoils. When all was over Watt Grayson walked back to the spot where the rope was hanging. He caught the noose in his hand and said:

"You white men kill me now; no more money."

The old man was right. We had completely gutted the establishment. Next morning in the Younger Bend we counted out $34,000, but found to our disappointment that $12,000 of that sum was in Confederate greenbacks.[9]

Harman[10] corrects the date to November 19, 1873, but does little more than add assumptions of his own: The loot consisted of thirty thousand dollars in gold coin, which Grayson had secured "by a system of official thievery from tribal funds"; he had hidden it in the mountains during the war, afterward burying the coin under his house to prevent members of his tribe proving "his malfeasance"; the robbers learned the hiding place of his "ill-gotten lucre" by "stretching him off the ground seven times," then throwing the noose over the head of his wife, she being "elevated three times." Harman names only three robbers: Jim Reed; Dan Evans, "who made the assertion that he was one of Reed's pals in the job;" and "a man named Wilder," the only member of the trio made to suffer the penalty.

From these Fox-Harman yarns, various interpretations of Myra Reed's involvement have been presented.[11] Contemporary newspapers and court records support none of them.

The *Fort Smith New Era* of November 26, 1873, the *Fort Smith Herald* of November 29, 1873, and the *Tahlequah Cherokee Advocate* of November 29, 1873, carried brief accounts of the robbery, estimating the amount of money stolen at "less than $4,000." A more detailed account, headed "Outrage on the Frontier" and bearing a Parsons, Kansas, November 24 dateline, appeared in the *Little Rock Daily Arkansas Gazette* of November 25:

Walt Grayson, a Creek Indian farmer and stock dealer living near here, was robbed Friday night of over thirty thousand dollars, most in gold and silver, by a party of three white man. One of the men had been at Grayson's and about his premises for two or three days under the pretense of buying horses. His confederates arrived Friday evening, well mounted and heavily armed, and Grayson was immediately seized and his money demanded. He refused to deliver it, whereupon he was hanged to a tree until nearly insensible. He still refused, and the hanging was repeated six or seven times and not until the robbers threatened to hang his wife did he reveal the place of its concealment.

Several half breed Indians and negroes were about the house but most of them were confined in the upper rooms, and all were intimidated to such a degree they offered no resistance. The robbers have been traced to a point a few miles south of the Canadian, where they separated, one going south, the others going north.

A reward of fifteen hundred dollars is offered for the apprehension of the robbers, which would doubtless be greatly increased if the men were captured and the money recovered.

Grayson is an old man, nearly sixty-five years of age, and is now lying very sick from the effects of his maltreatment.

The morning after the raid, Grayson posted two letters at North Fork, one going to his son Edmond, who operated a store at Eufaula:

My Dear Son.

On last night I was robbed of every dollar I had in the world by three white men. You will please get a Marshal and come forthwith to my aid in searching for them. I will give an ample reward for them of twenty five hundred dollars.

Your father
Watt Grayson

The second letter went to W. H. Rogers, a friend who obviously owed Grayson money:

Mr. W. H. Rogers
    Dear Friend,
        I am sorry to inform you that on last night I was robbed of every dollar I had in the world and I think took your note which I hold, but have not had time to look carefully for it. Notify all U.S. Marshals to be on the lookout for three men. One riding a Bay mare with white spots on her sides and perhaps a star in the forehead. The man light complexion, with sandy hair and whiskers. Another, with Brown eyes, Brown hair and whiskers, with a roman nose, wearing gray clothes rather worn. Age about 30 or 33. The third light hair and little whiskers same color. Low and tolerably heavy set. For recovering of men I will pay 2500 Dollars.

Your friend in haste
Watt Grayson

Look out for the note and should it be presented take the man holding it.

W. G.[12]

On November 24, Edmond Grayson swore out a writ before U.S. Commissioner James O. Churchill at Fort Smith, stating that "three white men (names unknown) and not Indians by birth, marriage or adoption, did willfully and feloniously steal, take and carry away from the lawful possession of the owner Watt Grayson three thousand seven hundred dollars in Gold and lawful currency of the United States."[13] Commissioner Churchill issued an order for their arrest.

A tentative identification of the robbers was made nearly three months later. On February 14, 1874, Deputy Marshal L. E. Bracken signed a writ before U.S. Commissioner Edward J. Brooks at Fort Smith, declaring: "I do solelmnly swear and believe from reliable information in my possession that Cal Carter, Robert Reed and John Boswell, white men and not Indians, did in the Indian Country . . . feloniously steal, take and carry away from the lawful possession of the owner Watt Grayson three thousand seven hundred dollars in lawful money of the United States."[14] Bracken did not reveal the source of his "reliable information" but listed Watt Grayson and a Grayson employee named Gilbert as witnesses. Possibly he settled on Reed because the description of the robber with brown hair and whiskers and a prominent nose had been used by Texas and Arkansas authorities. Cal Carter, of course, was one of Reed's old pals from the John Fisher gang. "John Boswell," it turned out later, was an alias for Fisher gang member Charles Bush.

Grayson provided details of the raid in a deposition made before the clerk of the U.S. District Court at Fort Smith:

On November 17 the robber believed to have been Carter rode up to his ranch, inquired about some ponies that might be for sale, and asked to board with the family for a few days. Shortly after sunset on November 19, Reed and the man believed to have been Bush came to the house, asking if a stranger was staying there. Grayson replied that he was "in the next room," and Reed entered the room and returned with Carter, carrying a couple of Grayson's shotguns. Reed, Carter, and Bush then assembled the Grayson family and a few hired hands in one room and announced that they were after money. Reed took a purse containing some keys from Grayson's wife, Susan, and while Carter and Bush held the victims at bay with the shotguns, opened a trunk containing more than $2,000 "in gold and silver, but mostly currency." Leaving Bush to guard the others, Reed and Carter then took Grayson outside and demanded the remainder of his money. Grayson replied, "I have no more," whereupon the Indian was taken near the stable, about fifty yards away, where Carter kept his horse, bridle, and saddle. The outlaws tied Grayson's hands behind his back. Then Carter removed the rope from his saddle, looped it around the Indian's neck, and tossed it over the limb of a tree. "Now, old man," Reed said, "if you don't tell where your money is I am going to kill you." Again Grayson replied, "I have no more money," and they hung him from the tree until he lost consciousness and was let down. They shook him until he regained his senses. Still he maintained he had no more money, and the outlaws again swung him by the neck. Grayson "knew very little" after his second hanging. He remembered lying on the ground "a long time" and the outlaws saying, "The damn old rascal isn't going to tell" and "Believe he is dying now." They sat him up, but he "fell over" and Grayson heard them say, "We'll hang his wife." At this juncture, he told them, "Wait till I come to myself, and I will tell where it is." Reed and Carter began "rubbing" the old Indian, and after he was able to stand they untied him. Grayson led them to the gold buried under the house, and Reed removed two kettles containing $30,000. The gold from one kettle was put in two sacks, the remainder in Susan Grayson's purses. The outlaws put some of the coins inside their boots. Keeping Grayson's shotguns, the trio "departed on their horses." The old Indian was too ill to go after the robbers himself, but some of his men and others pursued them across the Canadian into the Creek Nation and a short distance beyond North Fork on the road to Fort Gibson, where the trail was lost.[15]

Chu he maula, Creek Indian neighbor and member of the posse, made a sworn statement attesting to the rope marks on Grayson's neck and how the bark was rubbed off the tree limb where the robbers had pulled him up and let him down. Cox Hale, another neighbor, made affidavit that he found Grayson in his home the next morning, suffering from the effects of his ordeal, and saw the empty kettles and a hole beneath the house.[16]

No member of the Grayson family, none of the hired hands, and none of those who pursued the outlaws mentioned a woman, dressed as a man, taking part in the robbery. Within a few months, the alleged involvement of Charles Bush and Calvin Carter also would be discounted.

8 The Austin-San Antonio Stage Robbery

After the Grayson raid, according to the Fox[1] opus, the Reeds fled back to Texas, Jim going into hiding near Paris and Myra rejoining her relatives at Scyene. Fox's writer devotes a chapter to her trip and a performance at Bonham, where, dressed as "a smart young lawyer" and forced to seek lodging because of inclement weather, she sleeps with a Judge Thurman of Dallas, who has boasted that, despite "any disguise she might assume," he would recognize her anywhere. "Flossie"[2] repeats this story with a slightly different denouement. All of which Rascoe[3] discounts as "a masterpiece of erotic inventions . . . lifted intact and embroidered upon" by nearly every newspaper feature writer for fifty years afterward.[4]

At the same time, Rascoe[5] claims — and Hicks[6] and Scott[7] acquiesce — that Jim Reed stayed in hiding near Scyene while Myra took quarters in the Planters' Hotel in Dallas, hired a maid to care for her children, obtained the best horse and carriage that Grayson gold could buy, kept a riding horse and stud in the stables behind the hotel, employed a Negro as her special hostler and groom, and resumed her "spectacular" behavior. She wore beaded and fringed buckskin costumes with a "necklace of rattlesnake rattlers" or dressed in a tight black jacket and flowing black velvet skirts, high-topped boots, a man's Stetson turned up front and decorated with an ostrich plume, and a cartridge belt from which hung twin holstered revolvers. She drank in the bars, her boot on the brass foot rail like a man, or occasionally she "might spend a day" trying her luck at dice, cards, and roulette. Sometimes she dashed through the streets at breakneck speed, scattering pedestrians to the sidewalks, whooping and blazing away with her pistols at the sky and building tops "for the hell of it" without being

molested. Despite the knowledge that her husband had a
fifteen-hundred-dollar price on his head and she was "known
to be in contact with some of the worst desperados in the
nation," there was no warrant for her arrest. The constabulary
"maintained its distance"; the "whole town was afraid of her,"
and she "gloried in being pointed out as the Bandit Queen."[8]

Admittedly, Dallas was wide open and booming. The Houston and Texas Central Railway had arrived in 1872, providing
connections with the Texas and Pacific to the west and the
Katy through Indian Territory. The town vied to "turn one
hundred thousand head of cattle" from other shipping points
in its direction. "Experienced farmers and planters of the older
States seeking to better their broken fortunes by taking up the
virgin lands of Texas" arrived daily, "most of them accompanied by their families . . . so numerous that there was not
a sufficiency of hacks, wagons and omnibuses to transfer them
to the hotels, boarding houses, or over to the Central depot,
where the greater portion of them went, preparatory to push-
ing out for the various counties they selected in which to make
their future homes." Merchants and professional men came to
stay. Eighteen brick stores and four banks had been erected,
"nine edifices of the same material" were in the course of
construction, and "scores of frame buildings have gone up and
are going up every day." In three years, Dallas had leaped
"from an obscure frontier town of twelve hundred inhabitants
to a brilliant city of twelve thousand."[9]

Crime was as rampant as the spirit of activity and trade.
The *Dallas Daily Commercial*[10] boasted that the town had "as
efficient a police force as any city her size in the South," and
while it thought there was "not a sufficiency of men to effec-
tually preserve the peace and the salary now paid the officers
not sufficient to maintain men decently," available court dockets give lie to the claim that the city marshal and his limited
staff were inclined to back down from any individual or situation. The columns of the *Commercial* and the *Dallas Herald*
for the first months of 1874 are replete with cases of crooked

gambling, prostitution, drunkenness, robberies, and murder, with no mention of Myra Reed. Her "spectacular" exploits, had they indeed occurred, could have escaped neither the official registers nor the facile pens of reporters.

Actually, Myra disapproved of criminal life and the path Jim Reed had chosen. She left Reed after returning from Indian Territory and moved with her children into her parents' home at Scyene. This was not the real cause for the rift in their over seven years of marriage, however, as the *Dallas Commercial* explains:

Many were the bold and daring robberies committed in which this modern Dick Turpin [Reed] figured, and like his noted predecessor, he was not less renowned in love. In February, 1874, he seduced a young girl named Rosa McComus and fled with her to San Antonio, joining on the way three of his pals . . . Cal H. Carter, Jack Rogers, from Bates county, and J. K. Dickens, of Vernon county, Missouri.[11]

The *Commercial* describes Carter and Rogers as follows:

Cal Carter about 30 years old, five feet eleven inches high, blue eyes, light hair, heavy mustache, and imperial running down to the points of his chin. Is naturally light complected, but is now badly sunburnt; speaks a little Mexican; weighs about 135 pounds; wears No. 7 boots. Is a native of Butler, Missouri, where his relatives now reside.

Jack or Wm. Boswell, alias Jack Nelson alias Rogers is about twenty-four years old, about six feet high, weighs 185 pounds, well built, very strong, fleshy and awkward, light brown hair, reddish gray eyes, sandy mustache and goatee, wears No. 10 boots. He is a nephew of Carter's, and his relatives live in the same place.

Reed and his pals, the *Commercial* continues,

rented a house and all lived together in common, as one household, in San Antonio, the men frequenting as a loafing place, Price's saloon, watching the banks and waiting for an opening from February until the first of April, passing under the assumed names, respectively of William Jones [Reed], Chas. Farmer [Carter] and J.C. Nelson, Dickens alone passing under his own name.

On the first of April, Dickens, with his wife and Rosa McComus came to San Marcos, and on the day following they were joined by the other three men, their diabolical plans having already been concocted.

On Saturday the three men left town, and on Tuesday following [April 7] the San Antonio stage was robbed two miles east of the Blanco in open daylight.

First news of the holdup was dispatched to Dallas from Austin on April 8:

Last night about dusk, the stage bringing the United States mails and eleven passengers, of whom three were ladies, was stopped about twenty-three miles from here by three armed men, who cut the front horses out, made the passengers get out; took all their money and jewelry; broke open their trunks, gutted the mail bags, taking one of them and three of the stage horses.

Among the passengers were Bishop Gregg and Mr. Brackenridge, President of the National Bank of San Antonio, from whom they took $1000. They secured about $3000 from the passengers. The stage was the regular four-horse stage from San Antonio to Austin. It did not reach Austin until 4 o'clock this morning.[12]

Further pertinent details appeared in the *Austin Daily Democratic Statesman* of April 9:

About sunset Tuesday evening, when the stage was nearly two miles on this side of the Blanco, three men approached and drawing their six-shooters on the driver, Bill Anderson, well known in this city, ordered him to stop. . . . The stage had on board nine passengers, viz: Mssrs. McLemore, O'Neal, Waters, Brackenridge, Frazier, McDonald, Wells, Munroe and one lady, Mrs. Lloyd. . . . All were ordered to alight and seat themselves in a row. . . . Two of the robbers stood before them . . . a six-shooter in each hand cocked, and ordered them to give up their money, watches and other valuables.

After having collected . . . from the passengers, they proceeded to cut open and rifle their trunks, taking such articles of value as they could get away with speedily; and lastly came the United States mails; after cutting open the sacks and rifling them of their contents, they left them lying scattered around with the exception of one, which they took with them. After this they proceeded to cut the horses loose from the stage and rode off, leaving the bewildered and frightened passengers to proceed on their journey the best as they could. The driver returned to the nearest stand, about three miles back, and getting fresh horses proceeded to this city, where he arrived about

The Austin–San Antonio stage robbery. From an illustration

in Frank Leslie's Popular Monthly, *June, 1903.*

daylight Wednesday morning. No violence was offered to any of the passengers and they all conceded that the robbers went to work like men who knew their business.

The amount taken from the passengers was about $2500 in United States currency and four gold watches. As soon as the Legislature met yesterday a joint resolution was passed authorizing the Governor to offer a reward of $3,000 for the apprehension of the robbers; to this Mr. Callahan, United States Mail agent offers $3,000 more, and Mr. Sam T. Scott, manager of the stage line and senior partner of the S. T. Scott & Co., added $1,000, making $7,000 in all . . . and we trust this most daring and outrageous crime may be ferreted out.

The first report of the holdup had listed Bishop Gregg of the Diocese of Texas among the passengers.[13] The *Waco Daily Examiner* of April 15 noted:

Bishop Gregg, we are glad to learn, had left the stage at San Marcos, and was not of the party robbed a few miles east. . . . This was a narrow escape, and we hope the eminent preacher will be long in falling into the hands of the cavaliers of the road.[14]

Although every type of crime, particularly the murder of men for gain, had been prevalent in Texas since the war, stagecoach robbery was new, and it provoked considerable excitement throughout the state. The *Waco Examiner*[15] thought "the plan of offering large rewards a good one, and police officers of each county . . . should be stimulated to extra watchfulness"; another idea, the *Examiner* said, would be to "employ a reliable detective . . . shrewd enough to ferret out the rendezvous of the gang." The *Austin Statesman*[16] suggested in a strongly worded editorial the enactment of a "general law" offering a suitable reward for the capture and conviction of such offenders. "All experience proves that what is everybody's business is nobody's. When men are offered rewards it is quite a different matter. They make it a business."

The seven-thousand-dollar reward "induced quite a large posse to start after the gang" with hopes that "they may be speedily overtaken."[17] The robbers were tracked east toward Lockhart. "After reaching this place, they turned, and doubling their tracks, went in a northwesterly direction," where the trail was lost; "a large quantity of mail matter was found . . . containing drafts that could have been used by them, but they were too cautious to attempt it."[18]

Major Thomas F. Purnell, U.S. marshal for the Western District of Texas, took charge of the manhunt. On April 17 he furnished this information to the *Statesman:*

It is now definitely settled that the robbery was perpetrated by three men from Missouri, as follows: James Reed alias "Bill Jones" . . . Cal H. Carter and Nelson alias Jack Rogers . . . In Dallas county Reed seduced a girl named Rosa McComus . . . promising to marry her in San Antonio . . . where they went with J. M. Dickens, from Vernon county and his wife, making in all a party of six persons. . . . [On April 2] they camped together on the banks of the beautiful San Marcos. Here Reed, who seems to be an enterprising cuss, traded horses with a citizen by the name of Woolfork, he agreeing to pay Reed twenty-five dollars to boot in cash for [to give to] his wife. On Monday, the women and Dickens moved to Woolfork's, and in the evening the three other men left town, and on the next evening, the San Antonio stage was robbed. . . . The horses which the parties rode from San Marcos returned there the next day, as the robbers had turned them loose, preferring the spirited animals belonging to S. T. Scott & Co.'s stages to their jaded ponies. Dickens, his wife and the girl McComus are still in San Marcos, Dickens having rented a farm and gone to work; but a strict surveillance is kept over them, and they will be brought to this city to-day to be examined before the United States Commissioner to elicit further facts, if possible. As well as possible to divine, the robbers are traveling in a northwestern direction, keeping between the settlements and the Indian country. They have told some parties whom they met, that they were going to Arizona, and others that they were going to the Indian Territory. Reed has a friend in the Territory, to whose house he goes whenever he gets into trouble, and it may be that he is making for that place now, but he is said to be very fond of the girl whom he seduced, and it may be the lodestone that will draw him back to Texas.

Rascoe[19] says Major Purnell was a victim of the "wily wit of our Belle"; that "Rosa McCommas, not McComus," was "a schoolmate of Belle's at Scyene . . . of Belle's own age," whom Belle disliked because of "her superior position" as the daughter of Elder Amon McCommas; that while Belle was "little more than plain," Rosa was "very beautiful and became, in time, the legitimate wife of Jesse Cox"; therefore, Belle "decided to use Rosa's name among the many aliases she used at the time." Which apparently moved Drago[20] to comment on Purnell's "remarkable ignorance . . . 'Rosa McComus' was an alias for Belle Reed, the bandit's common-law wife . . . knowledge he could have acquired on any Dallas street corner."[21]

Both writers are mistaken on every point. Myra Reed used no aliases. She and Rosa McCommas were not schoolmates of the same age — Rosa was eighteen and Myra twenty-six — and Myra was not Reed's common-law wife. Rosana McCommas, Rosa's aunt, married Jesse Cox. Rosa McCommas was the daughter of James B. McCommas, eldest son of Amon Mc-Commas, and was living in the household of her grandfather, a minister of the Campbellite church.[22]

A little more than three months after the holdup, the *Dallas Commercial*[23] carried this dispatch from the *San Antonio Express*:

> We have been shown the daguerreotype likeness of Reed and of the girl he seduced about Dallas, and brought to San Antonio with him. He left her at San Marcos about the time of the stage robbery, and we learn that she has made her way back to Dallas. He lived with her here in San Antonio for several weeks, and the others were with him, immediately preceding the stage robbery. He has a wife and children, who, we believe, are somewhere about Dallas.

Later, the *Commercial* again made a separate and distinct reference to "the poor girl whom he [Reed] had ruined."[24]

On April 20, Dickens and Rosa McCommas were examined before U.S. Commissioner Price at Austin. The *Statesman* reported:

> No further facts were elicited than have already been published, but both parties were bound over to appear before the United States District Court; Dickens in a bond of $2,000, and the girl in a bond of $1,000.[25]

The U.S. Commissioner and U.S. District Court case records for this period are missing, and Texas newspapers made no further reference to the matter. Evidently the charges against Dickens and the girl eventually were dropped, since neither participated in the holdup.

9   Reed "Hands in His Checks"

The day Dickens and the McCommas girl were arraigned at Austin, Major Purnell received "positive information" that the stage robbers were "making toward Dallas, and that their destination was Indian Territory."[1] Purnell notified Dallas authorities. The *Herald* of Tuesday, April 28, published the results:

On Saturday evening Marshal Peak [June Peak of Texas Ranger fame, former deputy sheriff and now city marshal of Dallas] . . . chanced to stop in the hotel on Main street, east of the Central road, kept by Mrs. Rollins. A face in the crowd seated around attracted his attention, and . . . it suddenly flashed upon him that the man was none other than one of the bandits . . . photographs of those "gentlemen of the road" having been furnished the sheriff of this county. Satisfied that one of the men was before him, he quietly informed him that he was his prisoner and at once lodged him in jail. He gave his name as W. D. Wilder, but from papers found on his person there can be no doubt but Wilder is an assumed name, and that he is the notorious . . . Reed. Later in the evening, Marshal Peak arrested another suspicious character, who gave his name as Bidwell, and who answered in part another photograph in possession of the marshal, but he was released in about an hour, [Peak] not thinking that there was sufficient grounds for detaining him. Subsequent developments disproved the judgment of the marshal, and he at once dispatched Officer Crabb and ex-Officer Phares in search of him. With the usual success which attends the efforts of these gentlemen, they found Bidwell three miles this side of Scyene, fast asleep or feigning slumber, in a grove of timber near the public road. Taking him in custody they brought him to this city, and placed him in jail.

There seems to be no question in the minds of the sheriff and the marshal that they have got the right "birds." Everything found upon them, papers, books, letters and many other things form almost flawless links in the chain of evidence against them. Immediately on their arrest, Sheriff [James E.] Barkley telegraphed the United States marshal at Austin, and received a reply that he would be in this city today.

The *Dallas Commercial* of April 27 noted the arrests but doubted that Wilder "is Reed, the man who made a happy family circle at Scyene desolate by robbing it of its brightest jewel and abandoned his true wife and little ones."

The *Herald* of April 20 reported the "Release of Wilder and Bidwell":

After a careful review of the statements of the above two men and a comparison of all the facts in the premises, it was the opinion of United States Marshal Purnell that the fabric of the evidence was not strong enough to justify the further retention and incarceration of the prisoners and they were released by Sheriff Barkley on Tuesday night. After their liberation, Wilder, at the request of Major Purnell, accompanied him as far as Scyene, where the wife of the brother of Reed, the principal in the robbery, resides, and from whom it is thought some light may be obtained as to the whereabouts of the bandit chief.[2]

Which of Reed's sisters-in-law still resided at Scyene is not known. Most of his brothers had returned to Missouri since their widowed mother brought them to adjoining Collin County ten years before. Possibly this was the wife of Sol Reed, who was still dodging a Texas warrant.

From the Scyene trip, Purnell learned that Rosa McCommas was visiting at the home of John T. Morris, former peace officer and distant relative of Reed now farming in Collin County about five miles south of McKinney. The Morris home was put under surveillance by three U.S. "detectives," in the hope that Reed eventually would try to see the girl. On Saturday, May 23, Reed and a member of his gang arrived, supposedly to spend the night. A posse of twenty-five men, including the detectives and Collin County sheriff's deputies, surrounded the house. The plan was to capture the two desperadoes the next morning. The *Dallas Herald* of May 27 described the "unfortunate affair" which transpired:

During the night . . . the detectives became impatient and concluded to go up to the house and arrest the men . . . a deputy sheriff urged that the different parties surrounding the house should be notified . . . the detectives, however, did not think this warning necessary. As they approached, they were halted by some of the other parties and gave the countersign, but unfortunately it was not understood by the parties hailing, and they fired a volley . . . severely wounding one and slightly wounding another of the detectives. Subsequently, it was ascertained that the robbers the party was in search of were not in the house, but were camped a short distance off, and, on hearing the firing, took to their heels.

The *Herald* identified the wounded detectives as Herseberg and Martin: "Herseberg will probably die, as he received nine buckshot in his back. Martin received a wound in his leg, but is able to get around with the aid of crutches." The *Denison Daily News* of May 27 reported the "death of Deputy U.S. Marshal Herseberg."

The identity of the stage bandits also was amended slightly. On June 5 the grand jury for the U.S. District Court for the Western District of Texas at Austin brought a bill of indictment against "Jim Reed, otherwise called William Jones and Robert Miller, Cal Carter, Wm. Boswell, otherwise called William Rogers and William Nelson," charging that "on the 7th day of April . . . they feloniously assaulted William Anderson, a carrier of the United States mail, and robbed him of said mail, effecting said robbery by the use of dangerous weapons putting in jeopardy the life of said Anderson." Listed as federal witnesses were "William Anderson, Mr. Brackenridge, [J. M.] Dickens and W. W. Woolfork."[3] On June 30 a capias was issued for Reed, Carter, and Boswell—the trio accused of the Watt Grayson robbery in the February 14 writ signed by L. E. Bracken before Commissioner Brooks at Fort Smith, Arkansas.[4]

News of the indictment appeared in most Texas, Indian Territory, and Fort Smith papers. It was probably from this source and the descriptions given that Deputy Marshal C. R. Stephenson of Indian Territory swore out still another writ on June 21 before U.S. Commissioner Floyd C. Babcock at Fort Gibson, accusing "Calvin C. Carter, Reed alias Jones alias Miller, and Charles Bush alias Boswell" of robbing Watt Grayson of "thirty one hundred dollars."[5]

After escaping from the Morris home in Collin County,

Reed and companion fled to Indian Territory, where, three weeks after the Stephenson writ was filed, the gang descended upon the William Harnage residence in the Cherokee Nation. The tactics employed, according to the *Tahlequah Cherokee Advocate* of July 18, were similar to those in the Grayson raid:

Last Monday night, 13 inst., Mr. Wm. Harnage of Going Snake District was robbed of about $1,600. Mr. Harnage was from home at the time. From his account of the affair, it appears that two men came to his house about night fall and asked to stay all night. They were permitted to stop, and a while after supper the tramp of horses feet was heard, and pronouncement by some one of the family to be Mr. Harnage, or the Sheriff, who had promised to be there that evening. In a few minutes instead of Mr. Harnage or the Sheriff, several strange men made their appearance, seized a hired man, conducted him into the house with a pistol presented and bade him not to open his mouth under penalty of death. They then proceeded, eight in number, to burst open the trunks and chests, to drag the bedding upon the floor and to search the premises generally. They succeeded in getting all the money about the place except forty dollars in gold lying loose in a trunk. It is believed by the family that there were others on the outside of the house keeping watch while those within did the robbery.

Those who were in the house were pronounced to be white men.

A July 16 letter from John B. Jones, U.S. Indian agent at Tahlequah, to the U.S. deputy marshal at Fort Gibson[6] was more specific:

Sir:

On Monday night last Mr. Wm. Harnage in Going Snake Dist. was robbed or rather his house was robbed of about $1,600 or 1,700 dollars in gold and $25 or 30 in Greenbacks, an Enfield Rifle gun, a fine double shawl for ladies, a hat & a ladies satchel, & a very peculiar powderhorn.

Mr. Harnage's hired man, Thomas Madras, was at the same time in the same house robbed of saddlebags, a revolver & some clothing.

The deed was done by eight men. They were seen by Mr. Harnage's family & they can identify four of them surely. It is thought that the description given suits Cal Carter, Bill Fisher, Reed & one other of that gang.

Mr. Harnage wants you to send a force to cooperate with Y. R. Wright, Sheriff of Going Snake Dist.

He wants another force to Briartown to take them there as they are supposed to go there. It is thought that they take refuge at Tom Starr's & his son Tuckey's.

Please act promptly and bring these men to justice.

The above is written at the request of Mr. Harnage.

I have the honor to be
Very Respectfully
Your Obdt. Servant
John B. Jones
U.S. Indian Agent

The Indian Territory officers were no more successful than the Collin County posse. The gang was surrounded, the *Advocate* noted, by U.S. deputies and Cherokee police at "the house of an Indian named Star, a short distance from Muskogee, but they managed to escape." Reed himself returned to Texas, this time taking refuge at the home of a friend, Henry Russell, in Lamar County about twenty miles northwest of Paris.[7]

On August 9, 1874, two startling dispatches appeared in Texas newspapers:

Paris, Texas, Aug. 6—Jim Reed, the San Antonio stage robber, was shot and killed by J. Morris, of McKinney . . . this evening, about fifteen miles northwest of this city.

Morris has followed Reed for three months, and had succeeded in capturing him . . . they were traveling together and stopping at a farmhouse for dinner. Morris asked Reed to surrender, and he said he would; Morris told Reed to get up, but instead of doing so he ran under the table and raised it up between him and Morris and started out the door with it. Morris shot two balls through the table. The third shot killed Reed almost instantly. Morris then brought the body to Paris.

———

McKinney, Aug. 8—Last night the remains of Jim Reed, the mail robber, arrived here from Paris, near which place he had been apprehended and shot; and were buried today after having been fully identified by those who knew him. . . . Much praise is bestowed on Morris for his bold and successful undertaking . . . [he now] is in hot pursuit after Cal Carter and John Boswell, Reed's desperate companions . . . and justly entitled to the pro rata reward . . . offered for the three.

Reed's body had become very much decomposed, particularly about the head, having been shot just between the nose and right eye. The drayman, in carrying him to the potter's field mistook the place, and in returning, with the breeze to the windward of the corpse, he took sick, and was compelled to abandon it on the roadside. It was, however, taken charge of by the sheriff, and finally interred.

According to the *Denison News*,[8] U.S. Marshal Purnell and Sheriff William Merritt of Collin County provided Morris authority as a special deputy to "work up the case" and Morris "finally got so far into the confidence of Reed as to enter into a plot to kill and rob an old man in Arkansas [and] they were on their way . . . to carry out the proposed robbery when Reed was killed." The pair stopped in late forenoon and asked a northeast Lamar County farmer named Lowery the directions to Slate Shoals, twenty-some miles east, where the Red River ran shallow over a rock formation, providing a natural ford into Indian Territory. They rode on three miles and stopped at the home of S. M. Harvey.

Morris realized that his special deputy's commission would be worthless once he crossed into the Territory and that this might be his last opportunity to capture Reed. His statement at the coroner's inquest in Paris was published in the *Dallas Commercial* of August 10:

TRAGIC DEATH! THE MOST NOTED OF
AMERICAN ROBBERS! HANDS IN HIS CHECKS!

My name is John T. Morris. I came up with the deceased yesterday about 10 o'clock at Henry Russell's about 20 miles northwest of Paris, in this county—was well acquainted with the deceased—we staid [sic] all night at Russell's. This morning we started for Arkansas together, traveled on until dinner time, when I proposed to stop and get dinner, to which he agreed. We stopped at Mr. S. M. Harvey's house for dinner. When dinner was ready, we went out into the dining room and sat down to the table. I got done eating before Reed and went back into the main room, and explained to Harvey, Reed's character, and asked him to assist in his arrest, which he agreed to do. Mr. Harvey and I went out to the horses . . . took the pistols off of Reed's and my horse. We went to the dining room where Reed was still eating. I said to Reed, "Jim, throw up your hands," he said he would do so, but ran under the table, and raised up with the table and ran towards the door with the table in advance. I shot two holes through the table. After he dropped the table I shot him in the right side. He ran his hand in his pocket to draw a cylinder as I thought. I shot at him four times, and hit him twice, once a scalping shot in the head and once in the right side.

Deceased left his pistol on his saddle at my suggestion. He had an extra cylinder which he carried in his pocket. After he got out of the house, he ran up to me and grabbed me—my pistol refusing to fire— and as he rushed against me, I fell and he fell too. I then called upon Mr. Harvey to assist me in his arrest, which he did and we thus secured him. He has acknowledged to me often that he was one of the San Antonio stage robbers.

He showed me his two purses, which contained, by his count, forty-nine twenty dollar gold pieces, remarking that was what he had made since he saw me. He came to my house to see his wife who was visiting at my house. It was at that time that the policeman was shot by mistake, an account of which was published at the time.

The deceased deposited with Henry Russell all his money except three twenty dollar gold pieces, which I now have in my possession.

Russell is an old acquaintance of Reed's and Reed had been staying with him since last Thursday.

I live four and one-half miles south of McKinney, Collin county, Texas, and am duly authorized by Maj. T. F. Purnell, United States Marshal, and also William Merritt, Sheriff of Collin county, to make the arrest. The way that I found out his whereabouts was through a letter he wrote to his wife and myself, and sent by Russell, which he delivered to her and then came to my home with the letter to me. I came back with Russell to his home where we found Reed. His wife did not accompany us—she played sick—she is not his real wife, however.

(Signed)   Jno. T. Morris[9]

On August 19, Deputy Marshal T. M. Wright charged Henry Russell as an accessory in the San Antonio stage robbery and took him before the U.S. commissioner at Denison "to determine whether jurisdiction should rest with the State or Federal government since the case involved looting the United States mail."[10] During the examination,

evidence disclosed more or less the adventures of Reed and associates, together with the details of his tragic death, as given by Morris. . . .

It appears that Reed had been stopping at Russell's house under the name of Williams—and Russell went to Collin county after Rosa Mc-Comus, the girl seduced by Reed, and with whose picture the detectives are all familiar as she appears from a San Antonio photograph standing by him. The evidence disclosed that Reed frequently walked in open day through the streets of Paris and rode about the neighborhood without disguise. He had just left Russell's house in company with Morris, with whom he had planned a robbery in Arkansas—when Morris, awaiting his opportunity, shot him—and now claims the reward—the whole amount; State, Stage Co., and Government rewards amounting to $11,000.[11]

Russell was bound over to U.S. District Court for the Eastern District of Texas at Tyler under one thousand dollar bail. Tyler court records for this period were destroyed by fire in 1878, and contemporary newspapers do not note a disposition of the case. It is likely that Russell was not convicted.

Morris made return on the Austin capias for Reed, Carter, and Boswell: "I hereby certify that in obedience to the within writ I arrested the outlaw named J. C. Reed and on his attempt to escape I was compelled to kill him, which I done in Lamar Co. Texas. Thomas F. Purnell, U.S. Marshal, by Special Deputy." The warrant bears Major Purnell's scribbled notation: "Came to hand at Austin June 30 1874—within named Cal Carter and Boswell not to be found in my district, James Reed being killed by Morris near Paris."[12]

Since two of the robbers remained at large, Morris received only one thousand seven hundred dollars of the reward money.[13] Judge Thomas H. Duval of U.S. District Court at Austin issued a new capias for Boswell on February 23, 1875, after the fugitive reportedly was sighted in a Texas county.[14] However, Boswell did not return to Texas after the Harnage raid in the Cherokee Nation. The capias was returned four days later with Purnell's notation: "After diligent search I am unable to find Boswell alias Wm. Rogers alias Nelson, but we are informed that he was drowned in Kansas in crossing a river—his body was fully identified and there is no doubt of his death."[15] The following entry appears in the Austin court's criminal minutes of January 9, 1877: "On this day came the attorney of the U.S. and suggests the death of Carter one of the defendants herein—on motion the case is ordered dismissed as to him."[16] How Cal Carter lost his life is not related.

Before this, however, new developments in Indian Territory convinced Major Purnell that Carter and Boswell had not been Reed's companions in the Watt Grayson robbery. Early in May, 1874, William H. Anderson, one of Purnell's deputies, became intrigued with the similarity in the descriptions of Boswell and Dickens, released on bond with the McCommas girl, and how W. D. Wilder, released a few days later, strongly resembled the daguerreotype of Cal Carter. In a sworn disposition before U.S. Commissioner Ben Long at Dallas, Anderson stated:

> From the best information I could get . . . the Grayson robbers came in the direction of Texas. . . . I wrote to Grayson, who gave me their description and also described some shotguns taken by them [and] some purses that contained a part of the money. I afterwards found one of the purses in the possession of a lady of this County who said it was given her by Reed [and] was identified by Watt Grayson as belonging to his wife . . . also found that the two shotguns taken at the time of the robbery were sold in this county a short time later . . . by W. D. Wilder and Marion Dickons [J. M. Dickens] alias Burns. I then went to Eufaula, Indian Territory where I met Grayson . . . told the facts to him. He then employed me to arrest the robbers if possible and bring them to justice, and to recover any money that I might find in their possession.[17]

The old Creek Indian already had employed A. J. King to track down the bandits. King, an Ohio native, had lived in the Choctaw Nation four years and had worked for Grayson in various capacities. He was selling some of Grayson's cattle in St. Louis at the time of the robbery. King took the bandits' trail "four weeks later and could easily have secured Wilder shortly afterwards, but was anxious to secure the other two men, Reed and Dixon, whose true name I since learned was Dickens."[18]

On September 14, King swore a writ in U.S. District Court at Fort Smith against Wilder and Dickens for theft of "Thirty Five Thousand Dollars in Gold and Lawful currency of the

United States" from Watt Grayson.[19] He obtained a warrant
for their arrest and secured an appointment as special deputy
U.S. marshal.

Meanwhile, Anderson had

trailed Dickens alias Burns, about three hundred miles South West
of Dallas and West of San Antonio . . . where [Dickens] stopped a
short time and then went into Mexico beyond reach of my process.
I have not heard of Dickens since. . . . I then arrested W. D. Wilder
in Bosque County on the frontier of this State.

The *Denison News* published this brief account of the capture:

W. D. Wilder, no less desperate and notorious than Reed, was
corralled at Coon creek, Bosque county. With him was a woman supposed to be his mistress, and a confederate supposed to be . . . in
the Grayson robbery. All three fought to the bitter end, particularly
the woman, who fought with the fury of a tigress.

Wilder was shot three times before he surrendered. He was put in
irons, and to-day, the 6th [October], was taken to Fort Smith in
charge of deputy marshals W. H. Anderson and T. M. Wright.[20]

The return on the capias, signed by A. J. King, shows that
Wilder was arrested September 26 and delivered to U.S. Marshal J. F. Fagan at Fort Smith on October 9 by W. H. Anderson, with Henry Minehart and G. B. Holland as guards.[21]
King made further affidavit that Wilder told him after the
capture that

Reed & Dixon [Dickens] had applied to him in Texas to aid them
[in the Grayson robbery]. That they had assured him that Grayson
had between thirty and forty thousand dollars in gold, which they
promised to divide equally . . . but Reed took all the money himself
and made a division of part of it about twenty miles from North Fork
on the road to Fort Gibson, when Reed gave Wilder Seven Hundred
and fifty dollars and said that would do for small change for present
use, that when they reached their rendezvous in Texas they would
make a final division of the rest, but that he Wilder never got any
more.[22]

However, the officers had recovered "at least two thousand
dollars," and King had "no doubt but that the money he

brought back was part of what was taken from the [Grayson] trunk."

Wilder was examined before U.S. Commissioner Brooks, "identified by Grayson as the man who adjusted the rope around his neck and by other witnesses as one of the robbers," and committed to jail to await action of the grand jury.[23] The jury brought three indictments against him. The first, dated November 17, charged theft of "three thousand dollars in currency and seven hundred dollars in gold coin" from Watt Grayson; the second, dated November 27, accused Wilder, Dickens, and the deceased James C. Reed of stealing gold and silver coin "to the sum of thirty two thousand dollars"; and finally, a true bill dated November 30 charged "William D. Wilder and one Burns [Dickens] . . . first or christen name unknown" with stealing $32,000 from Watt Grayson. A penciled notation states, "Burns dead"; the circumstances of his death are not known.[24]

Judge Henry C. Caldwell of the Eastern District of Arkansas presided at Wilder's trial. The Fort Smith judge, William Story, his less than fourteen months' tenure attended by incompetency and corruption and the judge facing a strong case of bribery and impeachment proceedings in Congress, had resigned in June, 1874. Judge Caldwell was ordered to Fort Smith for the November term and was to remain there until the vacancy could be filled.

Wilder was found guilty on December 8, 1874, and on December 12 was sentenced to imprisonment in the Arkansas Penitentiary at Little Rock "at hard labor, for the term and period of one year, and that he pay to the United States . . . a fine of One Thousand Dollars together with all their costs in and about this prosecution laid out and expended."[25] He was delivered to the Arkansas prison on December 14; on January 6, 1875, the court ordered the U.S. marshal to collect the fine and $300.25 costs. The order was returned April 7 with the certification: "No property could be found within the limits of this district on which to levy the written execution."[26]

In April, Isaac C. Parker, former state's attorney, judge, and representative to Congress from the Twelfth Judicial Circuit of Missouri, was appointed to the Fort Smith bench by President Ulysses S. Grant. Judge Parker opened his first term of court on May 10, 1875. Eighteen persons were tried for murder; fifteen were convicted, and eight of these sentenced to the rope. One was killed attempting to escape, and because of his youth, the sentence of another was commuted to life imprisonment by the president. The six remaining men — three whites, two Indians, and one Negro — died on the Fort Smith gallows as a sextet on September 3 and launched Parker's undeserved worldwide reputation as the heartless and bloodthirsty "Hanging Judge."

One of the white men who were hanged was an insolent twenty-year-old braggart named Daniel Evans of Bosque County, Texas. In November, 1874, he accompanied another Texas youth, William Seabolt of McKinney, into Indian Territory, where he murdered Seabolt for his horse, clothing, and other property. Evans was apprehended in the Creek Nation near Eufaula in possession of Seabolt's fine bay horse and its new saddle and wearing the victim's fancy-topped, high-heeled boots. When he was sentenced, his lips warped in a scornful smile and he said flippantly, "I thank ye, Judge." Asked on the gallows if he had any last words, he stared defiantly at the marshal and shook his head. In a newspaper interview a few days earlier, however, he had laughed and joked about riding with various "scouts" and claimed to have assisted Reed and Wilder in robbing Watt Grayson of his gold. He claimed to have held burning pine torches to Grayson's bare feet to make him divulge the hiding place of his money and said he was nearby at the time Reed was killed.[27] All of which was untrue.[28]

The Grayson affair continued, finally to involve Myra Reed. After Wilder's conviction, Watt Grayson realized he had little chance of recovering any of his money. On January 23, 1875, he employed John B. Luce, a Fort Smith attorney, to pursue

Isaac C. Parker, Fort Smith's "Hanging Judge," who sentenced Sam and Belle Starr to brief terms in the House of Correction at Detroit, Michigan.

the possibility of adjustment under Section 16 of the Act of
Congress of June 30, 1834, regulating trade and intercourse
with Indian tribes, which provided that

where, in the commission, by a white, of any crime, offence, or misdemeanor within the Indian Country, the property of any friendly
Indian is taken, injured or destroyed, and a conviction is had for such
crime, offence, or misdemeanor, the person so convicted shall be
sentenced to pay to such friendly Indians to whom the property may
belong, or whose person may be injured, a sum equal to twice the
just value of the property so taken, injured or destroyed. And if
such an offender shall be unable to pay a sum at least equal to the
just value or amount, whatever such payment shall fall short of the
same shall be paid out of the Treasury of the United States.

Attorney Luce filed his claim package with Commissioner
of Indian Affairs Edward P. Smith on February 2. It was forwarded to Secretary of the Interior Columus Delano on February 20, then transmitted to the speaker of the House of
Representatives. Besides the statements of Grayson and his
family, the package included the depositions of Grayson's
neighbors Chu he maula, Cox Hale, and A. J. King, all supporting allegations that the thirty-two thousand dollars did
exist. Congress took no action. In December, 1875, Luce submitted additional evidence in defense of a point raised by
Commissioner Smith: that the claim "did not satisfactorily establish that the money could not be recovered from the offenders." Among the evidentiary documents was a certified copy
of the execution stating that no property of William D. Wilder
could be found against which to levy. Strengthening the claim
was this testimony by Myra Reed, sworn on December 16
before U. S. Commissioner Long at Dallas:

I, M[yra] M[aybelle] Reed, do solemnly swear that my place of
residence is at Scyene, Dallas County in the State of Texas, that I
am the widow of Jas. Reed who was killed Paris Lamar County in
this said State of Texas on or about the 6th day of August A. D.
1874. That during the life time of my husband . . . while we were
stopping on the Canadian River in the Indian Territory he told me
that Watt Grayson a Creek Indian living on or near the Canadian

River had over Thirty Thousand ($30,000.00) in gold, and that he meant to have it, and that said Reed came to me in company with W. D. Wilder and Marion Dickons alias Burns on or about the 16th day of November A. D. 1873, and that on that day Wilder parted, and on the second day the other two, Dickons and my husband parted, and said that they were going to rob the said Grayson of his money and that on or about the 20th day of November A. D. 1873 in the morning, they returned all together, the above named Reed, Wilder and Dickons alias Burns and came near where I was stopping and stopped in the woods and sent for me. I went to them and they told me that they had accomplished their object and had the money to show for it, and they sat down upon the ground and began count-ing it. I saw they had a large amount of gold, they counted it and divided it in my presence, and to my best recollection they had about Ten Thousand ($10,000.00) in gold apiece making $30,000 in gold. They also had some currency, as well as I remember, about Five hundred ($500.00) or Six hundred ($600.00) apiece, making about Fifteen hundred ($1500.00) or Eighteen hundred ($1800.00) Dollars in currency—all of which they said they took from Watt Grayson the night before. That my said husband was killed near Paris Lamar County in this State on or about the 6th day of August A. D. 1874 while resisting an attempt made to arrest him on charge of robbing the United States mail. That of the amount taken from Grayson, I know of no part that could be recovered, my said hus-band having spent or disposed of all that he had and having left me in a destitute condition.

M. M. Reed[29]

Myra's testimony was substantiated by Deputy Marshal An-derson, who had "made it his business" to

inquire if any of the money taken could be secured and became satisfied that it had all been gambled off and otherwise spent. They [Reed, Wilder, and Dickens] had been seen gambling in gambling houses in this place [Dallas] with large sums of gold, and I learned that in one instance Wilder lost $3,000 in gold on one horse race, at another time he paid $1,500 in gold to release one of their gang from an arrest. They were all notorious for horse racing, and often lost large sums of money in that way. I am quite sure that the effects of all three of them together that I know of or could find would not bring 1,000 dollars.

W. H. Anderson[30]

In January, 1876, Luce enlisted the aid of Representative William W. Wilshire of Arkansas to withdraw the Grayson claim package from the speaker of the House for submission to the Committee on Indian Affairs. Still no action was taken. On August 1, 1878, Watt Grayson died. His last will and testament, recorded in the clerk's office of Gaines County, Choctaw Nation, the previous March, bequeathed his ranch and "all moneys that he might die in possession of" to his wife, Susan. His livestock was given to various relatives and friends. Luce, attorney for the estate and acting for the Grayson heirs, addressed a new petition to Congress; it was received by the Commissioner of Indian Affairs in June, 1880. With no action forthcoming, Luce submitted another claim package, covering all important aspects of the case, to the chairman of the Committee on Indian Affairs on January 18, 1881. In December, 1882, Representative J. E. Cravens of Arkansas withdrew the papers from the House; the claim was approved by the Committee on Indian Affairs, but Congress failed to appropriate money for its payment. U.S. Senator A. H. Garland of Arkansas pushed the matter in 1883 without success. Representative John Rogers of Arkansas withdrew the claim papers from the House for the third time in 1884. On December 16, 1887, the claim was listed in the schedule that Treasury Department accounting officers reported to the Forty-ninth Congress, and thirty-two thousand dollars was included in a deficiency appropriation bill for the fiscal year ending June 30, 1888. After lengthy debate, the bill was approved March 30.[31]

Myra Reed's testimony in the congressional records and the evidence in the Grayson robbery developed by federal marshals in Texas and Indian Territory show that she was no more than a bystander.

10   The Mystery Years

How Myra fared the year following her husband's death is revealed in her letter to the Reed in-laws postmarked August 10, 1876, and addressed "F. M. Reed, Metz P. O., Vernon County, Missouri":

Dear Mother and Brothers and Sisters: — I write you after so long a time to let you know that I am still living. Time has made many changes, and some very sad ones indeed. My poor old father has left this world of care and trouble. He died two months ago today. It seems as if I have more trouble than any person. "Shug" got into trouble here and had to leave; poor Ma is left alone with the exception of little Eddie. She is going to move away from here in a few days and then I'll be left alone. Eddie will go with her, and I don't know that I shall ever see him again. He is a fine, manly looking boy as you ever seen and is said to resemble Jimmie very much; he is very quick motioned, and I don't think there is a more intelligent boy living. I am going to have his picture taken before he leaves and I will send you one; would like for you to see and know him. I know you would love him for the sake of the dear one that's gone. Eddie has been very sick and looks pale and wan, but I think my boy will soon mend up. Rosie is here in Dallas going to school; she has the reputation of being the prettiest little girl in Dallas. She is learning very fast. She had been playing on the stage here in the Dallas theatre and gained a world-wide reputation for her prize performance. My people were very much opposed to it but I wanted her to be able to make a living of her own without depending on any one. She is constantly talking of you all, and wanting to visit you, which I intend she shall sometime.

Jno. L. [sic] Morris is still in McKinney, at large. It seems as if justice will never be meted out to him. Pete Fisher is in Colin City, where he has always lived. Solly hasn't the pluck and love for Jim I thought he had. I have Jimmie's horse Rondo yet; I was offered $200 for him the other day. If Sol had come to Texas, freely would I have given the horse to him if he had sought revenge.

I think Brocks are in Montague county. I will realize nothing from my farm this year. Brock rented it out in little pieces to first one and another, and none of them tended it well, so I made nothing. I am going to sell it this fall if I can.

I am far from well. I am so nervous this evening from the headache that I can scarcely write.

The letter bore no signature, "a most peculiar trait of this peculiar woman," says Harman,[1] never to sign or date her letters or record the address whence they were written. He says he copied the original on October 4, 1898, for inclusion in his book. It was written on the stationery of Dallas County Sheriff James E. Barkley, and it appears authentic.

Myra's youngest brother, Cravens (John Allison or "Shug," sometimes called "Doc"), was now eighteen.[2] The nature of his trouble is not known, but apparently it was serious enough for him to leave Texas. As noted, Myra had been training Pearl for the stage. According to Harman, "the little girl gained much local [not worldwide] renown as a dancer, but in the autumn of 1876 during a performance she was overcome by a sudden rush of blood to the brain and for a time death was feared; on her physician's advice, Belle thereafter kept Pearl away from the theater." Pete Fisher was a member of the clan involved in the Shannon feud at Evansville, Arkansas, where Scott Reed was killed. Obviously, Myra had expected Sol Reed to avenge the death of her husband, but "Solly . . . appreciated a safer course," not to mention that he was still wanted in Texas for questioning in the Bosque County murders. After John Shirley's death at Scyene in June, 1876, Eliza Shirley disposed of the farm and moved to Dallas, but she did not take Eddie as predicted. Myra sent the boy to Rich Hill, where he lived with his Grandmother Reed until he was twelve years old. Shortly afterward, Myra made a trip with her daughter to Conway, Arkansas, where she visited a few months with an old schoolmate from her Carthage days.

The next three years of Myra Reed's life are a mystery, but undaunted biographers have found a wealth of "facts." Four popular stories, cribbed in part from the Fox opus, are basically Harman:[3]

Belle leaves Pearl at Conway and returns to Dallas, where she "began to exhibit her former roving disposition." On a cold, windy day she goes for a ride with a girl named Emma Jones, who is "as wild as herself." The pair stop to warm themselves in a small prairie village; Belle makes a fire at the back of a small store, the wind whips the flames into the building, and the merchant's goods are destroyed. During Belle's trial for arson at Dallas, a wealthy stockman named Patterson, who had known John Shirley and "heard of Belle's nervy action at her husband's bier," enters the courtroom. He falls in love with Belle at first sight, secures her release, and gives her a large sum of money. "Whether he expected to make her his wife cannot be stated authoritatively." Belle goes to Conway, takes Pearl to the bank of a small stream, and counts out the wealthy Patterson's gift. "Baby," she tells her child, "here is enough so you and I will never want again, mamma will go up into the Territory and fix up a nice home and have lots of music and nice horses and then come and get her baby and we will always be happy." Of course, "none of the stockman's gift was ever used in fixing up the nice home mamma intended."

Short of money again, Belle "decks herself in raiment suitable for appearance in a civilized community," adopts a "silver-toned voice," and has no difficulty "ingratiating herself with the best society . . . in one of the stirring Texas cities." One of her admirers is a middle-aged bachelor who is cashier of one of the leading banks. Belle enters the bank one day while he is alone, and after "murmuring away in sweetest tones, pulling at his heart-strings at every breath," she suddenly slips an "ugly-looking .45 pistol" from the folds of her skirt and forces the surprised and frightened man to place thirty thousand dollars in a sack beneath the flap of her basque. "Now, dear," she warns him, "don't make any outcry; your life depends on it; good bye sweetheart; come and see me when you come up into the Territory." Whereupon she proceeds to a livery stable nearby where she has left her horse, vaults into the saddle, and is "away like the wind."

About a year later, Belle, who has spent most of her "intervening time" in Indian Territory, is arrested and jailed at Dallas on a charge of horse stealing. However, she soon "wins the heart" of a deputy sheriff who is guarding the jail. He elopes with her but returns "to the bosom of his family a month later, his infatuation, for some cause, having cooled."

Finally, Belle gathers about her "a set of male admirers as reckless as herself, to each of whom she was at one time or another especially gracious and who was for the time counted as her lover." Among these "lovers" are "Jack Spaniard, Jim French and 'Blue Duck,'" ready and willing to obey the wishes of "the woman they admired yet feared, who could out ride . . . and out shoot them all." She becomes known as the "Prairie Queen" and "Queen of Desperadoes." Blue Duck borrows two thousand dollars from Belle, goes to Fort Dodge, Kansas, and loses "his mistress' money" in a crooked poker game. When he tells Belle what happened, she "swears a string of oaths" and heads for Fort Dodge. Entering the gambling hall, she covers the players with "her pistol" and grabs up the entire stakes of seven thousand dollars, saying: "Gentlemen, there is a little change you're due; I haven't time to give it to you now; if you want it come down into the Territory." The gamblers never call for their change.

After the Fort Dodge incident, concludes Harman, "she spent two years in Nebraska, and in 1880 Belle became the wife of Sam Starr [securing] a claim to which she was then entitled as a citizen of the Cherokee Nation."

The Fox-Harman stories have been elaborated upon by most Belle Starr biographers.[4] Jack Spaniard and Blue Duck would play minor roles in Myra Reed's life years later, but in the late 1870s they were considered law-abiding citizens of Indian Territory. Bluford Duck, whose Cherokee name was Sha-con-gah Kaw-wan-nu, was still in his teens and living with his family on Rogers Creek west of present Oologah. Jack Spaniard was one-quarter Cherokee, twenty-six years old. His proper name was Sevier (from his grandfather on his father's side); he had been given the name Spaniard while growing up on Spaniard Creek between Muskogee and Webbers Falls. Orphaned when a child, he was raised by a relative, Andy Gourd, and attended school at Webbers Falls and at Texanna, Creek Nation, where he lived with an uncle. Jim French, another Cherokee youth, still lived with his father, Tom French, a well-to-do citizen of Fort Gibson. He began his criminal career by shooting a Creek youth named Joseph Ceaser in a crap game on April 28, 1889; he was charged with assault to kill an Indian officer in October, 1892, and robbery of the U.S. Mail in September a year later; in 1894, he rode with the infamous Cook gang of train bandits and was slain February 7, 1895, while attempting to rob a store at Catoosa. So it is not strange that none of Myra Reed's alleged "Queen of Desperadoes" exploits made the contemporary press.[5]

In her letter of August 10, 1876, Myra announced intentions of selling her farm at Scyene. To whom and when the transaction was made is not known, but one can assume that with the proceeds she did no more than idle her time between daughter Pearl in Arkansas and son Eddie and the Reed in-laws in Bates and Vernon counties, Missouri. The Fox opus suggests that during this period Myra visited her hometown of Carthage and old friends around Nevada City and Joplin, finally taking up with Bruce Younger:

> Bruce, a cousin of Cole's, a gambler and a good looking, good-for-nothing fellow, was deeply enamoured of Bella, and would frequently present her with his winnings, or purchase for her valuable pieces of jewelry. But she inwardly despised his tricky nature, and could not possibly bring herself to love him. . . . However . . . certain it is that the pair found their way to Younger Bend, and there resided for a while as man and wife . . . when Bruce, becoming sorry of his bargain, struck out one night leaving Bella in possession of the premises.[6]

The "Bandit Queen" saddled her horse the following day,

trailed him "across the Kansas border" and overtook him at Baxter Springs, where she procured a license and a preacher and, threatening to "blow his brains out," forced Bruce to marry her in the presence of "at least twenty witnesses." The ceremony concluded, "Bella sent for a keg of beer for the by-standers, while Bruce slunk away and disappeared." She never saw him again.

The *Fort Smith New Era* of February 22, 1883, carried an article about Belle, which stated in part: "It is claimed she was at one time the wife of Bruce Younger, the notorious horse thief and desperado." Rascoe[7] concludes it was from this story that the Fox writer "got the name 'Bruce' Younger as one of Belle's early suitors" and that he knew Cole, Bob, Jim, and John had no brother named Bruce, "so he made this mythical Younger a cousin."

There is an element of truth in the Fox account: Bruce Younger was not a mythical character. A half-brother to Cole's father, he hung out in the rough-and-ready mining camp of Galena, Kansas, a few miles west of Joplin, and made his debut as a suspect in the James gang's train holdup on the night of July 8, 1876, at Rocky Cut, near Otterville, Missouri. The *Joplin News* of August 7 reported:

Sunday night [August 6] about ten o'clock a party of mounted men rode into Joplin and visiting the Centennial saloon, arrested Bruce Younger, hand-cuffed him and placed him in a buggy and drove rapidly out of town toward Granby. Since that time rumors of all descriptions have been in circulation, and all kinds of crimes fastened upon Younger by the fertile imagination of public gossips.

The squad that made the arrest was headed by Jack Gardner of Granby, and he stated that Younger was arrested on suspicion of having been indirectly concerned in the late train robbery of the Missouri Pacific. It is also reported that he had been concerned in a mail robbery, and was maturing a plan to rob the Joplin bank, all of which, by far, lack confirmation.

On last Saturday, a man named Carey was arrested in Granby and it is supposed from him came the clue that led to the arrest of Younger. It is claimed the names of a whole gang of organized rob-bers are known to the officers, and that these are but the beginning of a number of arrests soon to be made. . . . In a short time after the arrest of Younger the whole party mounted their horses and rode away. They expected to ride some twenty miles by tonight and there make additional arrests, an object they will probably have accomplished by morning. . . . Albert Carey is well known among the boys in Joplin as "Hobs" Carey.

When taken into custody, Carey confessed that the Jameses, Youngers, and several other noted outlaws halted the train and rifled the express safe of more than seventeen thousand dollars, all of which Jesse denied in a letter to the *Kansas City Times* on August 14, offering to prove "by eight good, well-known men of Jackson County" that he was not present. Bruce Younger also had an alibi; he was released and returned to Galena.

Riley Robinson, a retired Joplin miner whom Shackleford[8] interviewed in 1938, recalled that "Belle appeared in Galena about 1879" as a brunette of medium height, about one hundred and thirty pounds, and shapely; she "dressed like other women . . . nothing loud or flashy," but soon gained a bad reputation because she "run around with Bruce Younger." Galena was booming, full of money. Mine laborers "run around with big rolls of bills in their pockets." Bruce was a "tinhorn gambler" and frequented the biggest honky-tonk in town, the Round Top. Most of the saloons, dance halls and gambling joints were on Redhot Street; Belle and Bruce were "well known on Redhot Street . . . lived together in several places here in Joplin, but mostly they stayed at the Evans Hotel in Galena." Asked about their marital status, Robinson did not think they were legal, but "people like them didn't get married much in those days."

Shackleford also interviewed Sam Evans, former sheriff of Cherokee County, Kansas, whose father owned the hotel at Galena. The old man did not care to discuss Belle because "too much damn' foolishness had been written," but he finally acknowledged that Bruce Younger "lived in the hotel while Belle was there." Evans did not know whether they were man and wife because "people minded their own damn' business

in those days. . . .Belle's mother was with her part of the time
. . . also her brother, Doc, that some people called Shug. And
her daughter Pearl was there for a while . . . she was about
eight or nine years old. . . . Belle was a mighty good-lookin'
woman, well-educated, quietly dressed — not tough like the
newspapers made out."

Galena's seventy-year-old police judge, W. L. Lumbley, told
Shackleford he saw Belle and Bruce often when he was a
boy. People talked about them a lot, he said, but "Belle was
always well behaved." There were plenty of tough characters
around Galena; Bruce and Belle were "no worse than the rest."

Apparently, Harman and the writers who followed him
knew nothing of the Belle–Bruce Younger affair. "Flossie"[9]
wrote in 1933:

> There is one episode in Myra's life during these years that has
> never been known except to a few. The name of Younger has been
> connected with that of Myra a great many times. Myra Reed was
> married to Bruce Younger about 1878. She was never married to
> Cole Younger. But in about the year named she met Bruce Younger
> in Coffeyville, Kan. and they were married. They did not live to-
> gether very long.

In his family narrative, Richard H. Reed states that after
brother Jim's death in Texas "Maybelle lived with Bruce Younger, a cousin of Cole, and from this association Rosie Lee
became known as Pearl Younger."[10]

Fred W. Allsopp of Little Rock, Arkansas, was aware of
the Bruce Younger connection. In his 1931 *Folklore of Romantic
Arkansas*,[11] he mentions "Sam Starr, her *third* husband," and
after Sam was killed, "Belle became a widow for the *third*
time."

There may be truth also in the Fox writer's claim that Myra
and Bruce "resided for a while at Younger Bend." About
this time, Myra renewed her acquaintance with the Starr clan,
particularly old Tom's son, Sam.

Sam Starr was no mangy-looking renegade. He was three-
quarters Cherokee, handsome, and appeared much older than

Myra Maybelle Reed about the time of her marriage to Sam Starr in 1880.
Courtesy of Thomas Gilcrease Institute of History and Art, Tulsa,
Oklahoma.

Sam Starr on horse-
back. Artist's sketch
from Samuel W.
Harman's Hell on
the Border.

Marriage record of Samuel Starr and Mrs. "Bell" Reed, from Cherokee
Volume, 1-B, *page 297.*

he was. He was not as tall and muscular as his father, but he
was magnificent when mounted on his fine bay pony. Except
for long black hair cut off below the neck and tied with a
scarlet ribbon beneath a black, broad-brimmed hat, he dressed
like a white man and wore a well-kept, white-handled revolver.
His noticeable feature was his eyes, which, despite their hawk-
ishness, were friendly and magnetic. In the early summer of
1880, he and Myra were married in the Cherokee Nation.
The entry in Cherokee Volume, 1-B, 297, "Marriage Records,
Bills of Sale, Court Records, Permits to Non-Citizens,"[12] appears as follows:

Starr & Reed

> On the 5th day of June 1880 by Abe
> Woodall—District Judge for Canadian
> Dist. C. N. Samuel Starr a citizen of
> Cherokee Nation age 23 years and Mrs.
> Bell Reed a citizen of United States
> age 27 years.
>
> H. J. Vann, Clerk[13]

Exercising a woman's prerogative, Belle came out of the ceremony five years younger. Pearl and Eddie had a new and unusual parent, Belle the appellation under which she would begin the period of her life that is more consistent with her biographies.

11   Belle Among the Starrs

For a short time after their marriage, Sam and Belle lived in a little box house a mile or two south of present Porum. Then Sam took an allotment of forest and bottom land in the extreme southwest corner of the Cherokee Nation on the north side of the Canadian.[1] It was not Sam's land, however. Cherokee lands were held communally. A member of the tribe could choose a site not granted to some other member; if the selection was approved, he had possession of it as long as he lived. He owned such improvements as he might make and could transfer title to them should he settle elsewhere. In event of Sam's death, the improvements would go to Belle. As an intermarried white, she was now a citizen of the Cherokee Nation and a ward of the U.S. government.

The allotment was a picturesque spot nestled between low-lying inaccessible hills sixteen miles below Eufaula, six miles west of Briartown, and about the same distance from Tom Starr's place on the same side of the river. To the north rose Hi-Early Mountain, where the Jameses and Youngers rendezvoused during the war. Ten miles downstream and three miles south of Briartown across Tilden Cramp Ferry on the river in San Bois County, Choctaw Nation, lay Whitefield (designated "Oklahoma Postoffice"). Between Briartown and Whitefield and partly encircling the Starr lands wound the great elbow of the South Canadian—its yellow waters implacable, writhing among its quicksands—called Youngers' Bend. Along the south bank, caverned precipices provided concealment and lookouts for the six-gun gentry who slept by day and rode by night. The only approach to Sam's and Belle's place was through a narrow canyon leading from the river to the uplands off the old Briartown-Eufaula Trail. Its walls were so steep and boulder-strewn that a wagon could barely pass between them. Most of the year, the trail was passable only on horseback.

The house has been described as a fortlike palace or castle filled with sumptuous wardrobes and fine furniture freighted in from St. Louis, plus a grand piano secured at great expense from Fort Smith.[2] The piano, at least, would come later. Actually, the house was a cedar log cabin with a clapboard shingle roof, built by an Indian named Dempsey Hannell shortly after the war, and was occupied for many years by a Cherokee full blood called Big Head, who supposedly buried ten thousand dollars in gold coin on the premises and died without telling anyone where it was hidden. Old-timers in the area used to claim that Belle and Sam spent most of their married life digging holes all over the place, hunting for Big Head's treasure.

The cabin stood on a rocky knoll, facing south, was within fifty feet of dense timber, and overlooked a wide meadow, where a stranger could be sized up easily coming off the canyon trail in daylight. The original room was about fourteen feet square, with an old-fashioned fireplace on the west side. The rafters were seven feet high, the puncheon floor laid as straight as an axman could lay it. A small window at the right of the door let in enough light to dispel the shadows. To the rear was attached a lean-to kitchen, divided into two small rooms, beneath which was a cellar. A veranda, or porch, stretched across the front of the house.

Belle papered the interior with cloth after the Cherokee custom. Most Indians used cheap, bright-hued muslin, but Belle chose white calico with a little flower design. There were a couple of beds, a table, several chairs, a good lamp, and portraits of herself, her family, and friends. Bearskin rugs covered the floor. The antlers of a prairie deer occupied a prominent place above the mantel. And the intellectual tastes of John Shirley were represented by a crude shelf of some of the best books of the era.

Water for the cabin came from a never failing spring near

Belle Starr's old home of cedar logs at Youngers' Bend with the lean-to kitchen at left and a later addition on the right.

a stream, called Belle Starr Creek, two hundred yards away. The narrow cut leading up from the river was called Belle Starr Canyon.

To these surroundings Belle brought Rosie Lee, now eleven, giving her the name Pearl Starr. The child readily took to the freedom of the wilderness, as happy as she was isolated and innocent. Belle wanted her to be a lady, and called Pearl her "Canadian Lily."

The first year, Belle helped Sam clear about three acres of land for a corn field and vegetable garden. Bass, catfish, perch, and crappie from the Canadian and deer and wild turkey

Front view of Belle Starr's cedar log cabin at Youngers' Bend.

The spring on Belle Starr Creek at Youngers' Bend.

from the timbered slopes of Hi-Early Mountain supplemented the family larder. They added a frame room to the east side of the cabin and constructed a smokehouse, a corncrib, and corrals for their milch cows and horses. The canyon meadow provided good grazing.

They were almost surrounded by members of the Starr clan, either direct descendants of James Starr or people who married into the family. A few miles northeast lay the settlement of the West clan, of whom John C. West and his youngest brother, Frank, were to play important roles in Sam's and Belle's lives. Much of the country within a radius of fifteen miles was leased by cattlemen or an occasional white sharecropper or renter.

Belle did not associate much with her neighbors, nor did she care to. It was her intention then, she wrote years later in a short biographical sketch to John F. Weaver of the *Fort Smith Elevator,* to live a quiet life, a credit to her sex and her family. She wrote:

On the Canadian River . . . far from society, I hoped to pass the remainder of my life in peace. . . . So long had I been estranged from the society of women (whom I thoroughly detest) that I thought I would find it irksome to live in their midst.

So I selected a place that few have ever had the gratification of gossiping around. For a short time, I lived very happily in the society of my little girl and husband . . . but it soon became noised around that I was a woman of some notoriety from Texas, and from that time on my home and actions have been severely criticized.

Notwithstanding some of the best people in the country are friends of mine. I have considerable ignorance to cope with, consequently my troubles originate mostly in that quarter. Surrounded by a low-down class of shoddy whites who have made the Indian Territory their home to evade paying tax on their dogs, and who I will not permit to hunt on my premises, I am the constant theme of their slanderous tongues. . . .

My home became famous as an outlaw's ranch long before I was visited by any of the boys who were friends of mine. Indeed, I never corresponded with any of my old associates and was desirous my whereabouts should be unknown to them. Through rumor they learned of it.

Jesse James first came in and remained several weeks. He was unknown to my husband, and he never knew till long afterwards that our home had been honored by James' presence. I introduced Jesse as one Mr. Williams from Texas.

The time of Jesse's visit to Youngers' Bend is conjecture.[3] For three years after their escape at Northfield, Jesse and Frank James hid out in Kentucky, Nebraska, West Texas, and Mexico before returning to their old grounds in Missouri. On October 7, 1879, the Chicago and Alton express was flagged at Glendale Station in central Jackson County and robbed of thirty-five thousand dollars. On July 15, 1881, the Rock Island and Pacific express was held up at Winston, Missouri. On September 7 the same year, another Chicago and Alton train was robbed at Blue Cut, Missouri. Then the gang disbanded. Bob Ford, who was familiar with the James boys' operations, had met secretly with Governor Thomas F. Crittenden at a Kansas City hotel and agreed to "go after Jesse" if the State of Missouri would dismiss certain charges against his brother, Charley, and if the reward of ten thousand dollars offered for Jesse would be paid for taking him dead or alive. Jesse could have visited Sam's and Belle's ranch after the Blue Cut robbery in September.[4] In October, 1881, he made a brief visit to his home at Kearney, where he met Charley Ford and agreed to shelter him. In November, Jesse moved his family to St. Joseph, Missouri. Charley and Bob Ford were his house guests. On the morning of April 3, 1882, while the renowned outlaw was standing on a chair brushing the dust off a wall picture, the "dirty little coward" Bob Ford entered the room and sent a pistol bullet crashing through Jesse's brain.

In any event, Jesse's visit to Youngers' Bend provided the springboard for much novelistic nonsense. Afterward, according to Belle's biographers, so many of her old friends found the Starr ranch such a handy retreat that she was forced to fit up a cave on Hi-Early Mountain into a habitable abode and built two additional log cabins for their accommodation. Often as many as a half-dozen hard-ridden mounts stood in her corrals; the gangs she harbored stole horses, committed petty robberies, and sold whiskey to the Indians. The inaccessibility of Youngers' Bend and the prestige of Belle's father-in-law and the powerful Starr clan prevented unheralded visits by the Indian police and federal marshals.[5]

A favorite tale perpetuated by newspaper feature writers is how Belle and her gang preyed on peddlers, or drummers, who traveled the Cherokee Nation. Belle supposedly stationed her desperadoes on a bald hill a mile southeast of present Inola, today an Oklahoma landmark called Belle's Mound. The treeless hump rises several hundred feet above the flat prairie and a maze of brushy gulches. On its summit stood a rock tower the gang used as a lookout. It has been torn down bit by bit until little remains, but tourists still drive out of their way to gaze at the barren formation and enjoy the vicarious thrill of imagining lynx-eyed guards up there keeping vigil for easy victims or federal marshals approaching in time to sound the alarm for a getaway.[6]

Twelve miles west, on the Little Verdigris near the mouth of Spunky Creek, stood the boom town of Catoosa, a crossroads of two important cattle trails and end of track on the Frisco. Tulsey Town (Tulsa), a few miles southwest on the Arkansas, had grown up around a Creek Indian village and was a trading point for cattle outfits in the Cherokee Outlet. Tulsey was a wild town, but Catoosa was a hellhole of vice, drunkenness, and murder. Cattle shipped to St. Louis markets from the Creek Nation, southwestern Indian Territory, and parts of Texas were loaded onto trains at Catoosa, and the drovers always went on a spree. Since saloons were prohibited, dance halls and pool halls with back rooms for card games and smuggled liquor were the masculine centers of amiable profanity. And the town was full of fences. Allegedly, Belle disposed of her stolen chattels here more easily than at any other place in the Territory, and she found an excellent outlet for the moonshine whiskey made in the bend of the South Canadian.

We are told that Belle set up horse-stealing stations fifty miles apart, where animals stolen from a hundred miles north were exchanged for those stolen the same distance to the south. A blacksmith at Briartown claimed he once nailed shoes on Belle's mare backward to deceive a posse attempting to pick up her trail![7]

Ouachita National Forest and the Kiamichi Mountains cover a large part of southern LeFlore County, Oklahoma (old Scullyville and Sugar Loaf counties in the Choctaw Nation). Peaks resembling the Blue Ridge Mountains of Virginia rise two thousand four hundred feet and higher and extend from east to west for seventy miles. Winding Stair, the best know mountain of the group, takes its name from the old Military Road, constructed in 1832, leading up and across it from Fort Smith to Fort Towson. In these mountains not far from Cedar Lake is Horse Thief Spring, another station where Belle and her cohorts are said to have "rested, exchanged and sent on into Texas" horses stolen from Arkansas.[8]

Her most celebrated station — today a holiday haven for both Oklahomans and out-of-state visitors — is Robbers Cave, a foreboding recess extending inward from a sheer sandstone cliff virtually hidden in the rugged San Bois Mountain wilderness of northern Latimer County above Wilburton. The natural-beauty spot is in an 8,400-acre game preserve, replete with some seventy campsites, two youth camps, and twenty-three beautifully furnished housekeeping cabins, including huge wood-burning fireplaces, on a mountainside overlooking Lake Carlton, a 52-acre body of water created by damming Fourche Maline Fork of the Poteau River.

Outlaw legends began to grow around Robbers Cave during the Civil War when it was used by deserters from both Union and Confederate forces. After the war, guerrilla bands and gangs of robbers made it a rendezvous between raids on stores and payrolls. Down the Fourche Maline within pistol shot of the cave runs Robbers Trail, used by the Starrs in the 1850s and 1860s and by the Jameses and Youngers on their trips to and from Texas. Youngers' Bend is thirty-five miles to the north.

"When Belle Starr and Jesse James were trying to get out of the public's view they hid out in the cave; afterwards, the glamorous gunmoll . . . lost no time picking it as her private territory," the journalists write. During her reign, "a posse led by a deputy U.S. marshal beseiged part of the James band of outlaws in the cave for two days, killing one and capturing others after they were 'smoked out.'" Stories of hidden treasures in the cave "still lead to searching and exploring parties."[9]

Although some Robbers Cave stories have a basis in fact, the exploits attributed to Belle are wholly unsubstantiated. A fix she was not, for she had neither money nor acquaintance for influencing federal administrators of the law in the Western District of Arkansas. After her marriage to Sam Starr, Belle did not appear in contemporary reports or official records until July 31, 1882, when she and Sam were charged in U.S. Commissioner's Court at Fort Smith with the theft of a horse belonging to Andrew Pleasant Crane of the Cherokee Nation.

12   A Trip to Detroit

Belle's biographers err on many points in their versions and interpretations of the Crane affair.[1] The facts are in *United States v. Sam and Belle Starr*, Case No. 2370, U.S. District Court, Western District of Arkansas, Fort Smith. On July 31, 1882, Cassius M. Barnes,[2] chief deputy U.S. marshal at Fort Smith, signed a writ before U.S. Commissioner Stephen Wheeler, declaring: "I do solemnly swear and believe, from reliable information in my possession, that Sam Starr and Belle Starr did, in the Indian Country . . . on or about the 20th day of April . . . feloniously steal, take and carry away from the lawful possession of Pleasant Andrew [Crane], a white man, one horse of the value of eighty dollars." Listed as government witnesses were "Pleasant A. Crane, G[eorge] A. Crane, John West, Al[fred] Harper." A capias was issued the same date and sent to L. W. Marks, a deputy marshal for the Vinita District, Indian Territory. Marks's return on the warrant shows he did not serve it until "the 21st day of Sept. 1882, at Bird Creek, Cherokee Nation, by then and there taking into custody the within named Sam Star, Belle Star."

The delay of nearly eight weeks was explained by Mrs. Fannie Blythe Marks, the deputy's widow, during an interview at Vinita in 1937:[3]

Belle Starr's story has been told and re-told many times . . . but this is the only authentic account . . . of her first arrest.

L. W. Marks . . . was given a writ for the arrest of Belle and Sam Starr for horse-stealing. They were reported headed for the Osage hills . . . then, as now, a safe and favorite rendezvous for desperadoes. . . . Marshal Marks made a determined effort to arrest her and her husband, but he was often confused by the conflicting reports of people along the way [as the pair fled north to the vicinity of Catoosa]; sometimes it was a man and a boy he was trailing, sometimes a man

152

and a woman. Finally he came to where they had stopped for the night with a negro family away out west [on Bird Creek near the Osage border]. The marshals camped too, and concealed themselves. . . . Presently Sam Starr and a negro boy came leading their horses to water. The officers arrested and disarmed Starr, chained him to a tree to look as if he were just standing there, then sent the negro boy under threat of death with a message to Belle to come down as Sam wanted her. The ruse worked. . . . She being a woman, the marshals did not want to use violence so they hid behind trees on opposite sides of the path and stepped out as she passed, each catching an arm. . . . Under the drapery of a pannier overskirt was a six-shooter; and concealed in the bosom of her dress were two derringer short pistols. She fought like a tiger and threatened to kill the officers . . . she meant it, too.

In those days transportation was slow and tedious. The marshals, to make their trips, had to take wagon outfits and camping equipment, traveling overland, picking up offenders of the law along the way, and a trip lasted for a month or six weeks.

Belle Starr was the most exasperating prisoner that the marshals ever dealt with. She would drop knives, forks, blankets or anything else that she could reach as she rode along in the wagon, and the loss was not discovered until the article was needed. Her one object . . . seemed to be to irritate and annoy those having her in charge. Because of her sex the officers were as considerate and forbearing as possible, until patience ceased to be a virtue. . . .

The outfit camped near Muskogee at the old fair ground. Here the prisoners were left under guard while the marshal and his posse went in pursuit of other criminals for whom they had writs. Just as they were returning to camp for dinner, they heard a shot and saw Belle running around the tent, a smoking revolver in her hand, in hot pursuit of the guard.

She had been alone in her tent eating her dinner when the side blew up, disclosing the guard seated on the outside, his pistol in his scabbard, with his back toward her. It was but the work of an instant for her to seize the pistol; she intended to kill the guard, liberate the other prisoners, her husband and herself. Unfortunately for the success of her plans . . . the timely arrival of the officers saved the day. She cried with disappointed rage when she was disarmed, but thereafter, for the safety of the others, she was chained.[4]

Belle and Sam engaged the services of a Fort Smith law firm, Cravens & Marcum, hoping to win in the preliminary hearing before Commissioner Wheeler on October 9. The testimony

United States of America,

WESTERN DISTRICT OF ARKANSAS.

Before STEPHEN WHEELER, United States Commissioner.

UNITED STATES,

VERSUS

Sam Starr & *Larceny*
Belle Starr

SEE COMPLAINT FILED HEREWITH.

On this *9th* day of *October* 188*2*
came the United States of America, the Plaintiff in this cause, by WM. H. CLAYTON, Esq., *Geo A Goom Act* U. S. Attorney, and the Defendant in *their* own proper person, in custody of the Marshal and by *their* Attorney *Cravins & Marcum* when the following testimony was heard and proceedings had, to wit:

Andrew P. Crane being duly sworn, deposes and says: I reside at *Cherokee Nation* and know the defendants in this cause, *I lost a horse; he was a large bay horse with a star in his forehead and a rope mark around his left fore leg. 5 years old last spring. not branded that I know of. about 16 hands high, he was not shod. His gate was a fox trot or single foot as some call it. One of my neighbors raised the horse, he was worth $85. He was*

Complaint in United States *v.* Sam Starr and Belle Starr *for the larceny of the Crane horse, filed at Fort Smith, Arkansas, October 9, 1882.*

not only provided facts, it reflected conditions and attitudes of the region and people who would affect Belle's life in years to come:

ANDREW P. CRANE being duly sworn, deposes and says: I reside at Cherokee Nation and know the defendants in this cause. I lost . . . a large bay horse with a star in his forehead and a rope mark around his left fore leg, 5 years old last Spring, not branded that I know of, about 16 hands high, he was not shod, his gait was a fox trot or single foot as some call it. One of my neighbors raised the horse, he was worth $85. He was running about 5 or 6 miles from where I lived when taken. He had been out there about a week and I went to hunt for him and could not find him. My father went with me. It was about two weeks before I got any information as to where he was. . . . I went to defendants to see them about it. Mrs. Starr said she would try to get my horse for me. She said she knew the man that rode him, his name was Childs, and that she would do all she could to get him or get pay for him for me. I went to her again about it, we had a right smart talk . . . she finally told me to go to John West and if he would pay $30 on the horse that she and the rest would satisfy me . . . she did not take the horse . . . that if I had her and Sam brought down here that Sam would not be a bit too good to waylay my road. I told her that if I found out who took my horse that I intended to report them. I went to John West and told him what Mrs. Starr told me. I then went back to Mrs. Starr and told her that John brought out an oath and said he'd be damned if he would pay for something he did not get, that they had been trying for some time to get him into something of that kind. Mrs. Starr then said he ought to go to hell in a minute, he got $40 of the money. I then told her that if they would satisfy me for my horse I would go west to keep down a fuss. She then said she would go to Muskogee and would send me $30 in a letter but that I must not claim it as hush money . . . it was for the purpose of giving her time to get my horse and her witness to prove it on the other side. I never got the money or any letter. Sam told me once that he did not steal my horse but that he almost knew who took it . . . he could not swear to it. The horse was taken about the last of April. I am living in the Cherokee Nation as a white people, pay a permit there. Sam Starr is Cherokee. Mrs. Starr is a white woman. The defendants live 6 or 7 miles southwest of me & 3 or 4 miles from where the horse ranged.

CROSS EX.: I never heard Mrs. Starr claim to be an Indian woman. . . . My mother claims to be a Cherokee but has never proven it.

My mother has claimed that her father Zack Downing was a Cherokee. My mother's name is Caroline Crane. She has black hair, and is dark complexioned. I was born in the state of Arkansas. I lived in Sebastian Co. Arkansas before I went to Cherokee Nation. I will be 25 years old the 6th of next month and have lived in the Cherokee Nation 8 or 9 years. My father bought a place in the Cherokee Nation but did not prove his rights and left it 5 or 6 years ago. He never voted there, they would not let him vote. My horse was running near John Wests when I lost it . . . about the 10th of April . . . I hunted for the horse and could not find it, then went to John Wests house to inquire for it. Mrs. Starr . . . always told me that she never took the horse . . . told me that as I was a poor boy and a crippled boy she had rather give me $30 than to give it to these big lawyers down here. I told Mrs. West that someone waylaid my road while I was hunting my horse and I thought they burst a cap at me. I told her I did not know who it was. I did not tell her that I thought it was John West . . . did not tell who I thought it was.

JOHN WEST being duly sworn says: I live in Canadian Dist. Cherokee Nation . . . 5 or 6 miles from defendants. On the 20th of April 1882 about dusk I went out to stake a horse and . . . Mrs. Starr wanted to see me. I went out to where she was & she said she wanted to pen some horses. She said she was going down to McAlister. . . . I asked where her horses were. She said Sam was with them out behind the lot. I told her to bring her horses around and pen them. I opened the gate and they penned them. She said she was going to take that horse and ride it 3 or 4 days. I told her that if I was in her place I would not take the horse that it belonged to Andrew Crane, that he was a cripple. . . . She answered God-damn the horse, she did not want to steal him. They caught the horse, I helped them catch it. Sam led the horse out and when they got ready to start she told Sam to go back and get Campbell's mare, that her horses back was sore and she would ride hers as far as home. About 9 days from that time Sam came back. I asked him if his wife had got back, he said no, asked him what she was riding, he said . . . Campbell's mare. About a week or 10 days after that he came back after his step daughter to go up home and drop corn for him. He asked me what I thought he had best do about the horse. I told him that the best thing he could do was to go and bring those horses back and turn them loose. He said he was afraid to go . . . afraid they would kill him. He asked me if I had a big pistol I could lend him. I told him I had and I let him have it, and he pulled out a fine pocket pistol and gave me and told me that if he never came back I could keep it that he stole it from a man named Childs. He then said he would go down to his fathers and get some money to bear his expenses and would start. He came back the same evening and said he had got a letter from his wife saying she would be back in a few days with the horses. He asked me what I thought about his wife going off with that man [Childs]. I told him that was not for me to say. I asked him what he thought about it, he said he just thought she was laying around with him . . . if his wife did not bring Andrew Crane's horse back he was going to give Andrew his horse for the one she had taken. He never opened his mouth about Campbell's horse. When they left my house with the horses they rode off on the horses they came on, Mrs. Starr leading Campbell's gray mare and Sam leading Crane's horse. Both horses had been running on the range there, they were not in my care. I do not know what has become of the horses. . . . It was 3 or 4 weeks . . . before I saw Mrs. Starr again, Sam and Childs was with her. Crane passes for a white man.

CROSS EXAMINATION: Sam is a Cherokee Indian. Campbell is a Cherokee. I never heard Mrs. Crane claim to be a Cherokee. Andrew Crane and his father voted once up there. The horses had been running about there a month or two. Campbell's mare was heavy with foal and in a condition that I thought she could not travel very fast . . . I saw Crane looking for his horse after it was gone. I did not tell him . . . the last I saw his horse [it was] penned in my lot. . . . The last time I saw Childs was when I saw him with Belle & Sam as I have stated. They stayed on my premises that night at their wagon. . . . I never received any money from Childs . . . don't think I ever had any business transactions with him whatever. He was never at my house but the one time. . . .

GEORGE A. CRANE being duly sworn says: I know Dfts. Mrs. Starr has been there in the settlement about two years. I went to them about my son's horse. Mrs. Starr told me if I would give her 3 weeks she would bring the man back that got the horse . . . and the man would tell who he got him from. I waited about the 3 weeks and went back to see them and they told me they did not find the man and the horse and they wanted a little more time. . . . I gave them more time but did not go back . . . and they never brought the horse back. I told them if they would tell me who took the horse would promise to be witness against him . . . but they would not tell me. . . . I went to the Nation from Sebastian Co. I was born in Smith Co. Tenn. I am a little past 52 years old. I was only 10 years old when I left Tennessee.

CROSS EXAMINATION: I went with my son to hunt for the horse.

We went by John Wests. We inquired of West about the horse and I think he told us he had not seen him for a couple of weeks. . . . About the time the horses were taken I understood that Starr was at home sick. The first time I saw him after the horse was taken he looked badly.

SAMUEL CAMPBELL being duly sworn says: I know Dfts. & know Crane. I lost a gray mare. She was running close to John Wests. I never got it back. I think Mrs. Starr came from Texas to that neighborhood. She is generally known as a white woman. If Starr and his wife took my horse they took it without my knowledge and consent.

ADJOURNED TO OCT. 10, 1882
TUESDAY OCT. 10, 1882

The following witnesses examined for defendant.

ELLEN LOWRY being duly sworn says: I live at Briartown, C. N. have lived there since '70. I know Dfts. I live just one short mile from Uncle Tom Starrs. His family took the measles the last of March. Sam was taken with the measles about the second week in April and was sick with them but a short time but had a relapse and was then sick over a month. I visited the family often during his sickness, sometimes twice a day, sometimes once a day, sometimes every other day, and sometimes I staid all night. They were all sick there. From the time Sam took sick until he was able to go about I think it was over a month. My husband died the 30th day of March last & there was so much sickness along about that time that I cannot exactly keep dates, but Sam was sick the second week after my husband's death.

CROSS EXAMINATION: I am sister to Tom Starr's wife . . . Sams aunt. I don't know of Sam being away from home about the time he got well. I was sick about a month. Dr. Redding attended him. The whole of Starrs family had the measles, it got in among the children first. I heard of the horses being taken down at Wests soon after they were taken. I think I heard it about the last of April. Sam came from his own home to Uncle Toms and was sick there. While I was going back and forth to Uncle Toms during their sickness I don't remember ever having missed Sam from home. He was in bed part of the time. . . . Belle Starr was backwards and forwards between her house and Uncle Toms. I saw her nearly every day. When she was there she waited on Sam. She was there most of the time.

THOMAS STARR being duly sworn says: I live at Briartown, I. T. Sam Starr is my son. I had the measles in my family last Spring. Sam took the measles in March, and had a relapse about the 12th of April and was down sick with them until the last of May. He took them about the first of March. On the 20th of April he was sick at my house. Belle Starr was there and back and forward to her place.

CROSS EX.: I remember the dates because I was there and plowing. . . . Sams place is about 5 miles west of my place. It is out of the way to go by Wests in going from my place to Sams. I have known Crane 7 or 8 years. Crane does not vote up there, he failed to prove his rights. I did not know Mrs. Crane's father. Lewis Downing told me that Mrs. Crane was his cousin. Lewis Downing was once Chief of our Nation. I don't know what day of the month this is. Indians don't keep the day of the month like white people. We keep it by the moon. I was down to Muskogee along last May, last Spring. Corn was away up then. We generally plant corn in March & April. I think it was in June when I went to Muskogee.

GEORGE A. CRANE recalled by Plf. says: I went to Tom Starrs about a week after the horses were missing. I went there to inquire . . . about my horse. I ate dinner there. I didn't see Sam there at all nor Belle. It was in April when I was there. . . . I was not in all the rooms . . . saw Sam at church after that.

SAMUEL CAMPBELL recalled by Plf.: I heard that they had the measles at old man Starrs along last Winter sometime but I don't remember what month it was. It was all over the settlement. Sam and I are not altogether friendly.

JOHN WEST recalled by Plf. says: They had the measles in that neighborhood about the middle of January—at Mrs. Davis' first. We had a ball at my house on the 18th of January and Jeff Davis a son of Mrs. Davis came out there & my children took the measles from him . . . next I heard of it Sam Starr had them. This must have been between the first and 15th of February. I was not up there but I heard that he was tolerably bad off. . . .

ALFRED L. HARPER being duly sworn says: I know Dfts. I live about 5 miles from their place. I met Mrs. Starr some time in July and in a conversation with her . . . she said if old Crane had kept his mouth shut about the horse he might have had it by this time, that it was through sympathy for Andrew Crane that she proposed to get the horse back for him. This was at Mrs. Lowry's house. I have seen Cranes horse but don't know who took it. Last Saturday Mrs. Starr came out on me with a tirade of abuse and said if she ever got out of this she would make it hot for us fellows up at Briartown.

CROSS EX.: I am old man Cranes son in law. . . . Mrs. Lowry was not present when Mrs. Starr made the statement . . .might have been about the place somewhere. I think Mrs. Starrs words were "Crane the damned old Arkansas hoosier, if he had kept his mouth shut would have had his horse by now."

Commissioner Wheeler ordered Sam and Belle held for "appearance at District Court on November 6" and "in default of finding bail in the sum of one thousand Dollars . . . they stand committed." On October 10, Tom Starr and his brother James, Jr., signed a recognizance for "twelve hundred dollars," listing assets "over and above all debts and liabilities and . . . exempt by law from execution . . . 70 head of Cattle worth $560, 10 horses $400, 160 head of Sheep $240." Sam and Belle returned to Youngers' Bend.

On November 7 the Fort Smith grand jury found "a true bill of indictment . . . for Larceny in the Indian Country." The original recognizance stood, and the government subpoenaed for additional testimony "Geo. Paul, Burt Brown and Frank West." The Starrs hired an additional lawyer, Colonel Benjamin T. DuVal. On November 9, DuVal and Cravens & Marcum filed an application for witnesses:

Said defendants state that they . . . cannot safely proceed to trial without the testimony of the following, viz: Dr. Henry Redding, James Beck, Tobacco Smallwood, William Crump, Thomas Starr, Ellen Lowry, Russel Childs & James C. Woods.

They can prove by said Redding that at the time of the alleged larceny on the 20th day of April 1882 the said defendant Sam Starr was confined to his bed with the measles & was absolutely unable to leave the house. That he first took the measles in the month of March last & on or about the 10th day of April following he took a relapse & continued sick & unable to travel till in the succeeding month of May & that during his said sickness the said Redding was his attending physician. He can also prove the same facts by the said Tom Starr & Lowry, James Beck, Smallwood & Crump.

They can show by the said witnesses that said defendant Sam Starr during his said sickness was at the house of his father a distance of about five miles from the place where the larceny is alleged to have been committed, the time & place of said larceny having been specifically fixed by the testimony of the main prosecuting witness in his examination before the Commissioner.

They can prove by said Childs that he purchased the horse alleged to have been stolen from John West . . . about the time the said horse was lost by the owner for the consideration of forty dollars in cash.

Defendants believe that the said Smallwood, Beck & Crump will swear specifically & positively to having seen the said Deft. Sam Starr at his fathers on the said 20th day of April 1882 & that he was then and there confined to his bed by reason of sickness.

Said Redding, Beck, Crump, Tom Starr & Lowry reside at & near Briar Town Cherokee Nation in Canadian District. Said Woods is in said Nation [Cherokee Outlet] near Caldwell Kansas. Said Childs resides as Defts are informed & believe at the mouth of Kiamitia on Red River in the Choctaw Nation.

Defts. believe said facts to be true. That this application is not made for delay but that justice may be done. That they have not the means & are actually unable to pay the fees of said witnesses.

Wherefore they pray that said witnesses may be summoned at [expense of] the United States.

Between November, 1882, and January, 1883, Deputy Marshal Marks made service on all witnesses except Childs. He noted that Childs had "fled to Texas" (never to be seen again).

The case came to trial before Judge Parker on February 15. It aroused somewhat more than passing interest along the border but did not make the big eastern dailies.[5] A single account appeared in the *Fort Smith New Era* of February 22:

> In the U.S. district court last week the case of Sam Starr and Belle Starr, his wife, of the Cherokee Nation, charged with the larceny of two horses on the 20th of April, 1882. . . . The very idea of a woman being charged with an offense of this kind and that she was the leader of a band of horse thieves and wielding a power over them as their queen and guiding spirit, was sufficient to fill the courtroom with spectators. . . .
>
> As an equestrienne, Belle Starr is without rival, is said to be an expert marksman with the pistol, and it is claimed that she was at one time the wife of Bruce Younger, the notorious horse thief and desperado, and while she could not be considered even a good-looking woman, her appearance is of that kind as would be sure to attract the attention of wild and desperate characters.

The trial lasted four days, and Belle did not take the witness stand. According to the *New Era,*

Federal courthouse in Fort Smith, Arkansas, with basement jail, where Sam and Belle Starr were tried for horse thievery in 1882. A new addition to this structure was authorized by Congress in 1886 and completed in 1889.

she would frequently hand notes to her attorneys, and it was a subject of remark that they paid strict attention to the contents. A devil-may-care expression rested on her countenance . . . and at no time did she give sign of weakening before the mass of testimony that was raised against her. Once, when allusion was made to Jim Reed, her former husband and the father of her child, tears welled up in her eyes and trickled down her cheeks, but they were quickly wiped away and the countenance resumed its wonted appearance.

Later, when Sam Starr was testifying and became confused from verbiage he could not understand, District Attorney William H. H. Clayton, a vigorous prosecutor, ridiculed his illiteracy. Belle was infuriated. "If looks had been killing, the prosecutor would have dropped in his tracks."

On the third day, the government rested. DuVal and Cravens & Marcum presented the defense. DuVal, an authority on the early history of the court and the struggling days of the city of Fort Smith, first worked on the matter of citizenship: "The court had no jurisdiction in crimes committed by one Indian against another. Such offenses belonged in the tribal courts." Belle was legally "a white woman and not an Indian," ruled Parker. Her marriage to Sam made no difference. But Sam was out of the Campbell case, both men being Cherokee. "Crane is of Indian blood and probably a citizen of the Cherokee Nation," DuVal pointed out. Clayton was on his feet at once with proof that Crane was "living in the Indian Country as a white person." Sam stayed in the Crane case.

The defense then offered as an alibi that at the time of the thefts Sam was confined at old Tom Starr's with the measles and Belle was "at his bedside most of the time." Most of the defense witnesses testified to that. On cross-examination, however, Clayton found many contradictions. The horses had been stolen the third week in April. Wasn't this the week that Sam was at home before his "relapse"? Dr. Redding thought so, Sam's aunt "couldn't remember exact dates," and Tom Starr confessed that "Indians go by the moon."

The only avenue left was to blame Childs. Childs left the horses in the Starr pasture and when Belle sold the herd she didn't know that the Crane and Campbell animals were among them. But John West stood firm. He had pointed them out to Belle, but she had "taken them anyway."

The jury returned its verdict within an hour: Belle was guilty on both counts, Sam on one. Their sureties were "released from the conditions of their recognizance" and the defendants "committed to jail to await final sentence."

The pair were brought before the court in custody of the U.S. marshal on the morning of March 8. Sam appeared "dull and morose"; Belle stared at the judge, "bold and fearless." Surpisingly, Parker was lenient. He gave Sam one year and Belle two six-month terms in the House of Correction at De-

*William H. H. Clayton, U.S. district attorney, western district of Arkansas,
Fort Smith, 1874–75 and 1889–93.*

troit, Michigan, with an opportunity for release in nine months, under prison rules, for good behavior. He took into consideration the fact that it was the first conviction for both defendants and expressed hope that they would "decide to become decent citizens."[6]

In the brief time Belle had to arrange her affairs, she thought only of daughter Pearl. After the commissioner's examination, she had sent Pearl to live with Mrs. "Mamma Mc" McLaughlin, an old friend from her Galena-Joplin days, whose family operated hotels at Oswego and Parsons, Kansas. She had refrained from using her daughter as a defense witness, and now she determined to correspond with her as Pearl Younger for fear the prosecution might learn of her whereabouts and compel her attendance. On the eve of her removal to Detroit, Belle wrote a touching letter addressed to "Miss Pearl Younger, Oswego, Kansas." It conveys the strength of this woman's maternal instinct and family pride:

PANDEMONIUM, Feb. —, 1883

My Dear Little One: — It is useless to attempt to conceal my trouble from you and though you are nothing but a child I have confidence that my darling will bear with fortitude what I now write.

I shall be away from you a few months baby, and have only this consolation to offer you, that never again will I be placed in such humiliating circumstances and that in the future your little tender heart shall never more ache, or a blush called to your cheek on your mother's account. Sam and I were tried here, John West the main witness against us. We were found guilty and sentenced to nine months at the house of correction, Detroit, Michigan, for which place we start in the morning. Now Pearl there is a vast difference in that place and a penitentiary; you must bear that in mind and not think of mamma being shut up in a gloomy prison. It is said to be one of the finest institutions in the United States, surrounded by beautiful grounds, with fountains and everything nice. There I can have my education renewed, and I stand sadly in need of it. Sam will have to attend school and I think it the best thing ever happened to him, and now you must not be unhappy and brood over our absence. It won't take the time long to glide by and as we come home we will get you and then we will have such a nice time.

We will get your horse up and I will break him and you can ride John while I am gentling Loco. We will have Eddie with us and will be as gay and happy as the birds we claim at home. Now baby you can either stay with grandma or your Mamma Mc, just as you like and do the best you can until I come back, which won't be long. Tell Eddie that he can go down home with us and have a good time hunting and though I wish not to deprive Marion and ma of him for any length of time yet I must keep him a while. Love to ma and Marion.

Uncle Tom has stood by me nobly in our trouble, done everything that one *could* do. Now baby I will write to you often. You must write to your grandma but don't tell her of this; and to your Aunt Ellen, Mamma Mc, but to no one else. Remember, I don't care who writes to you, you must not answer. I say this because I do not want you to correspond with anyone in the Indian Territory, my baby, my sweet little one, and you must mind me. Except auntie; if you wish to hear from me auntie will let you know. If you should write me, ma would find out where I am and Pearl, you must never let her know. Her head is overburdened with care now and therefore you must keep this carefully guarded from her.

Destroy this letter as soon as read. As I told you before, if you wish to stay a while with your Mamma Mc., I am willing. But you must devote your time to your studies. Bye bye, sweet baby mine.

BELLE STARR.

The letter was published first by Harman[7] with an appended note: "Copied from the original." He says it "was mailed at Fort Smith and, an unusual proceeding with [Belle], was signed with her full name." "Flossie"[8] used the letter after she "talked to people who say [Belle] wrote the letter and Pearl received it." It has been excerpted, but questioned, by later biographers.[9] However, it seems authentic.

The Marion mentioned in the letter was Francis Marion Reed, the Uncle Marion who later, according to "Flossie," took Pearl to visit relatives in Wichita, Kansas. Aunt Ellen, or "auntie," may have been Uncle Marion's wife. Riley Robinson of Joplin stated in 1938: "Pearl Starr lived at a hotel in Parsons, Kansas, run by a family named McLaughlin, while her mother was in prison. I saw her there in 1882 or 1883 — a pretty little thing, probably about fifteen years old."[10]

The "Feb. — , 1883" date is obviously Harman's, for the letter was written March 18. On March 19, Belle and Sam departed Fort Smith for Detroit in the regular railroad prison car, "Old Ten Spot," with five guards and nineteen other convicts. Belle was the only woman in the party. Two days later she and her husband were received at the House of Correction by Superintendent Joseph Nicholson.[11]

13   Belle's Piano

The Starrs' new home was a model institution stressing education and redemption as well as punishment. Several Indians who went there picked up trades and learned to read and write, but Sam was not interested in the white man's ways. He was assigned to hard labor. As for Belle's interlude, it is claimed that, when she was ushered into the presence of the warden, who heard many tales of this "terrible woman," he took one look at her and decided he needed an office assistant.[1] It is also claimed that she spent most of her leisure hours discussing current literature with the prison matron[2] and that she tutored the warden's children in French and music.[3]

Harman[4] wrote that, before the warden ever set eyes on Belle, her "V-shaped bodice quite *decollette*" style of dress had been replaced by an institution garment of "severer cut" and he conducted her immediately to the chair factory. As they passed through the bottoming department, stacked with frames ready to be given splint or cane, he said; "Take a chair." Innocently, perhaps with a gentle sadness, Belle replied, "No, thank you. I had much rather stand." The warden explained that he had meant for her to pick up a frame and be taught how to weave a cane seat for it. Belle smiled, embarrassed. She had never heard the invitation put that way. She soon gained favor with the matron and won many friends with her ladylike behavior; after the first month she was allowed the freedom of the place with "scarcely any tasks being assigned to her." Impressed by her "fine perception and a good flow of language, the warden offered to suspend the rules in her case and permit her the untrameled use of pen, ink and paper in return for her promise to write a book . . . upon what she saw and learned concerning the jail and its inmates."

Fox's writer tells us that she "entered upon a plan for the publication of her . . . autobiography and commenced a love story about an Italian bandit and a Spanish Gypsy heroine "which never developed beyond the twelfth chapter."[5] If Belle wrote anything, it did not appear in print, nor did she retain the manuscripts. At the end of nine months she and Sam were on their way back to Youngers' Bend.

Belle stopped in Missouri to spend Christmas with the Reeds and to pick up Pearl. Eddie, now almost thirteen and tired of his humdrum school days at Rich Hill, had gone to his Grandma Shirley's in Texas. An orphan girl named Mabel Harrison, who was related to the Reeds and had come to them after her parents had been "shot down before her eyes," was staying with Pearl. They had become great friends:

> Mabel Harrison was a beautiful little girl about 15 years old, with . . . lovely yellow hair. . . . Her father had a sum of money . . . to make the last payment on their little farm. Some men who claimed to be officers came and said they were there to search the house, planning to rob Mr. Harrison. . . . Of course he resisted them and Mrs. Harrison, who was sitting in line with the door [holding her young son, Will] was killed instantly. The men, seeing what they had done, fled.
>
> Belle asked Mabel if she would like to go home with her and live with Pearl. And today a frail little woman in Missouri can tell you more about the real Younger's Bend than perhaps anyone.[6]

Old Tom Starr had kept a man on the place during Sam's and Belle's absence. The corn and garden patches had been plowed and the livestock well cared for. Belle repapered the cabin and helped Sam get ready for spring planting. She had little interest in housework but could prepare an excellent meal when in the mood and took pride in making candy and passing along her favorite recipes to her friends. Pearl and Mabel did most of the cooking. They also attended the neighborhood school at Briartown.

> Tuition paid by the pupils kept the school. The students were mostly of Indian blood. . . . It was a carefree life and the girls could mount their horses and ride all through the country.

When Belle and Sam departed for Detroit they left three cats at the Bend. When they came home the cats began to spring up from everywhere, and exactly twenty-two kittens were counted. She and the girls laughed heartily many times as they thought of the kittens of all hues and sizes.

[Belle] wouldn't have a chicken on the place, because she preferred a garden. Wherever she went she brought back flowers and roots and seeds and the dooryard at the Bend [became] a veritable flower garden. And Pearl tamed two young fawns that played about. . . .

Books were [Belle's] delight. When some neighbor woman came who was tiresome to her, she would get a pillow and her books and maybe slip off and get in a wagon and there she would spend the day. And if Pearl came and said, "Why, Mamma, Mrs. — doesn't know what to think. You surely aren't going to hide out here all day!" Belle would say, "All she can talk about is pumpkins and babies! I can't stand such gab!"

Belle was capable of a warm, devoted friendship. But she felt that so few people merited it. In the last few years men have written defending her. [Although she blamed John West for her imprisonment] when a baby was born to John West's wife, Belle came by and found Mrs. West lying there depending on the older children for most of her care. Belle sent home for her clothes and stayed until Mrs. West was able to be up and around, even getting to name the baby. And today one of the West sons bears the name Belle gave him.[7]

Belle displayed much affection for children and delighted in telling them stories. Around Briartown and Whitefield, many a boy and girl grew to manhood and womanhood remembering the tales she related when she "came calling" and how she played and sang religious songs, such as "Jesus, lover of my soul, let me to thy bosom fly" or "There is a fountain filled with blood."

Prison life had put her on the plump side, but she still had a good figure, weighed about one hundred and forty pounds, and her movements remained quick and graceful. She could vault to the back of a horse with ease and danced well, especially to the fiddling of country breakdowns. She had lost some of her facial beauty. Thinning cheeks gave her long nose an aquiline appearance, and with her deep tan and long black hair she was often mistaken for an Indian. Her hands had broadened somewhat, but her feet were small and she was so vain of them that she wore only the finest, most expensive boots. She wore gold earrings, rarely other jewelry. On dress occasions she wore a black velvet riding habit and a man's sombrero with the brim pinned up by a bright feather. A small sorrel gelding and a fine black mare named Venus were her favorite mounts. Her expensive and highly decorative side-saddle became widely known as the Belle Starr saddle. When riding alone about the country, she usually buckled a Colt .45 around her waist; she called it "my baby."

"Belle was facetious," says Harman;[8] at times she "remembered her early training and demanded from the rough and uncouth dwellers of the plains the full courtesy due a lady in civilization." One day as she was crossing Scullyville Prairie near Fort Smith the wind blew her hat off. William Kayser, a cowboy, was riding by; she hailed him and asked him to retrieve it. Kayser refused. "Instantly grasping her pistol, she 'drew a bead' and with telling oaths commanded: 'Get down and pick up my hat!'" Kayser "hastened to obey," and Belle admonished: "The next time a *lady* asks you to pick up her hat, do as she tells you." Some biographers[9] and most journalists have credited this incident to Blue Duck, but it was Kayser who said he "never forgot the lesson in etiquette."[10]

In the same vein is a yarn, spun by a Fort Smith feature writer, about Felix LeFlore, grandson of Choctaw chieftain Greenwood LeFlore, who gave LeFlore County, Oklahoma, its name. Felix was leisurely riding along the road west of Fort Smith in the Choctaw Nation when Belle galloped up behind him. "Hurry it up, young man!" she shouted. Felix retorted: "I'll travel at any rate I please." Belle whipped out her six-shooter and sent a bullet flying over his head. Felix put spurs to his horse and, with Belle popping her six-shooter behind him, flew over the trail faster than he had ever traveled in his life.[11]

There were those who charged that when Belle came back to the Bend she opened the "suburbs of hell"; that her gang stole horses and buggies in Arkansas and Kansas; that the "whole community was wild for fear she or some of her pals would steal their livestock, or shoot them if they reported to the federal marshals, and surely had to play 'shut mouth' if you had to travel some long trail, or plow in the fields."[12] In a clearing about a quarter of a mile from Belle's cabin stood a lofty cedar, trimmed with only a small tuft of limbs at the top, called "the marshal's pole." When a luckless deputy fell into the clutches of her desperadoes, he was taken to this tree and forced to climb it; then, for their delectation, they "shot him out just like a squirrel."[13] There is no proof that this happened.

Belle allegedly frequented Fort Smith gambling halls and played for the highest stakes, but, unlike Poker Alice Tubbs, the female gambler of Deadwood, South Dakota, she did not smoke cigars—she did not "consider cigars feminine and . . . liked to keep her sex appeal."[14] She would drop in at the various saloons and play the piano for hours, or if the mood struck her, she would ride her horse on the sidewalks in the custom of the Wild West bad men. Small boys and girls haunted Garrison Avenue to glimpse the "flashy outlaw queen" with a brace of heavy revolvers buckled around her waist, yet one Fort Smith resident remembered that she "looked very modest on a horse, the most modest woman rider I ever saw."[15]

In the *Indian-Pioneer History* interviews collected by the Oklahoma Historical Society during 1937–38 and bound in one hundred and twenty volumes averaging five hundred pages each, at least one hundred old-timers recalled seeing or knowing Belle Starr or hearing relatives tell about her. Strangely, none of the escapades mentioned received contemporary notice, nor does her name appear in Fort Smith police registers. In fact, Belle's conviction for horse stealing garnered only three lines in an Indian Territory newspaper;[16] there was no blaze of interviews with reporters as she left for prison; no reporters were waiting for her when she returned. She had been all but forgotten.

Another point of controversy is whether Belle had a piano at Youngers' Bend. Some biographers[17] doubt it, but according to John Jetton,[18] Belle got the piano in early spring, 1884.

Jetton freighted between Newman (now Stigler), Choctaw Nation, and Fort Smith. One evening he unloaded some hides in a buyer's warehouse at Fort Smith and camped for the night. Not wanting to deadhead, he scouted about town next morning for something to haul back. He soon sighted a big crate on the sidewalk and a man circling it, "making quite a commotion." Walking closer, he recognized Icsam Perry, a young Choctaw who lived near Whitefield; inside the crate was an almost new Lingsburg Cabinet Grand piano.

Perry was recovering from a drunk. About daybreak he had run into a man with two teams and wagons piled full of household goods, the piano, his wife, and their children. They were moving to Texas, had come a long way, were out of money, and "kids plenty hungry." Perry felt sorry for them. The man wanted to sell the piano, so Perry gave him all the money he had—fifty dollars.

Belle galloped past while he and Jetton were talking, spun her sorrel horse and rode back. Perry told her: "Folks at Whitefield sent me to buy things they need. Now they be big mad. 'Fraid to go home—they raise plenty hell with Icsam. Can't carry piano back to Whitefield on pack horse either."

Belle dismounted. She examined the piano, lifted the keyboard cover and ran her fingers over the ivories. "Perry," she said, "did you get a bill of sale?" The Indian fumbled a piece of paper from his pocket. Belle read it, pulled a leather pouch from her dress, and shook several coins into his hand. "There is your fifty dollars, Icsam. Go buy whatever your folks sent you after; then skin for home."

"Got your freight rig in town?" she asked Jetton. Jetton nodded, and she offered him fifty dollars to haul the piano to the Bend. Jetton was "leery," but fifty dollars was a lot of money.

It was a grueling trip across the Poteau into the Choctaw

Nation, then west through Keota and Newman to Whitefield. Spring rains had made the roads boggy. The Canadian was up, and Jetton had to drive downstream a mile and use the Brassfield ferry to cross into the Bend country. Belle rode to the front and rear of the wagon like a scout, making small talk, giving instructions along the way. Shortly after noon the fourth day, he followed her into Belle Starr Canyon. The trail was "not too rough," but Jetton felt that from behind the boulder-studded walls and thick brush he was "being watched over the sights of a rifle." Finally they reached the cabin. A tall Indian came out on the porch, and Belle introduced her husband.

"Sam Starr was the most striking man I ever met," Jetton recalled. "He was over six feet tall, slim, broad-shouldered, face like a picture." Even his big revolver "seemed to fit." Belle told him she had bought herself a present and would explain later.

Jetton squared his rig with the porch, and Sam summoned a couple of "tough-looking dudes" squatting in front of a building nearby to help roll the piano off the wagon. The piano went through the cabin doorway "without a hitch." Belle pulled the leather pouch from her dress and shook out three twenty dollar gold pieces. Jetton said, "You only owe me fifty," but Belle insisted that he had earned the extra ten.

Jetton thanked her and climbed into his wagon. He heard her tell Sam to accompany him to the ferry, and the knots in his stomach "started tightening again." He knew of Sam's reputation as a bushwhacker and started to tell Belle he could make it himself, but he noticed the "two dudes" eyeing him and decided that Belle was sending Sam to protect him. Sam led off, riding "about twenty yards in front, didn't look back or say a word," until they reached the ferry. Then he "rode alongside and said, 'Thanks, Jetton. If you are ever back in this country, stop by.'" Jetton "just nodded," too relieved to think of anything to say. When he got back across the Canadian, he felt like "kissing the ground." But he could never believe that "Sam Starr was the devil some said he was."

Jetton recalled that Belle later hired Charley Williams, a young traveling music teacher, to give her children piano lessons. Pearl "tried hard, but had little talent"; Eddie "had some talent . . . but cared nothing for music."

Some time afterward, Dr. R. I. Bonds of Canadian, a settlement on the Katy Railroad twenty-some miles west of Whitefield, was summoned to the Bend by a Cherokee messenger to treat a patient and found Pearl suffering from a severe attack of the grippe. Dr. Bonds instructed Belle concerning the care Pearl should receive, gave her the medicine she would need, and left. During his brief visit he "saw a piano" in the cabin.[19] Mooney[20] says the piano was still there in 1888; his mother played on it many times and taught Belle a very popular song of the period, *Listen to the Mockingbird.*

Actually, 1884 was a relatively uneventful year for Belle. Mrs. Shirley came up to Eufaula from Texas on the Katy and spent a few days at the Bend. She brought little Eddie, and for the first time since the death of her lamented husband, Jim Reed, Belle and her children were together at home again.

Mrs. Nancy Middleton (Jim's aunt) and her four sons, Bill, John, Ike, and James, lived three miles west of Paris in Logan County, Arkansas, near Lower Short Mountain; Lee Reed (probably Solomon Lee) and his four motherless daughters, the youngest twelve, lived less than a mile from the Middletons in the same neighborhood.[21] Pete Marshall and family, old Missouri friends of Belle, resided at Chickalah in Yell County. Occasionally Belle would leave Eddie with Sam and Mabel Harrison, take Pearl, and visit the Reed relatives and Marshall family, with side trips to some sulfur springs near Dardanelle.

Hicks[22] thinks Belle "combined pleasure and health with business" by working out an "operating agreement" with a horse-stealing ring in the area; that it "is quite conceivable" that Belle and John Middleton "transacted quite a bit of business in [this] line"; and that it was hardly a coincidence that Mrs. Middleton and John's kid brother James came to Indian Territory "that very winter" and established a home near Briartown, where James began farming. In an interview at Briartown in 1937,[23] James Middleton said he came to Indian Territory in 1885.

> I was born in 1857 . . . settled in Younger Bend community on the Canadian river. . . . The old Tom Starr place was the most prominent settlement in this vicinity at that time. . . . The country was all open range and the cattle business was very profitable. As to farming, our principal crop was corn and we always disposed of our surplus farm products to the cattlemen.
>
> I became acquainted with Sam Starr and his wife, Belle Starr, when I first came to Indian Territory as I rented a place from them . . . four miles west of Briartown . . . the first year I was here.

In any event, Belle's year of tranquility was about to be broken. Just before Christmas, 1884, John Middleton, wanted for murder, with a price on his head and carrying a shotgun, knocked on her door.

14   Outlaw Middleton and a One-eyed Mare

Belle probably had met John Middleton in Arkansas, but his sudden appearance at the Bend must have surprised her. At twenty-nine he had become "widely known as one of the most daring outlaws in the land, able to cope with the best officers that could be put on his trail."[1] Of medium build, with a heavy sandy mustache and weathered complexion, wearing half boots, dark cassimere pants, a vest, and a dress shirt under a short winter coat, he was rather pleasing to look upon, except the tip of one ear was missing.

When a lad, Middleton visited a half-brother in Lamar County, Texas. The boys went to the home of a family named Chance, one of the sons being a friend, and asked to borrow Mrs. Chance's scissors to give each other a "foxy" haircut. The woman refused, so they obtained a pair of shears from the barn. As each youth's hair was being clipped, he would bleat like a sheep. As John's hair was being cut, the shears slipped and sliced a piece off his ear.[2]

Middleton made his debut as a criminal in Logan and Scott counties, Arkansas. At age eighteen he stole a pair of boots, some shoes, and several pocket knives and was sentenced to a year in the penitentiary. Afterward he returned to Scott County and "soon became a fugitive . . . charged with burning the courthouse at Waldron . . . fled to Texas and went to stealing horses, becoming very proficient in the business."[3]

Slate Shoals in Lamar County was a favorite Red River crossing for thieves who stole horses in Arkansas and Indian Territory to sell in Texas, and vice versa. One day a farmer near the Shoals, while repairing a fence to keep his livestock out of a heavy thicket, noticed two horses tied in the underbrush. Not recognizing their brands, he did not molest them.

177

Soon some men carrying shotguns came from the direction of the Territory and rode into the thicket. About dark, shots were heard, and the men and the horses vanished. Next morning a search party found the buckshot-riddled corpse of Dave Bowen, a resident of Indian Territory and known associate of Middleton. Middleton finally was arrested on a charge of bringing stolen horses into Texas and was jailed at Paris, where he suddenly became ill. On the advice of the county physician, he was placed in a room at the jailer's residence, apparently so sick that a close watch on him seemed unnecessary. One night in August, 1884, he disappeared.[4]

In November, J. H. Black defeated a man named Crook for sheriff of Lamar County. On the night of November 16 a rider appeared at the home of Sheriff Black and called him to the door. As the sheriff's big frame filled the opening against the lamplight, a voice shouted, "Here's a little present for you!" A shotgun blasted in the darkness. Black clutched his chest and fell to his knees. In the dim light he could not see the rider's face clearly, but he had recognized the voice. "Middleton—damn you—you've killed me!" he screamed, then toppled forward. Middleton drummed off into the night.

It was believed that Middleton had been hired by Black's political enemies, and former Sheriff Crook and one of his former deputies were jailed at Sherman as accomplices in the murder. Local rewards totaling five hundred dollars, plus three hundred dollars offered by the state, were posted for Middleton. Deputy Sheriff Polk Burris of Lamar County and John ("Jack") Duncan, the state detective known for tracking down John Wesley Hardin and credited with working up the case against Crook, pursued Middleton into Indian Territory.[5]

About Christmas, Burris and Duncan lost their quarry in the vicinity of Youngers' Bend. They made the acquaintance of John West, who "had risen to the dignity of Indian policeman."[6] West guided them through the country for several days, but they were unable to strike a new trail. The officers turned their papers over to West and returned to Texas.[7]

What John Middleton did during the next four months while hiding out on the South Canadian is not known. Fox's writer has Belle and the "residents of Younger Bend" (Middleton presumably included) visiting Wewoka and robbing John Brown, treasurer of the Seminole Nation.[8] This robbery having proved successful, "Bella determined on trying her hand once more" by robbing Sam Brown, treasurer of the Creek Nation. Subsequent biographers accept Fox and variously charge Sam and Belle Starr, Middleton, "Grant Cook," and Felix Griffin.[9] No substantive contemporary accounts or official records support them. "Grant Cook" does not appear in the annals of Indian Territory crime, and the participation of the Starrs, Middleton, or Felix Griffin in treasury holdups is folklore.

Felix Griffin was a regular visitor at Youngers' Bend, but he had no problem with the law at this time. Thomas, his brother, "had a bad record, though short." Both were raised at Webbers Falls; a sister married into the Starr clan. In the summer of 1882, Thomas "rendered himself notorious" by killing Santa Brewer, a prominent Cherokee. With a five-hundred-dollar reward on his head, he fled to Mexico, where he "robbed for two years," then "started for Nashville to have an operation performed on his mouth which was drawn to one side." He was captured on the train and returned to Webbers Falls for trial in an Indian court, but he escaped from Sheriff Stan Gray and "began scouting" between Eufaula and Okmulgee. Sheriff Gray was suspended, and Chief Dennis W. Bushyhead offered a private reward for Griffin's capture. Some four thousand dollars had been deposited at McAnnally's Store in Eufaula pending settlement of an Indian claim. About eleven o'clock on the night of August 16, 1884, "a noise was heard at the side door" by clerks Tom Lindsey and Ed Sanger, who were sleeping inside and guarding the money. "Both reached for a shotgun . . . Tom got it first . . . Griffin, through cracks between the double doors, slowly worked the bar until the end dropped, then stepped inside and scratched a match to light a small burglars' lamp he carried." A dozen feet away stood Lindsey. Griffin reached for his pistol. "Nine buckshot tore into his left arm on which hung his saddle bags and entered . . . his heart." His horse was found hitched fifty yards from the store with "his boots which he had taken precaution to remove" tied on the saddle. Next day the body was claimed and buried at Eufaula by Frost Starr and wife and Griffin's mother.[10] Felix Griffin lived at Webbers Falls but frequently had been seen with Sam Starr.

The Fox opus alleges:

> Middleton had loved Bella [from the time] he first laid eyes on her, and determined to win her if it were in his power. Bella herself was captivated. The comparison between Middleton and Starr was decidedly unfavorable to the latter. Though both were good-looking, the white man had much the advantage, besides being able to boast a good education. . . . That our heroine grew weary of her husband is certain from the fact that she eloped with Middleton, and camped with him for over a week in the Dardanelles mountains.[11]

Therefore, Rascoe assumes, with Sam gone from home dodging the marshals and Indian police, Belle was "left alone with Middleton." Her love for Sam grew "cold," Middleton "enkindled it," and finally the pair decided to "give Sam the slip."[12] Subsequent biographers follow suit.[13]

Actually, the tenacity of John West and his Indian deputies forced Middleton, not Sam Starr, to keep up an uncomfortable dodging from January through April, 1885. It is doubtful that he troubled his younger brother Jim for protection. Jim Middleton stuck to his farming, did odd jobs for his neighbors, including Sam and Belle, and hunted in the mountains. With a brother like John, he was careful to keep legitimate and keep his mouth shut.

On the other hand, a "close friendship" sprang up between Sam Starr and murderer Middleton.[14] Sam may have considered him a potential ally in future operations. More than likely, the bad blood between the Starrs and the Wests, resulting from John West's testimony that sent Sam and Belle to prison, moved

Indian policeman John West, Sam Starr's nemesis.

Sam to seclude Middleton in the wilderness of the Canadian
bottoms, thus defying the Indian policeman in his own baili-
wick.

West's untiring efforts were not to be underestimated, however. By spring, 1885, Detective Duncan was "sleuthing" the
country again, this time accompanied by Lamar County Deputy
Sheriff J. H. Milsap. In mid-April, Duncan, Milsap, and West
"raided the Belle Starr ranch . . . but the bird had flown."
Belle was alone. She "met them with her six-shooter belted
around her, and after giving John West a cursing for piloting
the officers to her house, she cooled down and laughed at the
officers . . . ridiculing them for imagining they could take
Middleton," even had she been harboring him.[15] But the bold
raid unnerved Sam Starr, and Middleton was "only too willing
to leave the country."[16] His problem was getting away from
the Bend safely.

Belle decided it was time she and Pearl made one of their
accustomed trips to Chickalah. Belle wanted to see the Pete
Marshall family again and visit the springs near Dardanelle.
"Her route would take them by the home of . . . Lee Reed,
where she would leave Pearl to visit with her cousins for a
few weeks."[17] They would travel in her covered "horse wagon,"
their favorite mounts tied behind and Middleton concealed
beneath the canvas, until they were across the Canadian and
past Whitefield. From there Middleton would take Pearl's
horse and proceed by a circuitous route beyond the settlements where he might be seen, cross the Poteau River, then
go directly east through Booneville to his old home in Logan
County. Belle and Pearl would follow the trail through Newman and Keota to Fort Smith, take the Arkansas River route
to Logan County, and pick up Pearl's horse before proceeding
to Chickalah.

On May 2, Belle and Pearl packed their effects in the wagon
and with Frank Cook (a boy Belle employed for odd jobs)
as driver, began their journey.[18] Eddie Reed and Sam accompanied them a short distance past Whitefield, where they

camped for the night. During the night, "some trivial act of Middleton's caused a falling out" between him and Pearl and Pearl "refused the loan of her horse."[19]

The morning of May 3, while the little company was at breakfast, Fayette Barnett, a white rancher who had married a Choctaw woman known as the "Widow Brooken," was out looking after his stock and stopped to converse with Belle. Middleton was hidden in the timber. Belle told Barnett they were in need of an extra horse, which Barnett agreed to provide. He "went out upon the range" and caught a sorrel mare, later described as "about fourteen hands high, branded '31' on the neck and a half circle, or 'rafter A,' on the shoulder." He did not tell anyone the mare was the property of Albert G. McCarty, another white rancher who lived nearby. Eddie Reed "took the horse to Middleton in the woods." Middleton was not pleased with the mare—she was without shoes and blind in the right eye—but he had no choice and paid Barnett fifty dollars for the animal. After Barnett had departed, Middleton "placed on the mare's back Pearl's saddle [which Belle had purchased for her at Eufaula], then, taking Belle's six-shooter and leaving his shotgun in the wagon," rode off toward the Poteau.[20]

Sam and Eddie turned back to Youngers' Bend;[21] Belle and Pearl drove toward Newman and Keota. Two of Belle's acquaintances, William Hicks and James Johnson, "met her on the road and nooned with her." After visiting several other parties along the way, Belle and Pearl reached Fort Smith the following evening, stayed all night at a hotel, and the next day continued their journey toward Logan County.[22]

On Thursday, May 7, Henry Tallay of Pocola, Choctaw Nation, found a sorrel mare, blind in one eye, tangled in the brush at the point of Poteau Mountain, twenty-five miles southwest of Fort Smith. She was bridled and saddled and from the saddlehorn hung a belt containing several cartridges and a .45-caliber Colt revolver. Mud and silt on the trappings indicated the animal had swum the river, and "in belief the rider had been drowned, a search was instituted." On May 11, tracks were discovered where the mare had entered the water. About two hundred yards downstream, washed up on the muddy bank, lay the badly decomposed body of a man clad in a vest, dress shirt, half boots, and dark cassimere trousers, his face and sandy mustache "half eaten away by buzzards." There was no identification, only two jackknives, a silver watch, and a ten-dollar bank note in his pockets. The remains were buried by the search party, and a description of the mare, trappings, the body, and the articles found on it was sent to O. D. Weldon at the *Fort Smith Elevator,* which carried an item relating to the discovery.[23]

Meanwhile, Albert McCarty had been making inquiries in the Youngers' Bend neighborhood for his missing mare. He furnished West and the Texas officers a description; they were already aware of Belle's and Pearl's sudden departure to Arkansas. "By some shrewd maneuver," Duncan learned of Belle's destination, and supposing that Middleton was connected, he and Milsap went by rail to Dardanelle to await her arrival. They saw the item in the *Elevator,* and "rightly surmising the dead man was the outlaw they were chasing, they wired John West to meet them at Fort Smith." Weldon joined them, and the quartet proceeded to the Poteau, where the body was exhumed and identified. "It had been buried in a box . . . after taking a good look at the man they had pursued so long, the dirt was again piled over the box, and the officers turned away." The river, easy to ford in normal weather, "was up and the current very swift" from recent rains, "but nothing daunted," and overestimating the stamina of the one-eyed mare, Middleton had "pushed into the stream . . . lost his life in the attempt to swim it . . . and thus justice was cheated of one of its ripest criminals."[24]

McCarty also saw the item in the *Elevator,* went to Pocola, and identified the estray. The saddle was "fully identified" as the one purchased by Belle at Eufaula. The Colt .45 was the weapon Belle wore at her waist when West and the Texas officers raided the Bend in April.

On May 18, Duncan, Milsap, and West reached Belle's camp near Dardanelle. They arrested young Cook for questioning and proposed to search Belle's trunk for additional evidence to link her with Middleton. "Belle grasped a pistol in each hand," writes Harman,[25] "and coolly informed them that if they broke open the trunk their souls would go speeding to the place of torment; the trunk was not opened." Belle had been "warned" of Middleton's death by one of the outlaw's brothers, and "on learning from the officers that the horse Middleton rode was the property of McCarty, she at once thought of the saddle . . . knowing that a charge of larceny would be trumped up against her."[26]

Frank Cook was taken to Fort Smith, where he gave a statement. If he was ever charged with anything, the case records do not show it.[27] Belle returned to Youngers' Bend without her revolver and Pearl's saddle.

Duncan and Milsap told Weldon they had been in "close pursuit" of Middleton and were about to take him when he and Belle "eloped" to Arkansas. In a dispatch to the *St. Louis Globe-Democrat,* Weldon referred to Belle as "the mistress of Middleton," and the local gossip that Belle was not always constant in her devotion to Sam Starr was fanned further when the *Muskogee Indian Journal* reprinted the story a few days later. This probably was the reason Belle's biographers used the Fox writer's alleged Middleton love affair as fact.[28]

15   Sam Starr, Fugitive

Sam was at home when Belle returned to Youngers' Bend. There is no record of his reaction to Belle's troubles or her version of Middleton's fate, but three weeks later he was hiding in the mountains—for the first time since their marriage, himself a fugitive from justice.

On June 15, 1885, three unidentified riders held up a U.S. Mail hack in the Cherokee Nation. A capias issued on the scanty information filed before U.S. Commissioner John Q. Tufts at Muskogee charged "robbery" and named "Sam Starr." A second capias, issued by Commissioner Tufts several months later, charged "attempt to rob the mail [by] Sam'l Brown & three others whose names are unknown."[1] The June warrant was never served, and no disposition of the case is shown, probably because Sam managed to stay a jump ahead of John West and his Indian deputies, and evidence that he participated in the holdup was lacking. However, by the time the second capias was issued, the federal government had charged Sam and two of his cohorts with an offense in which identification was more positive.

On the night of October 30, 1885, three men burglarized the Andrew J. Moore store and post office at Blaine above Pheasant Bluff seven miles northeast of Keota. The complaint filed before Commissioner Wheeler at Fort Smith on November 9 charged "Sam Starr, Felix Griffin and Richard Hays . . . in Choctaw Nation, I. T., did feloniously steal, take and carry away personal property of Andrew J. Moore [and] from the lawful possession of A. J. Short, Postmaster, United States currency . . . said money being P. O. funds and property of the United States." Listed as federal witnesses were "A. J.

186

Short, Leo Davis, A. J. Moore & Elliott Burns on the Canadian."[2]

A few weeks later Hays, Felix Griffin, and Felix's cousin,
Luna ("Loony") Griffin, were arrested by the Indian police for
horse stealing; they were convicted by a Cherokee circuit court
in session at Webbers Falls the last week in December, and each
was sentenced to four years in the Cherokee National Prison
at Tahlequah.[3] On January 14, 1886, the trio escaped in what
was "thought to have been a put up job."[4] Felix Griffin fled
back to Youngers' Bend, but he and Sam Starr "fell out and
had a shooting scrape, Felix getting shot in the right hand."[5]
Contemporary reports do not give a reason for their trouble,[6]
but when he was captured by the Cherokee authorities, Griffin's "left arm [had been] rendered useless by a gun shot [and]
his 'set to' with Sam about retired him from active pursuits
of any character."[7] He returned to his haunts around Webbers
Falls and afterward was seen running with Frank Palmer, another Falls ne'er-do-well who did odd jobs for Griffin's mother
and was a constant companion of Jack Spaniard.

Sam Starr kept to the Youngers' Bend wilderness, protected
by his many relatives. He ventured home on occasion but managed to avoid arrest. One afternoon John West met Belle on
the trail and asked her to persuade Sam to surrender. Belle
gave him another tongue-lashing, replying that the crimes laid
to Sam's door had been trumped up by his enemies, who
would not hesitate to swear him into prison if he stood trial.

Elias Rector[8] of Fort Smith told this story:

One day Belle learned that a posse of marshals had entered the Bend. Jim Cole and another deputy, thinking to
catch Sam at home, drove up the canyon incognito in a box
wagon and were surprised to find Belle expecting them. Belle
had nailed boards on a tree overlooking the river, "a kind of
ladder" that she could shinny up "to see who might be comin'."
When the wagon came close, she "advanced toward it." She
appeared unusually pleasant and agreeable and, squinting up
at the sun, said to Jim Cole: "I reckon it's approachin' the

noon hour. If you lawmen want to light, I'll cook up something to eat." While the deputies watered their team, Belle
busied herself inside the cabin. Soon they were seated at the
table, "partaking heartily" of the hot stew, corn bread, and
coffee she set before them. Strangely, Belle "didn't eat any of
the temptin' morsel." After the men had their fill and "squared
back to smoke and visit," she asked if they knew what they had
been eating. "Well," she said, relishing every word, "that was
an old rattlesnake I killed this mornin'. Now go out and puke
it up!" And they "exactly did."

Finally, the inevitable happened. West had continued his
investigation of the Middleton drowning in the Poteau. In mid-
January 1886, Belle "heard there was a writ out for her" for
stealing McCarty's mare. McCarty had signed the complaint.
Belle "did not propose to be dragged around again by some
federal deputy"; on January 21, she appeared in Fort Smith
and surrendered to the U.S. marshal.[9] She was indicted for
larceny. On February 8 she entered a not-guilty plea before
Judge Parker and filed an application for witnesses:

The defendant says . . . she cannot safely proceed to trial without
the testimony of the following . . . William Hicks and James Johnson
who live at Eufaula, Creek Nation, I. T. by whom she can prove the
day after said mare is alleged to have been stolen they fell in with
her on the road and nooned with her; and the next day she came
into Fort Smith and hired up her train at the wagon yard publicly
and stayed all night at a hotel where she registered in her own
name—that she was traveling in her horse wagon with her daughter,
that she did not have said mare in her possession at this time.

Edwin Reed who lives in Canadian district Cherokee Nation . . .
by whom she can prove that Fayette Barnett [was] in the country
near where said Albert McCarty lived—that he at the request of
Fayette Barnett took the horse to John Middleton out in the woods.
. . . That this defendant had no connection with the taking of said
mare nor anything to do with her after she was stolen.

By her daughter, Belle would show that

Pearl was in company with this defendant all of the time from long
before said mare was alleged to have been stolen until the death of

United States of America,

Western District of Arkansas.

IN THE DISTRICT COURT, *February* TERM, A. D. 1886.

UNITED STATES

VERSUS

Belle Starr

The Grand Jurors of the United States of of America, duly selected, empaneled, sworn and charged, to inquire in and for the body of the Western District of Arkansas, aforesaid, upon their oath present:

THAT *Belle Starr*

on the *3d* day of *May* A. D. 1885 at the *Choctaw* Nation, in the Indian Country within the Western District of Arkansas, aforesaid, did

feloniously steal, take and carry away, of the goods and chattels of Albert McCarty, a white man and not an Indian one horse, of the value of seventy-five dollars;

contrary to the form of the Statute in such case made and provided, and against the peace and dignity of United States of America.

WM. H. H. CLAYTON,

U. S. District Attorney, Western District of Arkansas.

Fort Smith grand-jury indictment in United States v. Belle Starr for larceny of Albert McCarty's mare, May 3, 1885.

Middleton in whose possession was reported to [have] been — and that this defendant never had such animal in her possession or anything to do with it.

"By David Moore and Joseph Hammon," whom Belle and Pearl saw after meeting Hicks and Johnson, "defendant would prove she did not have said mare in her possession," and "by N. W. Wagginer" she would prove that Fayette Barnett was "in the country where said Albert McCarty lived" at the time the mare was stolen. Parker approved the application and set trial for the September court term; Belle posted bond and was released.[10]

On her way back to Youngers' Bend, Belle visited Fayette Barnett and quietly told him, "I am innocent and can prove it." Barnett promised to lend every assistance and agreed to pay her attorney fees, fearing that she would turn the tables and prove the sale of the mare to Middleton by the rancher.

If John West thought the charge against Belle would smoke Sam Starr out of the brush, he was disappointed. The February 1 grand jury that indicted Belle also indicted Sam and Felix Griffin for the Blaine post office burglary; new capiases were issued February 8.[11] And on Saturday night, February 27, almost within the shadow of the Fort Smith court, an angry Sam Starr allegedly struck again.

Near Cache on the Canadian in Scullyville County, Choctaw Nation, Wilse W. Farrill and his three sons, Nick, Tom, and Gari Baldi ("Gar") Farrill, had established a farming settlement and reportedly had money. Three men brandishing rifles and six-shooters and "stating that they were deputy marshals" to gain entrance to Wilse Farrill's home "went through his trunk, getting about $40 in cash, $34 of which was the old gentleman's." They took a pistol at another house and stole a horse from the yard at a third residence.[12]

Farrill and his sons saw all three robbers but could not identify them. Neither could G. W. Tucker, Jack and Mary Burns, and Mrs. Elizabeth Loring, who witnessed portions of the action. Eighteen-year-old Lila McGilberry told a different story. She was alone at the Burns residence when one of the robbers, "a six-shooter in each hand, wearing pants and overcoat and a kind of white hat," came in and forced her into another room as a second robber "with a rifle, wearing a kind of grey overcoat," searched the house. Miss McGilberry, though "scared pretty bad," remembered that the bandit with the six-shooters "had nothing over the face . . . did not talk like a man . . . was a woman dressed like a man" and was none other than Belle Starr.[13]

An Indian police posse consisting of Billy Drew, John Drew, Carter Smith, William G. ("Billy") Robinson, John Lee, William Runnells, and John Toney assembled at Webbers Falls. A couple of nights later, John West and Sheriff William Vann of the Canadian District led the posse into Youngers' Bend. According to the *Muskogee Indian Journal* of March 11,

they made a raid on Sam and Belle Starr, where they found nine men, besides Sam and Belle. They captured one, a white man named Jackson, and after disarming him, released him. The others, the ones wanted, escaped, Sam Starr jumping his horse off a bluff over twenty feet high, and swimming the river. . . . These men are determined, however, to break up this band of cut-throats, robbers and horse thieves, and say they will never let them rest in peace. This is certainly a bad gang, and we would rejoice to know that they were out of the country. They [the officers] informed us that Belle Starr went to Eufaula a few days since and bought 100 rounds of cartridges, and from their [the gang's] maneuvers it is certain that they intended making a raid on somebody soon. Therefore, it is advisable for every merchant likely to be visited by them to be on his guard.

Evidently, full details of the raid were not furnished the *Journal* correspondent. After the "gang" escaped, the posse searched for the pistol and horse taken in the Farrill robbery but found only a peddler's pack containing an assortment of spectacles. Bill Vann, somewhat of a wag, saw Belle returning to the cabin and placed three or four pairs on his nose. As she rode up, he looked over the spectacles with owl-like wiseness and remarked sarcastically, "*Mistress* Belle Starr, I believe?" His companions burst into laughter. Belle's eyes flashed, in a rage that she was unable to express in words, as she reached for her revolver. John West was on her in an instant, snatching the half-drawn weapon from her grasp. Vann chuckled, perhaps a little uncomfortably; everybody laughed again. Then Belle put her face in her hands, sank down on the veranda, and cried. She was not arrested, but West kept her revolver. Years later he gave the gun to Jackson Ellis of Marble City, a long-time deputy marshal in Indian Territory.[14]

A complaint filed before U.S. Commissioner James Brizzolara at Fort Smith accused Belle of being "gang leader" in the Farrill robbery. A capias for her and subpoenas for "G. W. Tucker, Mrs. Loring, Jack Burns, Mary Burns & Lilley [sic] McGilberry" were issued March 10 and sent to B. T. (Tyner) Hughes, deputy marshal for the Choctaw Nation. Hughes made service on the witnesses, who gave sworn statements in U.S. Commissioner's court on March 24. Apparently he failed to locate Belle, for a notation on the capias shows it was "returned with no service, Tyner Hughes, Apr. 1, 1886."[15]

Hughes was successful with a new warrant issued April 27. At dusk one evening in mid-May he rode up Belle Starr Canyon with posseman Charles Barnhill and found his quarry. Sam Starr also was at home, says Harman,[16] but Pearl, "who had been outside," warned him that "officers were approaching a short distance from the house." Sam rose quietly, picked up his Winchester; Belle turned down the light, and he slipped from the house into the brush unobserved. Belle met Hughes and Barnhill, "each of them showing evident signs of nervousness," at the door. She "joked them about their chattering teeth and the condition of their clothing, showing, as she asserted, that they had crawled to the house on their hands and knees." She asked their mission, was shown the warrant in the Farrill case, and "consented to accompany the officers to Fort Smith. Pearl saddled her pony and accompanied her mother a matter of ten miles, and thereby, doubtless, prevented her stepfather, or 'Uncle Sam' as she always called him, from committing murder." Sam kept abreast of the party, but "every time he would attain proper range" for his rifle, "either his wife or Pearl would move between him and the officer he sought to destroy"; finally he "gave up the attempt." Pearl returned home, and Belle and the officers continued on their way to Fort Smith.

If Harman's story is true, Hughes and Barnhill were spared the fate which had befallen their comrade, Deputy Marshal William H. Irwin, a few weeks earlier. On Thursday, April 8, the Indian police surprised Felix and Luna Griffin near Walnut Town in the Creek Nation and captured Felix. Felix was brought to Webbers Falls on Sunday night and turned over to Deputy Irwin.[17] Irwin had intended to take him to Muskogee for examination before Commissioner Tufts on "an offense committed in the Cherokee country," but he carried subpoenas for several witnesses near Scullyville, south of the Canadian, and decided to take Griffin to Fort Smith to answer the Blaine burglary indictment and serve the process en route. He left Webbers Falls with the outlaw shortly after 1 P.M. on April 13, crossed the ferry where the Canadian River joined the Arkansas, and took the road to Pheasant Bluff. During the afternoon, several parties observed two men on the same road, trailing the marshal and his prisoner. The *Fort Smith Elevator* reported:

About dusk . . . W. W. Harris [who lived] a few hundred yards from Pheasant Bluff heard six shots down the road. . . . Early Wednesday morning a loose horse with saddle and bridle on was found near the house and Mr. Harris and other parties, thinking something was wrong, went down to where they heard the shooting, and about 300 yards from the house found the body of Deputy Marshal Irwin cold in death, having been shot in the left side, the ball ranging through the heart and out the right breast. Investigation showed that he had been followed by two men who waylaid and shot him for the purpose of rescuing the prisoner, Griffin. The first shot was the fatal one, which frightened the marshal's horse, and he carried his rider about 65 yards off the road, the murderers firing five more shots at him before he fell. . . .

His murderers did not disturb the body after their victim had fallen, as his pistol was found in its scabbard loaded all round, showing that he had been given no chance to draw it. His money and papers had not been taken. . . .

Mr. Harris and J. S. Forrest wrapped the body of the dead deputy up the best they could, placed it in a wagon and started for this place about twelve o'clock Wednesday, arriving here early yesterday morning. The body was taken to Birnie's undertaking establishment and prepared for burial where it was viewed by hundreds of people. . . .

The deceased . . . was appointed deputy marshal on the 1st of January. His mother resides in this city and he has two little children who live with her, he being a widower. His funeral took place from her residence.

Irwin was a brave and daring marshal, and it is hoped his murderers will be hunted down.[18]

Irwin's assassins were identified as Frank Palmer and Jack Spaniard, who had crossed the river that afternoon, "remarking to the ferryman, whom they knew, that they would get Griffin away from the marshal, even if they had to down him."[19] The government offered five hundred dollars' reward each for Griffin, Spaniard, and Palmer, and with Irwin's death so fresh in the minds of federal officials, who also knew that Griffin was a running mate of Sam Starr, Belle's reception at Fort Smith in the custody of Barnhill and Hughes was anything but cordial.

Undaunted, Belle again obtained the services of attorneys Thomas Marcum and William M. Cravens, denied the Farrill charge before Commissioner Brizzolara, and applied for half a dozen witnesses who would testify that on the night of the robbery she was attending a dance at Briartown. Then she gave bond and spent the next several days in Fort Smith visiting friends and shopping.

On Saturday, May 23, she "had her photo taken on horseback at Rhoeder's Gallery . . . for the [St. Louis] Globe-Democrat."[20] This photograph, used by almost every Belle Starr biographer, shows her with Deputy Tyner Hughes, mounted sidesaddle in her snugly fitting brocaded riding jacket, a light silk scarf around her neck, the brim of her hat pinned up with a bright plume, long flowing skirts reaching down the left side of her horse almost to the ground, her gloved right hand holding a rawhide riding quirt, and a white-handled pistol (lent by the photographer) in an open scabbard at her waist. On Monday, May 24, Belle "had another photo taken with Blue Duck, the Cherokee then under sentence of death, to be executed July 3rd."[21]

Blue Duck and William Christie, another Indian, were charged jointly with the murder, on June 23, 1884, of a white youth named Samuel Wyrick, who was plowing in the field of Martin Hopper in the Cherokee Nation. Evidence presented at the trial in January, 1886, showed that Blue Duck was "on a drunken rampage, determined on having blood." Christie's part in the affair was furnishing the whiskey. The jury acquitted Christie but found Blue Duck guilty. Blue Duck's attorney, Thomas Marcum, filed a motion for a new trial, which was denied. On February 27, Judge Parker sentenced Blue Duck to the gallows.[22]

As a last resort, Marcum obtained a volume of recommendations from the prisoner's many friends and relatives and appealed to the president of the United States for a commutation. With no report from Washington, Marcum thought to call fresh attention to Blue Duck's plight by having him photographed with the "notorious Belle Starr." He told Belle it would make Blue Duck "feel better" when he faced the noose. The appeal to Belle's vanity, perhaps, caused her to oblige. There is no proof that she was acquainted with Blue Duck before she met him in the Fort Smith jail,[23] and she did not see him afterward. Blue Duck's sentence was commuted on September 8, 1886, and on August 4, Judge Parker committed him to the Menard Branch of the Southern Illinois Penitentiary at Chester "for the term and period of his natural life." He served almost nine years, developed consumption; prison physicians gave him less than a month to live. On March 20, 1895, President Grover Cleveland issued a pardon, permitting him to return to Indian Territory "to die among friends."[24]

The hearing in the Farrill case (allowing time to subpoena witnesses) was set for the last week in June, and "Belle Starr left for her home on the Canadian River on Tuesday morning

Belle Starr and Deputy U.S. Marshal Tyner Hughes on horseback. Photo-graph by Rhoeder's Gallery, Fort Smith, Arkansas, May 23, 1886.

Belle Starr and Blue Duck, photographed together May 24, 1886, to renew attention to the convicted killer's plight and his attorney's efforts to obtain a presidential commutation to life imprisonment.

[May 25]. . . . Just before starting home she showed us a fine
pair of black handled Colt's revolvers, 45 calibre, short barrel,
which she had purchased at Wersing's the evening previous
for $29 cash."[25] Thus Belle replaced the two weapons taken
from her by Texas officers and the Indian police. Before she
left, however, she was "interviewed" by a correspondent for
several southwestern dailies. His dispatch, full of half-truths
and errors but the source of much Belle Starr nonsense, appeared in the *Dallas Morning News* of June 7:

THRILLING LIFE OF A GIRL.
_____

BELLE STARR, WHO SHELTERS OUTLAWS
_____

Her Romantic Career – Elopement at Fifteen.
Marriage on the Prairie – Visited by Jesse
James – Her First Taste of Outlawry.
_____

Fort Smith, Ark., May 30. – For the past week the noted Belle
Starr has been quite an attraction on the streets of this city. She
came to answer two indictments in the Federal Court, and expected
to have been tried at the present term, first for being implicated in
the stealing of a fine mare, the one ridden by the notorious John
Middleton when he was drowned in the Poteau River, twenty-five
miles above this city, in May, 1885; and second, on a charge of
robbery, in which it is claimed that Belle, dressed in male attire,
led a party of three men who robbed an old man named Ferrell
and his three sons, some forty miles north of here, in the Choctaw
Nation, about three months ago. Court adjourned on Monday last,
and her cases went over until August next.

Monday night Belle swung her Winchester to her saddle, buckled
her revolver around her, and, mounting her horse, set out for her
home on the Canadian. Before leaving, she purchased a fine pair of
45-calibre revolvers, latest pattern, with black rubber handles and
short barrel, for which she paid $29. She showed them to your
correspondent, with the remark: "Next to a fine horse I admire a
fine pistol. Don't you think these are beauties?"

Belle says she anticipates no trouble in establishing her innocence
in the cases against her, but thinks it terribly annoying to have to
spend her time and money coming down here to court five and six
times a year.

Belle attracts considerable attention wherever she goes, being a dashing horse-woman, and exceedingly graceful in the saddle. She dresses plainly, and wears a broadbrimmed white man's hat, surmounted by a wide black plush band, with feathers and ornaments, which is very becoming to her. She is of medium size, well formed, a dark brunette, with bright and intelligent black eyes.

A Romantic History.

While here she kindly granted your correspondent a long interview concerning her past life, but made it plainly understood that she had but little use for newspaper reporters, who she claims at various times have done her great injustice. Being asked for a brief sketch of her career she said in substance that she was born at Carthage, Mo., and was 32 years old last February. In 1863 her father, being a Confederate, removed with his family to Texas where he continued to reside after the close of the war. After the surrender of Quantrell's men they came to the locality and were at all times welcome guests at her father's home.

When less than 15 years of age she fell in love with one of the dashing guerrillas, whose name she said it was not necessary to give. Her father objected to her marriage and she ran away with her lover, being married on horseback in the presence of about twenty of her husband's companions. John Fisher, one of the most noted outlaws in the State of Texas, held her horse while the ceremony was being performed, her wedding attire being a black velvet riding habit.

Her First Captivity.

About six weeks after the marriage her husband, being an outlaw, was forced to flee from the country, and he went to Missouri, leaving her in Texas. Her father learned of his hasty departure, and in order to induce her to return home sent her a message that her mother was dangerously ill and her presence was requested in haste. She immediately went home, but found she had been duped, as her mother was not sick after all, and it was then she experienced her first captivity, for the old gentleman locked her up and kept her in confinement for about two weeks, after which he gave her choice of going to school in San Antonio or to a small place in Parker County. She was placed in school at the latter place and remained there for some time, but was not allowed to communicate with anyone outside of her family.

While there her husband came again to Texas, and after considerable trouble learned where she was and came after her.

Belle's First Taste of Outlawry.

By this time her admiration for him had become somewhat impaired, and at first she refused to go with him, but after considerable persuasion she borrowed a horse from a young fellow who was attending the same school, ostensibly to take a short ride, and meeting her husband after dark they struck out for Missouri, where her husband purchased a farm and made an effort to settle down and lead an upright life. He was harassed by enemies to such an extent that he could not live in peace, and finally they killed his brother, and in return he killed two of them after which they again fled to Texas, and from there went to Los Angeles, Cal., and remained in that State for some time. From there they again returned to Texas, and her husband was killed. Having followed the fortunes of an outlaw thus far, she has since been true to his friends and comrades, and she has continued to associate with men of his calling, having lived among the Indians nearly ever since, with the exception of two years spent in Nebraska.

Very Much Lied About.

In relating her experience during the past three years, she says since the return of herself and husband from Detroit, Mich., where they served one term of less than a year for alleged horse stealing, her name has been coupled with every robbery or other depredation that has been committed in the Territory, and in a spirit of mirth she said:

"I am the best guarded woman in the Indian country, for when the deputy marshals are not there somebody else is."

In speaking of her recent arrest by Deputy Tyner Hughes, she said she was never more dumbfounded in her life than when he rode boldly up to her house and informed her he had come to serve a writ. She was not used to that manner of approach, as the Marshals generally came into the Bend with a crowd of from twenty-five to forty men and crawled upon their hands and knees in the darkness.

"And whenever you see a deputy Marshal come in," said she, "with the knees of his pants worn out, you may be sure he has invaded Younger's Bend. Hughes is a brave man and acted the gentleman in every particular, but I hardly believe he realized his danger."

Denies the Robbery.

She says she never heard of the robbery of Ferrell until she was arrested as leader of the party who committed it, her accusers asserting she was in male attire. She admits that her husband is at all times on the scout to avoid arrest, and there are several charges of larceny, robbery, etc. against him, which have been trumped up by his enemies.

At Home.

When at home her companions are her daughter, Pearl whom she calls the "Canadian Lily," her horse and her two trusty revolvers, which she calls her "babies." The horse she rides she has owned for nearly five years, and no one ever feeds or handles him but herself, and it would be risky business for anyone else to attempt to ride him. She says she had been offered $300 for him time and again, but that $500 would not get him. He is a small sorrel horse, and when in good condition is a beautiful animal, but looked rather the worse for hard riding when here last week. Belle is a crack shot, and handles her pistol with as much dexterity as any frontiersman. No man enters Younger's Bend without first giving a thorough account of himself before he gets out.

Belle related many incidents of her life that would be of interest, and says she has been offered big money by publishers for a complete history of it, but she does not desire to have it published just yet. She has a complete manuscript record, and when she dies she will give it to the public. She spends most of her time writing when at home.

In winding up our interview, she said:

"You can just say that I am a friend to any brave and gallant outlaw, but have no use for that sneaking, coward class of thieves who can be found in every locality, and who would betray a friend or comrade for the sake of their own gain. There are three or four jolly, good fellows on the dodge now in my section, and when they come to my home they are welcome, for they are my friends, and would lay down their lives in my defense at any time the occasion demanded it, and go their full length to serve me in any way."

The correspondent may have been Albert A. Powe (pronounced *Poe*), who in 1890 became editor of the daily *Fort Smith Evening Call*. The *Dallas News* article, probably sent to Belle by her mother or a Texas friend, irritated her no end. A couple of weeks later when she appeared for the commissioner's hearing, Powe was seated in a penned-off space near the door where officers usually were posted to prevent the escape of prisoners. According to Miss Dymple B. Johnson of the Old Fort Smith Museum, who told the story often, Belle saw Powe and made straight for him. He was a dimunitive man who wore brass-rimmed spectacles. Belle seized the scruff of his neck, dragged him over the railing, lashed him with her riding quirt, and calmly marched into the courtroom to stand trial.[26]

The commissioner's hearing was brief. Nick Farrill was "not able to identify anybody." Wilse Farrill "seen three robbers . . . there was but one in the house at a time; two stayed in the door with Winchesters; could not tell who any of them were." G. W. Tucker, Jack Burns, and Mrs. Loring "could not identify any of the robbers." Lila McGilberry had "never seen defendant before that night." On cross-examination she stated that at first she "thought defendant was a man—a Cherokee," but defendant "did not talk like a man." On redirect examination she said: "I seen defendant here yesterday and knew it was her." On cross-examination, Wilse Farrill and Tucker described all three robbers as "good sized men" and did not think that "any of them was as small as this woman." Said Nick Farrill: "All [were] good sized men, none smaller than I am. Do not think there was any so small as defendant with men's clothes on." Belle's witnesses did not testify; it wasn't necessary. She was discharged on June 29.[27]

16   Belle Widowed Again

While Belle was in Fort Smith for the Farrill hearing, Sheriff Vann and Deputy Marshal Frank Smith, with possemen Simp Bennett, Jim Lowrey, Jim Cobb, and Bent Cobb, met Sam Six-killer of the U.S. Indian Police and Ed McCurtain with a posse of Choctaws at Briartown. They proceeded to Youngers' Bend "to clean out the gang of thieves there" and capture Sam Starr, Jack Spaniard, and Felix Griffin.[1]

Meanwhile, two men, one of them Bill Jackson, the outlaw Vann and his posse had captured and released in the March raid,

hired a buggy from J. M. Grant's Livery Stable at Oswego, Kans., to go into the country about four miles. The team not returning at the proper time, Grant sent a man to look for it, who tracked it to Tulsa, and [C. B.] Perryman of the U.S. Indian Police tracked the team and buggy from Tulsa . . . to Briartown, where he found that Deputy Marshal Frank Smith, Vann and Thompson Cooper, U. S. I. P. had just made a raid, captured Bill Jackson and his partner, and found the buggy all taken apart and hid in a tree-top on Belle Starr's place. [Jackson and his partner] were brought here [Muskogee] and then taken to Fort Smith.[2]

The Smith-Vann posse failed to find Sam Starr or Spaniard, but a few days later "the notorious Felix Griffin . . . was captured by Bullet Foreman," who operated a ferry on the Arkansas at the mouth of the Illinois River. "Foreman gets the five-hundred-dollar reward which the government recently offered."[3] Griffin was delivered to the U.S. marshal at Fort Smith on July 2, where he gave a *Daily Times* reporter this account of Deputy Irwin's murder:

I had just been turned over to Irwin by the Cherokee officers . . . and he had started here with me that morning. It was getting pretty late, nearly dark and we were riding pretty fast. Just as we got opposite Pheasant Bluff two men rode up behind us and called out to Irwin twice to throw up his hands. Irwin answered "all right," and reached for his pistol but before he could draw it, Palmer fired two shots at him. When he fired he turned and run west. I went the other way while Spaniard followed Irwin shooting four times at him before he fell. He then turned and overtook me. I asked him if Irwin was dead. He said he did not know but thought he was. We then rode to the mound [bluff] where Spaniard shouted several times for Palmer, but he did not come and we went on. Spaniard is a friend of mine but Palmer I had only seen a time or two. I had no idea they were going to attempt to rescue me.

Griffin admitted that the morning after Irwin's death he and Spaniard had gone some thirty miles northwest of Pheasant Bluff to the home of Martin Crowder on the Canadian and asked W. M. Wagner, Crowder's hired man, to put them across the river on the Cherokee side. Wagner told them he had only a small boat, that the Canadian was too rough and he was not willing to risk it, but that Belle Starr had a large boat about a mile and a half upstream. Wagner guided them to the point in the woods, hallooed, and Belle came across with Eddie Reed. Griffin and Spaniard took dinner at Belle's cabin.[4] Spaniard's black-and-tan hound, which had been seen with him and Palmer while they were pursuing Irwin, followed the men to the ferry but did not cross. The dog was taken by Wagner and turned over to Fort Smith authorities.[5]

Griffin was kept in jail until August, 1886, when the grand jury ignored the murder charge against him but indicted Spaniard and Palmer. Palmer left the country and was never apprehended. Spaniard sought refuge in the Creek Nation near Eufaula. On August 24, Griffin was indicted for the Blaine post office burglary; he posted bond and returned to Indian Territory.[6] The Fort Smith court did not see him again:

His time arrived on Tuesday night [April 26, 1887] . . . during an attempt to steal a horse from Robert Vann, who resides near Webbers Falls. Vann and Dick Scott, being aware that Griffin and several of his crowd were in the vicinity, had been guarding their horses. . . . Griffin and two others rode up within a short distance, hitched their horses and crept to the stable. Griffin was in the act of bridling Vann's horse when the two men opened fire. Griffin was instantly killed and it is supposed his comrades were wounded, though they made their escape but abandoned their horses. These were taken to Webbers Falls and proved to be stolen property. A large number of horses have been stolen in that section during the past few months, but it is thought the enterprise has received a set-back from which it won't soon recover.[7]

Two weeks after Felix Griffin gave bond, Belle appeared at Fort Smith for trial in the larceny of McCarty's mare. She still felt confident of acquittal and said as much to Amanda Jackson, who was attending court with her son, Lute Jackson. Lute had been subpoenaed before Judge Parker on September 10 to testify in a "sheep-killing" case originating on his ranch (near present Ringling) in the Chickasaw Nation, and Mrs. Jackson, a diminutive but spunky little lady wanting a piece of the action, had accompanied him.

The attorney who spoke for Lute and his cowboys combined legal talent with that of saloonkeeper, doctor, and sometimes preacher on Sunday. He expounded on the merits of the case for an hour. Judge Parker decided there was not sufficient evidence to hold the parties involved, and the cortege left Fort Smith before sundown. Belle and Mrs. Jackson visited most of the day, exchanging recipes and news of their respective sections of the country. Mrs. Jackson gave Belle her recipe for making sausage, and Belle gave Mrs. Jackson a couple of her favorites for making candy:

Sugar Candy—Six cups of white sugar, one cup vinegar, one cup water, teaspoon of butter, put in last, with one teaspoon soda dissolved in hot water. Boil without stirring one-half hour. Flavor to suit taste.

Cream Candy—Four cups sugar, two cups water, three-fourths cup vinegar, one cup cream or rich milk; piece of butter the size of an egg, two teaspoons vanilla. Let boil until it cracks in water, then work until white.

Mrs. Jackson was "very taken with Belle Starr." On the way home she kept telling Lute that this friendly woman could not possibly be guilty of stealing anything. She used the candy recipes many times and gave copies to friends and neighbors. The originals, in Belle's handwriting, are owned today by a grandaughter.[8]

Belle proved her innocence in the horse-stealing case, largely because Fayette Barnett testified that he was present when John Middleton paid "a stranger" fifty dollars for the McCarty mare. On September 30, the jury returned a verdict of "not guilty as charged in the within indictment."[9] Barnett paid Belle's attorney fees as promised, and, according to Harman, "deserted his Choctaw wife," went to New Mexico and "made a fortune in the liquor traffic."[10] Belle hurried back to Youngers' Bend. Sam Starr had been wounded badly by the Indian police.[11]

The evening of September 16, Sheriff Vann, Deputy Robinson, policeman John Toney, and Frank West sighted Sam in the Canadian bottoms; he was riding Belle's mare Venus through a corn field. Vann wanted to split the posse and take him from two sides, but Frank West, asserting that Sam would never surrender, leveled his revolver and fired several shots in rapid succession. Sam tilted back in his saddle with an astonished cry, his bullet-punctured hat flying through the air. One arm flew up as if grabbing for the saddlehorn. Then the mare screamed and went down, unseating him. He struck the ground, rolled over, and lay still.

The officers rushed to him. Venus was dead, shot through the neck. Sam lay unconscious between the corn rows, blood oozing from the side of his head and from another wound in his side. He appeared to be in bad shape, and the officers wanted to keep him alive if possible. Vann and West headed for the nearest farmhouse to borrow a wagon and find accommodations where they could dress Sam's wounds. Robinson and Toney were left to guard the prisoner.

The two guards decided to move Sam into the brush along a creek nearby, lest they be spotted by some of the Starr gang. They turned to place their Winchesters in the boots on their saddles. Although Sam's head wound looked serious, he had regained consciousness. From beneath his eyelids he saw the men with their backs toward him momentarily. Like a cat he sprang from the ground, snatching Robinson's gun from its holster, and soon had the pair disarmed and at bay. He gathered the reins of Robinson's mount and swung into the saddle without losing the drop. He grinned at their rigid forms and bitter faces, but his words reflected the hate inside him: "Tell Frank West he pay for killing Belle's mare!" Then he swung Robinson's black horse, rammed in the spurs, and dashed from the field into the timber. Robinson quickly recovered their weapons among the corn rows where Sam had flung them, but with only one horse to ride, they did not start pursuit until Vann and West returned.

A dispatch to the *Arkansas Gazette* at Little Rock on September 18 told how "police fired on Sam, killing his horse, without demanding his surrender" and said "fifty shots had been exchanged in the fight." The *Fort Smith Elevator* of September 24 described the clash with Indian officers as "a lively shooting match." R. P. Vann, Sheriff Vann's younger brother, stated in a 1932 interview that he was a member of the posse:

We saw Sam Starr go in a corn field and when he came out we hollered at him to halt. My brother first shot Sam in the side and then killed the horse. My brother's deputy was a white man named Robinson, an adopted citizen. Bill left Robinson and a fellow named Frank West to guard Sam Starr, but Tom Starr and his gang overpowered the officers and took Sam away with them.[12]

Contemporary accounts do not support R. P. Vann's version, nor do they mention his presence.[13]

Sam abandoned Robinson's horse in the river bottoms and made his way to the home of one of his brothers, where he had been hiding much of the time, and there Belle found him. She cared for her husband's wounds, cursed Frank West for killing her prized Venus, boasted of her recent victory in the Fort Smith court, and begged Sam to surrender to the U.S. marshal. Sam vowed to go to hell first, but Belle had a talking point. He would fare much better in the white man's court than in the tribal courts if the Indian police caught him. The Choctaw chiefs blamed old Tom Starr and his sons for much of the crime in their nation and hated them. Sam's chances of defending himself would be slim.

The only federal charge against Sam was the Blaine post office burglary. The most extreme punishment Judge Parker could hand out would be mild compared to death by the bullet or the scourging near-death of the hickory switch under Choctaw law. By surrendering to federal officers, he would be under the protection of the United States and the Indian police could not touch him. He would go free on bond—perhaps never convicted. Sam finally agreed. Belle notified Tyner Hughes, and on October 4 the deputy marshal took Sam into custody at Briartown on the old burglary capias issued February 6, 1886.[14]

Early on the morning of October 7, the citizens of Fort Smith were startled to see the long-hunted Sam Starr loping up the street to federal court, unarmed and escorted by Deputy Hughes. Behind them rode Belle, her revolvers belted at her waist and hat feathers waving in the breeze.

Sam was arraigned before Commissioner Wheeler on the grand-jury indictment for "breaking into Postoffice and larceny of postoffice money," and ordered "to find sufficient bail in the sum of one thousand dollars for his appearance at the District Court . . . at 10 o'clock A.M. the 1st day of November A.D. 1886. . . . In default of finding such bail he stands committed." Apparently, Belle had made bond arrangements before surrendering her husband to Tyner Hughes. Late in the afternoon, Alex Burns, a friend of the Starrs on the Canadian, and Frank J. Arnold (probably connected with the Reed relatives in Logan County, Arkansas) arrived at Fort Smith, each signing a recognizance. Arnold listed as assets a quarter section of land in Logan County, "1 span mules [and] 10 head cattle" worth $700; Burns "100 head Cattle, 8 head horses" worth $2,000.[15]

Sam Starr was a free man again, for the time being. Interviewed by an *Elevator* reporter concerning other crimes for which he might be wanted in the Nations, he replied that the Indian officers "had no charges against him . . . except for carrying a pistol, and he would have surrendered to the police the day they shot him if they had asked him to."[16]

Belle and Sam did not return to Younger's Bend immediately. The Seventh Annual Fair of Western Arkansas and the Indian Territory began at Fort Smith on October 12 and continued five days. Its principal attractions had been widely described by the *Elevator*[17] and the *Vinita Indian Chieftain*:[18]

A competitive military drill and sham battle in which ten or twelve military companies and two batteries will take part, the United States artillery company at Little Rock being one of them. . . . Gov. S. P. Hughes will deliver the opening address, and . . . the state militia will be properly organized for the first time in the history of the state and reviewed by [him]. . . . The attractions in the city will be grand illuminations, fireworks, trades procession, etc. Three race balloon ascensions take place, with a trapeze performer on each. . . . [Horse] races every day.

Belle wanted to enter the riding contests. When it was announced that she and Sam would attend the fair, last-minute arrangements were made to have them participate "in a sort of wild west show [which] proved a great [drawing] card."[19] Harman elaborates:

Judge Parker, always a public spirited man, requested [Belle] to take the leading part in a mock stage coach robbery; he offered himself as one of the passengers to be robbed. Belle consented and the affair was carried out to the satisfaction of the large crowd who came to the . . . Sebastian County fair grounds. . . .

Belle had sought to have District Attorney Clayton, also, as a member of the stage party but some accident prevented his taking part. . . . She [later] informed him that had he been an occupant of that stage coach she would have killed him; she intended having in her pistol one cartridge, not a blank, in order that she might avenge the attorney's ridicule of her husband's illiteracy.

Another amusing incident [involved] A. A. Powe . . . of the now defunct Fort Smith *Evening Call.* Powe was a "would be" politician, but was unpopular. While he was standing in a dense crowd, watching the races, some sports picked him up and threw him astride the horse on which Belle Starr was seated; she was equal to the occasion and putting spurs to her steed she dashed upon the track at full speed, making the circuit twice, while Editor Powe clung to her for dear life, dropping his hat and nearly losing his spectacles.[20]

Neither incident made the Fort Smith newspapers.[21]

Ward L. Schrantz, editor of the *Carthage* (Mo.) *News*, published an account of Belle's career in his edition of January 26, 1953, in which he states that "Carthage, in 1886, heard for the first time there was a connection between this city and Belle Starr . . . soon to become the most widely chronicled daughter of Carthage in history." Schrantz quotes from a report on the return of the Carthage Light Guard Band from the Arkansas fair with four hundred dollars in prize money:

> While in Fort Smith the Carthage bandsmen saw the noted Belle Star [*sic*]. Talk was that though she was under a sentence for outlawry as a result of a recent trial; being deemed trustworthy, was permitted to give a riding and shooting exhibition just the same. . . . Riding a horse bareback at full gallop, she broke clay pigeons and glass balls with rifle fire while in motion, varying the performance by leaping from the animal while moving at full speed, breaking more glass balls and clay pigeons from the ground with her rifle, then leaping back on her animal as it galloped past her again, still at full speed and continued her firing.

Apparently this was the extent of Belle's performance.

Harman must have overlooked the fact that M. H. Sandels, not Clayton, was Grover Cleveland's prosecuting attorney for the Western District of Arkansas from 1885 to 1889. Clayton was reappointed in 1889 by President Benjamin Harrison; in the interim he engaged in private practice at Fort Smith and, curiously, was one of Sam Starr's lawyers in the Blaine burglary-larceny case.

On October 18, "by his attorneys Clayton & Marcum," Sam made application for witnesses

> without whose testimony deft. cannot safely proceed to trial . . . to wit: Lon Workman, Jacob Horn, Pearl Starr, Thos. Shields & Jim Beck. . . .

M. H. Sandels, U.S. district attorney, western district of Arkansas, Fort Smith, 1885–89.

That said Pearl & Shields reside at Briar Town, Lon Workman resides at Wagner's Mills, Jim Beck resides at Texanna I. T. and said Horn resides at Winding Stair Mountains in the Choctaw Nation [by whom] deft. can prove he was at the house of Mrs. Ellen Lowry & some twenty five or thirty miles from the Blaine post office where the said crimes are charged to have been committed. . . .

The deft. says he has not the means & actually unable to pay the fees of said witnesses . . . wherefore prays that subpoenas issuing [be] at the expense of the United States.[22]

Judge Parker approved the application. Sam returned to Fort Smith for trial November 17, but because of a delay in locating witnesses for both prosecution and defense, his case was continued until February, 1887.[23]

Again Sam and Belle lingered in the city several days, this time with the hope of assisting old Tom Starr, now in the federal jail. For nearly a decade the names of various Starr clan members had graced the dockets of the Western District of Arkansas and commissioners' courts with liquor violations and livestock larceny. Case records of the U.S. Commissioner's Court at Fayetteville, Arkansas,[24] show that on June 9, 1884, Tom was charged with introducing into the Indian country five gallons of whiskey; a capias issued on March 2, 1885, by U.S. Commissioner E. B. Harrison was returned by Deputy Marshal Elias Andrews on October 1 with the notation that "defendant not found in my district." On December 15, 1885, Tom was charged with introducing and selling four gallons of liquor in the Indian country, was arrested by U.S. Marshal John Carroll the same day, and after pleading not guilty was bonded and released by Commissioner Harrison, "case pending." Smuggling whiskey from his former stomping grounds around Evansville was his favorite hobby, but his luck finally ran out. On November 2, 1886, he was apprehended bringing "one gallon of whiskey" into the Territory from Maysville and was arraigned before Commissioner Harrison the same day. He was "adjudged guilty" and "required to find bail in the sum of Three hundred Dollars, which requisition has not been complied with," so Tom was ordered conveyed to the federal jail at Fort Smith, "him there to be safely kept until he shall be discharged by due course of law."

The Fort Smith grand jury ignored the 1884 count but indicted old Tom in the other two cases. Arraigned before Judge Parker on November 23, he elected to plead guilty and Sam's attorneys could not help him. He was sentenced to one year in the Southern Illinois Penitentiary on the 1885 charge and to six months' imprisonment and a fine of fifty dollars on the 1886 charge, the latter sentence "to commence and date from the expiration of the one year term." On November 27, Tom Starr was delivered to the Illinois prison at Menard.[25]

Sam and Belle returned to Youngers' Bend. Bitter and despondent over his father's conviction, Sam was in no mood for further advice or consolation and even considered jumping bail. He blamed the Wests for all his woes since 1882 and wanted to even the score with them.

Mabel Harrison was spending the holiday season with the Reeds in Missouri. On Friday night, December 17, "Aunt Lucy" Surratt gave a Christmas dance at her home on Emachaya Creek near Whitefield. Thinking to relieve Sam's tensions, Belle suggested they attend and celebrate. Pearl and Eddie also had been looking forward to the annual affair, so late in the evening all four crossed the Canadian together.

A slow rain had set in that morning, turning to sleet and freezing drizzle by late afternoon. The trails were boggy, and the Starrs did not reach the Surratt place until after dark. Arvil B. Cole, a popular fiddler around Whitefield and Briartown, was on deck with a guitar picker who was too drunk to play. Cole welcomed Belle's appearance and asked her to accompany him on Mrs. Surratt's old-fashioned pedal organ. Soon they were whipping out *Billy in the Lowground.* The dancers swung and stomped, Pearl and Eddie among them. Sam Starr sat next to the organ near the front door.

The house stood on a low hill overlooking the Emachaya Valley. The Surratts had built a log-heap fire in an elm grove at the foot of the slope, and several guests stopped to warm themselves before coming up to dance. The hated Frank West had just arrived. Damp and chilled from the drizzle, he "squatted down" and was "holding his hands toward the blaze" when, according to the *Muskogee Indian Journal*,[26] a friend

came up and told him Sam Starr was at the house and that he had better go away to avoid trouble, but Frank said that would look as tho' he were afraid and that he would run from no man. About that time Starr came [outside] and, seeing Frank, accused him of shooting his horse at the time the Cherokee officers were trying to arrest him. . . . A few hot words ensued, when Starr pulled his revolver, and West drew his as soon after as he could, but not until he had received a mortal wound, from which he staggered; but, recovering, he sent a ball through Starr, and then fell dead. Starr staggered for about ten feet and then he, too, fell a corpse.[27]

Twelve-year-old Dan Folsom also was warming himself at the log fire. When Starr began accusing West, he knew that gunplay was imminent and made a break for the house. The bullet that passed through Sam's body tore into the muscles of Dan's jaws as he ran sideways, mouth open, up the hill. His wounds "healed in due time," but he carried the scars the rest of his life.[28]

A witness said "a Starr henchman" came in as the first dance was ending and whispered to Belle that West was "down at the log heap" and that Belle whirled to Sam, saying, "Go down and get the son-of-a-bitch," then turned back to the organ and began to play for the second dance. Moments later when the dance was interrupted by gunfire and a messenger burst in announcing wildly that both Sam and West were dead, Belle matter-of-factly inquired: "Why in hell don't you bring 'em in and lay 'em out?"[29] Others say Belle knelt beside her husband and held his head in her arms. There were no tears in her eyes, but her face was white and she cursed Frank West. However, that may be, both men died game within minutes after sighting each other.

A wagon was brought up, and West's body was taken home

to his wife and two children. The next morning, another wagon took Sam's body to his father's home for burial in the Starr cemetery southwest of Briartown, overlooking the Canadian.[30]

17 Belle's Triple Trouble

Some say Jack Spaniard moved in with Belle at Youngers' Bend before Sam was cold in his grave but she soon lost him to the Fort Smith gallows and took up with Jim French.[1] These writers are mistaken. French would not begin his criminal career until a year and a half later, and nothing was heard of Spaniard until the Cherokee fugitive was surprised and captured by Deputy Marshal James Pettigrew on the night of March 25, 1888, in a hideout seven miles from Eufaula in the Creek Nation.[2] Spaniard languished in the Fort Smith jail until his trial in April, 1889. The black-and-tan hound taken up by W. M. Wagner and kept at the jail for months by federal authorities proved his undoing. A jury found him guilty April 19. His attorney, Thomas Marcum, filed a motion for a new trial, which was denied. Judge Parker sentenced Spaniard to the gallows, Marcum's appeal to the president for commutation also failed, and he was hanged August 30.[3]

After Sam Starr's death and the dissemination of his criminal companions, things seemingly were quiet at the Bend. Trouble continued to pile up on Belle, however. It came from three sources.

First, the Cherokee authorities were opposed to her claiming the land at the Bend. Although her marriage to Sam had been perfectly legal, with Sam deceased she was no longer a Cherokee subject and should be removed from the nation as an intruder. The position of the Commissioner of Indian Affairs and his agents in Indian Territory was to take no action that would deprive such a person of improvements, or fruits of labor acquired by virtue of citizenship, without just compensation. An intruder's improvements should be appraised and the nation purchase same at the appraised value before dis-

A SHOOTING STARR.'

THE WESTERN ASTEROID, "JIM" STARR, ALIAS "JIM JULY," WHO RECENTLY GOT LOADED WITH LEAD AND DIED.

Bill July, alias James July Starr, Belle's last husband. From a portrait sketch in the National Police Gazette, *February 15, 1890.*

posing of them to its own citizens, the federal authorities said.

Belle quickly solved this problem. One of her "jolly good fellows" referred to in the *Dallas News* story was Bill July, a nephew of July Perryman of the Creek Nation and sort of an adopted son to old Tom Starr. Old Tom called him Jim July Starr. He was twenty-four, a fine-looking mixed-blood, mostly Cherokee, who wore his long hair cut below the neck as Sam had. He wasn't as handsome as Sam, but he had the same air of reckless indifference, which excited Belle, and he was not illiterate. Educated in the Indian schools, he could speak the language of nearly all of the Five Civilized Tribes fluently. At thirty-nine, Belle was no longer the beauty Jim Reed had married in Texas after the war or Sam Starr had married in 1880. Her face was almost mannish, her dark eyes hard, piercing; her thinning lips gave her wide mouth a certain cruelty, and her black hair was streaked with gray. Yet there was an aura of sensuality about her that caused July to accept her invitation to move in at the Bend and announce to all friends and sundry that he and Belle were cohabiting as man and wife—legal in every respect under an old Cherokee custom and good in the federal courts at common law.

Frederick Barde claimed the Starr name was "bestowed" upon July "by [Belle's] own legislative act" after he came to live in her cabin; he "was a common horsethief, had little nerve," and won his battles by "running instead of fighting."[4] Consequently, subsequent biographers assume he changed his name to please Belle and that he already was under indictment by a Fort Smith grand jury.[5] July's involvement with the federal court would come later.

Belle's second problem was her children. Pearl, now nineteen, and Eddie, nearly seventeen, were five and seven years younger, respectively, than their new "stepfather," and Belle was fifteen years older than her new husband. The situation grew sticky.

Eddie resented July's presence at the outset despite his mother's explanation of a forced arrangement to spare their

James Edwin ("Eddie") Reed, son of Belle Starr.

home from action by the Cherokee National Council. A husky, dapper youth cultivating a thin mustache, he exhibited all the wild characteristics of his father, and under the tutelage of Sam Starr he had gained a liberal education in scouting. He became involved in several minor outrages at local affairs, which added to his mother's public disgrace. Belle, always free with her riding quirt, whipped him, sometimes severely. Eddie made no secret that he hated her for her brand of punishment, yet he approved of the rough ways of her associates. In this matter Belle stood alone; certainly no help or guidance was forthcoming from young July.

Meanwhile, Pearl had become acquainted with a boy of her own age. Their friendship ripened into something more lasting, and "in August, 1885," writes Harman,[6] "the young swain asked Belle's permission to make Pearl his wife." Belle, taken by surprise, "entered a refusal saying, as she had so often told her daughter, that the man Pearl should marry must have at least property to the amount of $25,000." The youth replied, "Well, Mrs. Starr, you know I will never have one-tenth of that sum," and went his way. Belle promptly sent Pearl to visit the Marshall family at Chickalah. Pearl was "delighted" with the trip, expecting to return in a few weeks, but Belle kept her there for some time. "Fearing that Pearl's absence would not be sufficient to wean the youthful lovers, she wrote what purported to be a letter written by Pearl to the young man," in care of herself, and gave him the letter. "It was a series of farewells" and ended: "I was married last Thursday to a rich man who has lots of stock and $25,000 in the bank; so you see I have got that money just as mamma said. PEARL." The boy believed the letter. Heavy of heart that Pearl could forget him so soon, he turned to another girl, and when Pearl returned from Chickalah, she learned, "much to her chagrin," of his recent marriage.

During the spring of 1886 she met the young man several times but, "thinking of how quickly his pretended love had cooled, passed him by in cold silence, a stranger." Then the youth discovered Pearl was not married. He "persisted in his attentions until . . . about the middle of July, at a picnic, he met her face to face, seized her hand, and before she could break away, had forced a part of the truth upon her . . . both coming to a clear understanding of the mother's duplicity." Later the pair met again in a leafy nook for a "last talk." They realized it was too late to undo Belle's work; the youth offered to "seek a legal separation," but Pearl "refused to listen." However, "because of her very womanliness and the love in the heart of her companion . . . had now become like a heated furnace . . . the kind that knows no restraint—no shame . . . who can wonder . . . as they were about to separate . . . that she yielded?" About the time of Belle's hearing at Fort Smith in the McCarty horse-stealing case, Pearl discovered that she was pregnant. She feared that if Belle learned her condition, she would immediately suspect the young man and kill him.

Pearl confided her secret to Mabel Harrison. The fees she had received as a witness at Fort Smith, together with proceeds from the sale of several horses she had been allowed to hold in her name, amounted to two hundred dollars. By January, 1887, her intention was to leave home, go among complete strangers, never to communicate with her mother again. She also had a proposal of marriage from a Fort Smith liveryman she had met while attending court, but she could not accept without informing him of her condition, which could only result in scorn being heaped upon her.

Old Morris Kraft owned a store at Whitefield and ran a few head of cattle in the Canadian bottoms. On occasion he had provided bail for members of the Starr clan, had given Pearl her first red dress as a child, and otherwise had endeared himself to the girl and her mother. "One evening early in February 1887," Harman[7] writes, Kraft called at the Starr home. "While he and Belle indulged in a friendly chat, Pearl and Mabel were absent on an errand, and Belle proposed to procure a sheet, cover her head and play ghost." Kraft warned her against the plan because of the effect it might have on her daughter. Belle replied: "Pshaw! Pearl wouldn't be frightened if she saw a real ghost, let alone a make-believe." And the merchant asked if it was possible she had not discovered that Pearl was in a delicate condition. "In an instant Belle was like a thousand furies . . . and surmising that Kraft might be the author of her daughter's ruin, since he knew of it first . . . she began to berate him, but was met by a prompt and straight-forward denial." When the girls returned, Belle tried to wring a confession from Pearl. Pearl refused to name the father: "Not even if you were to kill me, mamma . . . I will never tell anybody."

For several days Belle "studied on a plan . . . Pearl accompanied her to Fort Smith . . . the infatuated liveryman urged his suit, and Pearl told him all. He was surprised, but did not give her up." He and Belle wanted her "to meet a noted Fort Smith physician," but Pearl "was afraid." There was only one alternative, Belle declared: Pearl must leave home and "never bring the child into my presence." Pearl packed her things, returned to Fort Smith and told her suitor she was "going away forever." He begged her to "place the child in a St. Louis foundling asylum and return and marry him . . . Pearl would not promise . . . the next train north bore her to the home of her grandparent in Missouri. She found her grandmother preparing for a trip to Siloam Springs, Ark., for the benefit of her health. Pearl accompanied her, and there, in April, 1887, Pearl became the mother of a pretty girl baby, which she named 'Flossie.'" Pearl and the baby returned to Rich Hill with the grandmother. She instructed the Reed relatives that should Belle write inquiring about her they were to reply that "she had left for some place unknown."

Harman provides no source for his details and dialogue, but later developments prove him basically correct. Subsequent biographers accept his story, variously identifying the child's father as "a neighbor boy, part Cherokee," "a young man who lived at Younger's Bend," "Bob, that was his name," "a young man, part Creek," and "a half-breed Cherokee boy."[8] "Flossie" says it was "a young man two years [Pearl's] senior, a part Cherokee from one of the best families," that she was born at Siloam Springs on "April 22, 1887," and was called "little Mamie," and that "Uncle Marion and Grandma Reed . . . kept [her] and Pearl always hidden until I was 16 months old."[9]

Belle expressed no immediate concern for Pearl's whereabouts, however, for another matter occupied her. John West had rounded up her new husband on a capias, issued by Commissioner Tufts at Muskogee, charging that "Bill July *alias* Jim Starr did in the Indian Country . . . on or about the 27 day of June 1887, take and carry with intent to steal one horse valued at $125, the property of J. H. McCormick, a white man and not an Indian."[10]

The hearing was held before Commissioner Tufts on August 30. A large black mare, nine years old, had been stolen from McCormick, a Coffeyville, Kansas, man camped at night twenty-five miles west of Okmulgee. July had been seen in the vicinity posing as a trader and gambler. When arrested he was riding a smaller mare "he got of Fox Taylor" near Fort Gibson. West found McCormick's mare at Taylor's place and developed evidence to show July had traded the mare for Taylor's animal and fifteen dollars. July was committed to jail at Fort Smith and ordered "to find sufficient bail in the sum of $500."[11]

Since Sam Starr's death, Belle had let it be known that her home was no longer a stopping place for fugitives from justice. Local residents had quit complaining to the marshals and Indian police about missing their horses and cattle, and on July 6, Robert L. Owen of Union Agency at Muskogee had written her a letter, which he caused to be published in Indian Territory newspapers:[12]

Mrs. Belle Starr
Oklahoma, I. T.

Madam: The complaint against you for harboring bad characters has not, in my opinion, been established and is now dismissed.

I hope sincerely that you will faithfully carry out your promise to this office not to let such parties make your place a rendezvous.

Yours respectfully,
Robert L. Owen
United States Indian Agent

Belle was proud of the letter. She publicly berated July and took no part in his defense. Friends obtained his release on September 5, pending his appearance in U.S. District Court on November 7, and July returned to the Bend. At his arraignment in November he pleaded not guilty, the original recognizance stood, and his case was continued to the following August.[13]

Nothing is known of Belle's activities for the next several months of her life.[14] Frederick Barde gives this assessment:

People knew her to be merely a harborer of thieves . . . even had a bit of sympathy for her. She was human to the heart, and in the thinly settled region where she lived, no woman was more generous to the sick and unfortunate . . . when the women in the neighborhood were ill and unable to care for their families, Belle Starr went to their homes and ministered to them with her own hands. . . . Her voice was soft and pleasing, and her manner polite and engaging when she was in good humor. Her language was not vulgar, nor was she profane save when angry. There are still persons living in old Indian Territory who feel that she was more sinned against than sinning . . . the victim of surroundings from which she could not escape.[15]

Belle spent the winter of 1887-88 quietly at Youngers' Bend with July and Eddie. Eddie loved his sister very much and constantly blamed his mother for her absence. Belle began to yearn for her daughter and addressed a letter to the Reeds at Rich Hill. They answered that Pearl had left for an unknown destination. In May, 1888, "when her baby was a little past a year old, Pearl moved to Wichita, Kansas, and found a home with a sister of her father, of whom Belle had not heard in years. . . . Pearl again left instructions that her mother should not be informed of her whereabouts."[16] However, developing events soon would bring Pearl back to the Bend.

For some time, against Belle's wishes, Eddie had been galli-
vanting about the country with Mose Perryman, a Creek Indian youth, who was a relative of Bill July. On July 21, U.S.
Marshal John Carroll swore out a writ before Commissioner
Brizzolara at Fort Smith, stating that Eddie and young Perryman "did on or about the 11th day of July 1888, feloniously
steal, take and carry away from the lawful possession of Jim
Lewis, a negro and not an Indian, one horse of the value of
thirty Dollars."[17]

James Lewis, known as "General Jim," lived about six miles
from the Grayson ranch in the Creek Nation. According to
the "reliable information" attached to Marshal Carroll's complaint,

Reed and Perryman left the neighborhood the same day and got as
far as Patrick Ferry on the Ark. River. Being near night, they couldn't
cross . . . went back to the point of Brushy Mountain to camp. . . .
After Ed Reed had gone to sleep Mose Perryman shot him in the head,
the ball entering near the nose and coming out at the ear. Perryman
then went to Philo Harris to stay all night, and Mrs. Harris discovered
the print of bloody fingers on his coat sleeve. She called his attention to it, and he, Mose said that while they were asleep some unknown party crept up and shot at them hitting Ed Reed. But Reed
swears Perryman shot him & wants a writ for him.[18]

Deputy Marshal G. G. Tyson, who investigated the affair,
appended this note:

Ed Reed's . . . statement is supported by Mr. Harris & wife, put
them down as witnesses. The negro Lewis came up day before yesterday and got his pony that was in Ed Reed's possession. Ed is now
at Mr. Wallaces house, badly shot.

The capias issued for Eddie went unserved for the time being.
Belle brought Eddie home to Youngers' Bend and, according
to Harman,[19] "sought for Pearl's whereabouts . . . failed . . .
forwarded $20 to the grandmother at Rich Hill, stating that if
Pearl wanted to see her brother before he died she must come
at once; she must leave her baby behind, but she could return
to it later. The money and message was sent to Pearl at Wichita,

and leaving her baby in care of her aunt, she started for home. She was received with open arms by this strange mother."[20] Pearl helped care for her brother two months before he recovered.

Meanwhile, on August 4, Deputy Marshal Tyson arrested Mose Perryman and took him to Fort Smith,[21] but Bill July and the Perrymans promised to help Eddie in every way possible and Eddie did not pursue his charges. While still at Fort Smith on August 7, July was surrendered by bondsmen on his old indictment and was committed to jail,[22] but he made a new bond the same date. His case was continued to February, 1889.

Eddie was arraigned before Commissioner Brizzolara on October 13. Testimony showed that when shot he was in possession of "a sorrel pony branded G. L. on hip & shoulder." General Lewis identified the animal as belonging to him. Eddie was bound over to a special grand jury that was considering other cases and was indicted on November 13.[23] Angry with July and his relatives, who had reneged in providing a defense, he moved to show that Mose Perryman was the thief and made application for witnesses:

Defendant states . . . he is indicted for . . . larceny and cannot proceed to trial without the testimony of Vicey Grayson, Nannie Grayson and Will Meek.

By Vicey Grayson & Nan Grayson he can prove that from Eleven until the middle of the afternoon on the day said pony was taken from General Lewis, which was taken about eleven o'clock in the day, this defendant was at their house and was riding a bay horse, the one alleged to have been stolen being a sorrel. . . .

By Will Meek he can prove that he [Meek] was present when this defendant made a trade with Mose Perryman and that Mose owed this defendant $25 and sold him the sorrel pony in payment of the Debt. That Perryman told this defendant that the title to said pony was good. This was in the Creek Nation about ten miles from Muskogee. . . .

Defendant is wholly unable to pay for the attendance of said witnesses. Wherefore he asks that they be subpoenaed at the expense of the United States.[24]

Judge Parker approved the application and set the case for the

March, 1889, term of court. Parker and District Attorney Sandels understood Eddie's situation, perhaps sympathized with
him, for the youth was released on his own recognizance.

Eddie returned to Youngers' Bend. He resented July more
than ever and disobeyed his mother openly and more frequently. Pearl continued to live at the Bend away from her
baby because Eddie needed her good influence, but there was
another reason: She still loved her mother.

Although Belle kept working on Pearl to put Flossie up for
adoption, at the same time she salved old wounds by promising to lead a better life herself. She even showed Pearl the
letter from Owen as proof that she was now in good standing
with federal authorities and the Indian police. During the last
week of September, 1888, while Eddie was still recuperating,
she and Pearl attended the International Indian Fair at Muskogee:

Last Thursday [September 27] began the chief day of the fair as
well as the time set for the shooting tournament, a goodly number
of Vinita people went down—the gun club included. . . . The trap
shooting occupied most of the afternoon and resulted very satisfactorily to the Vinita club. Two lady equestrian contests concluded the
day's programme . . . the daughter of the notorious Belle Starr was
one of the riders, and she used no saddle. . . . As the "wild Indians,"
so extensively advertised, did not show up, Belle was substituted as
the leading attraction.[25]

During the fall of 1888, Belle and Pearl attended several
dances around Briartown, Whitefield, and Eufaula. Eddie stayed
home, brooding and sullen, but Bill July accompanied the
women, dressed in his best white man's clothes, his long hair
braided down each shoulder, snake rattles tied at the end of
the braids. Like Sam Starr, he did not dance and would seat
himself inside the front door, two six-shooters within easy
grasp should harm threaten his womenfolk. It was like old
times, the past mistakes forgotten, and mother and daughter
seemed happy.

The hard years in Indian Territory had given Belle an un-
matchable shrewdness. Outwardly considerate and coopera-

tive, she was incomprehensible, conniving, and uncompromising. She did not give up on Flossie. She learned that the baby was with Jim Reed's sister in Wichita. Pearl wrote Aunt Mamie Reed and asked her to return the child to Missouri. According to "Flossie,"

Aunt Mamie [did so] immediately, then wrote my mother about the trip—how she had dressed me in a little blue frock, the color of my eyes. I have the dress locked in my trunk now.

But this letter, intended to comfort my mother, never reached her. Belle kept the letter, and told Pearl that I was to be placed in an orphanage. At this my mother began watching for a chance to slip away, but . . . it was not easy. Belle wrote letter after letter to the Reeds, and finally wrote that she would have me stolen and given to the gypsies. And this was the threat that won. Aunt Mamie took me to an orphans' home. At that time the gypsies were roving about, dirty and cruel . . . a real menace.

One day Belle Starr called Pearl to her and said, "I want you to sign this paper. The baby is in a Home." My mother told me that she cried out, "You can't make me sign it. You have done everything else to me, but you can't make me sign that paper!" Then she ran screaming from the room.

When she returned the paper was gone. And not until I took the paper out to her in Arizona, thirty-five years later, did she know what Belle had written or the location of the orphans' home in which I was placed. . . . The paper was signed on Nov. 19, 1888.[26]

Belle picked up her mail at Whitefield, and sometimes Pearl and Eddie accompanied her. William S. Hall and Jeff Surratt ran a store in Whitefield; in 1886, when Dr. Henry Redding (who had treated Sam Starr for measles) resigned as postmaster, Hall moved the office into the store and became acting postmaster until he was appointed by the U.S. Post Office Department on February 2, 1887. He remembered that Belle's mail consisted mainly of letters from "different States" and a few leading magazines and newspapers of the day. Belle instructed him that under no circumstances was either of her children to have access to it.[27]

One morning Hall was putting up the mail when Eddie came in and asked for all items addressed to his mother. Hall politely informed him of Belle's orders. Eddie drew his pistol and told him to hand it over; Hall complied promptly. Next day, Belle ushered Eddie into the store, strode down the aisle to where Hall was standing, and angrily demanded to know why the boy had been given her mail. When Hall explained, Belle "turned white with fury, drew her gun, levelled down on Ed and seizing a bull whip off the wall, literally cut the blood out of her son's back and shoulders," then warned him "to never, but never," show disrespect to Mr. Hall again.[28] It is probable that Eddie, at Pearl's behest, had hoped to intercept some of the correspondence to Belle from the Reeds in Missouri.

Pearl might have left the Bend at this time but for Eddie's sake. Furthermore, Christmas, 1888, was in the offing; February 5 would be Belle's forty-first birthday, which Belle had already promised they would celebrate with a trip to McAlester, and February 22 would be Eddie's eighteenth birthday. Too, Pearl was determined to stand by her brother at his forthcoming trial in March. Belle had refused to see Eddie's attorney or pay his legal fees, offering Pearl the excuse, "I've always told him not to steal." Harman[29] writes:

> Ed Reed was nearing his eighteenth birthday . . . [he] asked permission to ride [Belle's] fine black horse . . . which she prized very highly . . . to a dance several miles away. His request was denied and he stole the animal from its stable after dark and did not return until just before daybreak. . . . Belle awoke at his return . . . went to the stable and discovered that her favorite had been badly mistreated and ill cared for. She grasped her quirt . . . stalked to the house and into the room where Ed lay in bed asleep, and gave him an unmerciful whipping. His punishment greatly angered the boy, and he left home and was not seen for two weeks; it was said that he threatened his mother's life in return for her chastisement, and there was talk of his arrest.[30]

Eddie wasn't arrested, however. Early in December, "after a violent quarrel with his mother" (possibly over the whipping he received at Whitefield), he moved in with the Jackson Rowe family on the Choctaw side of the South Canadian.[31] Belle never saw her son again. Her third source of trouble since the death of Sam Starr would soon end her life.

18   Canadian River Ambush

More than a score of noncitizen farmers, or renters, had become Belle's neighbors in San Bois County, Choctaw Nation, south of the Canadian. Under Article 43 of the Treaty with the Choctaw and Chickasaw Nations of Indians, concluded and ratified, with amendments, at Washington, D.C., on June 28, 1866, the United States promised and agreed that "no white person, except officers, agents, and employes of the Government, and of any internal improvement company, or persons travelling through, or temporarily sojourning in . . . said nations . . . shall be permitted" in the Territory unless "formally incorporated and naturalized" by the nations of Choctaws and Chickasaws in accordance with their "laws, customs, or usages." The article did not affect adopted citizens or prevent the temporary employment of white teachers, mechanics, or persons skilled in agriculture. The legislatures of the respective nations could authorize "such works of internal improvement as they may deem essential to the welfare and prosperity" of their communities.[1]

Under terms of a bill enacted by the Choctaw General Council and signed into law by Principal Chief Allen Wright on November 20, 1867,[2] enterprising Choctaws who had laid claim to large tracts of rich bottom lands encouraged and even advertised for white tenants from the war-ravaged states of the South, offering virgin cotton land rent free under five-year improvement leases. The tenant was required to dig a well, construct a cabin and grain storage building, and clear, fence, and bring under cultivation a specified number of acres each year. At the end of the initial lease period, if the tenant wished to remain on the land, he paid the Choctaw claimant a share (usually one-fourth) of the corn and cotton production.[3]

By 1887 white immigrants outnumbered native Choctaws two to one. The General Council enacted additional permit legislation, approved by Principal Chief B. F. Smallwood on October 30, 1888, which reduced the lease period to "no greater nor less" than one year, required land claimants to make application to the county judge with the written endorsement of three responsible Choctaw citizens, and pay a five-dollar fee "for every farmer, or renter, so employed." Lease permits could be renewed from year to year if approved by the county judge upon proper endorsement of the issuing officers and payment of the annual fee.[4]

Among the largest claimants in the Whitefield area were Hiram and Jim King, Jackson Rowe, and Milo Hoyt, Jr. The King lands lay east of Whitefield along a branch on the Canadian bearing their name. Rowe and Hoyt occupied the river bottoms to the west, opposite and a little downstream from Youngers' Bend. Hoyt, a Cherokee, had married Harriet Folsom, a former teacher at Armstrong Academy in the Choctaw Nation, thus acquiring Choctaw citizenship. He claimed as much public land on the Canadian as he could manage, had about four hundred acres under cultivation, owned between three hundred and four hundred head of cattle and about as many hogs, and raised blooded horses which he entered in racing meets as far east as the Mississippi.[5] Under a Choctaw law of November 8, 1888, "no person or citizen" was allowed "to connect his pasture with that of another"; a passageway or lane "not less than twenty-five feet wide" was to be left between all such enclosures and kept clear for travelers.[6] A lane forty feet wide extending a mile and a half down the hill from the Hoyt home provided access to the south bank of the river. The young men of the Hoyt family frequently used it to exercise their horses.[7]

Early in January, 1888, a hard-faced man thirty-two years old, six feet in height, with blue eyes, red hair, and sunburnt whiskers, traveling with his wife in a covered wagon, stopped at the Hoyt ranch. He revealed nothing of his background except that he was "from Arkansas" and his name was Edgar A. Watson. He rented one of Hoyt's tenant farms on the west side of the land leading to the river, made a good crop of corn and cotton that fall, and asked to renew his lease for another year. Being a very mysterious sort of fellow, he had not mixed well with the natives and had difficulty obtaining the endorsements required under the permit law passed in October. Hoyt suggested he might rent some land from Belle Starr across the river and avoid the restrictions.

As an added source of income, since Sam Starr's death, Belle had allowed various white settlers to sharecrop her property. Watson set his sights on a piece of ground near the river which, with his know-how, could be made particularly productive. There was an aura of cruelty about him that Belle did not like, but he was decidedly good-looking, talked well, and apparently a man of exemplary habits. His wife was a young woman of more than ordinary refinement and quite chummy, and Belle saw in her a potentially good neighbor. She accepted their rent money; they could move onto the land in December.

Meanwhile, Belle and Mrs. Watson became close friends. On occasion Belle would ferry the Canadian and drop by the Hoyt tenant farm on her trips to Whitefield, and Mrs. Watson called at the Bend. They talked about their pasts, and one afternoon in a moment of confidence Mrs. Watson revealed to Belle that her husband had been charged with murder in Florida and had sought refuge first in Franklin County, Arkansas, then in Indian Territory.

Belle was not shocked. In fact, she was sympathetic. But, remembering the threat of Cherokee authorities and the U.S. Indian agent at Muskogee to expel her if she were caught again harboring fugitives, she began maneuvering to keep Watson off her property. At first she tried refunding the rent money. Watson refused. They had words. Indignant, Belle sent the money to him in a letter mailed from Eufaula, stating that she had made arrangements with Joseph Tate, a newcomer to Hoyt

Bottom south of the river, to sharecrop her ground. Watson went to Tate and informed him that so many Indian police and federal marshals visited the Bend there was no telling when she might be sent away to prison again and he might even be suspected of aiding in her lawless activities. Tate promptly advised Belle that he could not go through with their agreement.[8]

Belle's temper flared. In late November, Watson came to discuss the Eufaula letter. Belle cursed him for interfering with her business affairs, then added, scornfully: "I don't suppose the United States officers would trouble you *but the Florida officers might.*" Watson flushed as he realized that she had wormed from his wife his dark and terrible secret. Wordlessly, he mounted and rode away. Pearl, sitting in the cabin, had "overheard the conversation and chided her mother for being so careless . . . but Belle laughed and forgot the circumstance."[9] She saw nothing more of Watson. In January, 1889, he moved into one of Jackson Rowe's tenant cabins near the corner of the Hoyt ranch.

On Saturday morning, February 2, Bill July set out for Fort Smith to answer the old charge of horse stealing. Belle needed to pay a bill they owed at a little store on King Creek about ten miles from Youngers' Bend on the south side of the river, and so she went with him on horseback. At the store she paid in full their account of seventy-five dollars and decided to ride some distance farther with July. They spent the night at the home of one of her friends, Mrs. Richard Nail, on San Bois Creek twenty miles east of Whitefield. The following morning, Sunday, the two parted. July rode off to the court of Judge Parker, and Belle started back to the Bend.

Belle reached the King Creek store shortly before noon, fed her horse, and ate lunch with the proprietor and his wife. At the table, she appeared depressed.

"What's wrong, Belle?" inquired the merchant.

"Oh, it's just that things haven't gone so well for me lately," she replied gloomily, then added abruptly that she feared being killed by one of her enemies. She did not elaborate.

The merchant tried to cheer her. "Why, Belle, thunder and lightnin' couldn't kill you!"

Belle grimaced. She asked for a pair of scissors. Then, removing a large silk handkerchief, she cut it in two, diagonally, and gave half to the merchant's wife as a keepsake.[10]

She left the store at half past one. About four o'clock she arrived at the house of Jackson Rowe. Robert C. Barnes and his wife, Jerusha, and their several children were camped in the yard.[11] Barnes was a Rowe tenant before December, 1886, and was at Lucy Surratt's the night Sam Starr and Frank West gunned each other down. Mrs. Barnes was preparing supper for her brood. Belle was very fond of corn pone and wanted a piece of the sour corn bread that the woman was widely known for making. She also hoped to see Eddie, who had been living with the Rowes since moving there before Christmas.

The Rowe home was a popular Sunday gathering place for the tenant families of Hoyt Bottom. Besides the Barnes family, other visitors that afternoon included William England; Tom, Sliger, and Peeler Ellison; and a Mr. Hare. Edgar Watson sat on the porch. Eddie Reed had been there but left for the home of Andy McAntz, a mile and a half across the river, before his mother arrived. As Belle rode up, Watson left immediately, going in the direction of his cabin, about one hundred fifty yards away.[12] Belle got her piece of corn bread, chatted with Barnes and his wife nearly half an hour, then rode on. That was the last anybody remembered seeing her alive.

The trail led around Watson's place and intersected the Hoyt lane near the corner of another field three hundred yards from Watson's cabin. Apparently, Belle did not see the sinister figure crouched in the corner of the rail fence. She was munching the piece of corn bread, still in her apprehensive mood. She passed the fence corner and turned into the river lane, pocked with water puddles and mudholes from a heavy rain two days earlier. A shotgun bellowed at her from twenty feet. A charge of buckshot struck her in the back and neck and knocked her

THE ASSASSINATION OF BELLA STARR.

The assassination of Belle Starr. From an illustration in the National Police Gazette, *February 23, 1889.*

from the saddle. As she tried to lift herself from the mud, the assassin leaped the fence and fired the other barrel of the shotgun. This time a heavy charge of turkey shot struck her in the shoulder and left side of the face.

Milo Hoyt's twenty-two-year-old son, Milo Ard Hoyt (nicknamed "Frog" because of his long legs), was returning from a visit in the Cherokee Nation and had just reached the north side of the Canadian. Finding the ferryboat tied to the bank, unattended, he spurred his horse into the water, swam across, and sat down on the south bank to dry himself. Within minutes Belle's riderless mount, sidesaddle askew, dashed madly past him, leaped into the river, and swam to the opposite shore. Realizing that something unusual had happened, Hoyt rode rapidly in the direction from which the animal had come. He testified later:

The sun was about half an hour high. Passed Alf White's place. About half a mile from the ferry I seen [Belle] lying on her face stretched out across the road. I heard no shots . . . thought the horse had thrown her . . . never went up to her, but turned around and went back to boat. Miss Pearl was at the boat . . . just landing on this side.[13]

According to Pearl, her mother's horse

came home with the saddle on . . . about six o'clock in evening. Swam the river. I went to river, crossed over & met Milo Hoyt. He told me about Belle lying [in] road. I got behind him on his horse & he took me to Alf Whites & from there I went to body alone. It was almost dark when I got to her. She was not quite dead. She never spoke. She was lying on her side & face, kind of across the road. Her whip was in her hand. She was shot in back with buckshot & left side of face & arm with fine shot. The buckshot came out on right side of her neck. . . . There were three buckshots in her back close together. She had left home on Saturday morning with her husband Jim Starr.[14]

Martha (Mrs. Alf) White remembered seeing

Belle & Starr pass up the road on Saturday. On Sunday about 5 o'clock heard the report of two guns or two reports. I was inside the house, doors were open. When I heard shooting I went to door

. . . in a few minutes seen horse with sidesaddle running up the road to the ferry. There were no men folks at house. Mrs. Pierson was there with me. Milo Hoyt told me about Belle being killed . . . brought [Pearl] to my house.[15]

Alf White was visiting at the Benjamin Statham place:

When I came home about sundown my wife told about a horse passing with a sidesaddle on him. Directly Milo Hoyt came up & told us about Belle being killed. . . . I and Mr. Pierson went down with Miss Pearl to where her mother was, and in a little while got a wagon & took [body] up to my house.[16]

Benjamin Statham heard two gunshots that evening

about half a hour by sun. Then about dark Charles Acton & Mr. White came to my house & told me about Belle being dead & I went up there & helped take her up & put her in wagon & take her to Mr. White's.[17]

Charles Acton lived on Belle Starr's place. When he

heard she was killed . . . I got a horse & went to where she was. Found her in road & helped Miss Pearl to lift her up out of the mud. I then went after a wagon & took her to Mr. White's house. She was shot with a shotgun, with buckshot & small shot.[18]

Alice (Mrs. Joseph) Tate, who lived a mile from the ambush scene and half a mile from Edgar Watson,

heard two guns [shots] in the evening about half an hour by sun. My husband & Billy England were standing out back of house talking when guns fired. Ben Statham came to our house about dark & told us, & me & my husband & Fayette Vaughn & Billy England went down from our house.[19]

William England recalled that Watson was at Jackson Rowe's home Sunday afternoon:

He left before I did. I staid there 15 or 20 minutes, maybe a little longer & went to Tates. I heard two guns [shots] while at Tates. They sounded like they were off about half a mile.[20]

Ray England, who lived two miles from the White place and a half a mile from Watson, was well acquainted with Belle, but he had not seen her for a month until I seen her dead at Alf Whites. Fayette Vaughn on the 3rd day of February 1889 at after dark came to my house to let me know she had been killed and wanted the neighbors to go & take care of her. Me & Jack Rowe went over . . . found Belle Starr dead, laid out on a bed. . . . I sat up all night with her & in the morning me, Jim Cates & Ed Reed went down to where she had been shot. Found tracks where someone had stood in fence corner. We followed tracks about 100 yds southwest. This is as far as us boys tracked him. [Turner] England got in ahead of us boys & followed tracks. The tracks were six or seven [size shoe]. While we were following the tracks Watson came up where we were. He was walking. He had no [fire] arms. He owns a shotgun, a double barrelled one. He had nothing to say . . . staid there two hours. Never seen him after this.

On Febry 3/89 on Sunday heard report of two big guns. They were about a mile from me at the time. I was on my way home from old man Morrills. . . . When I got within 100 yds of Watson's house I heard someone calling hogs. When I got past house, someone halloed to me & I took it to be Watson. The sun was near down . . . he would have had time to have done shooting from the time I heard shots until I seen him at house.

It was muddy at the fence corner. It looked like person had been there a few minutes before he did the killing. This corner was about twenty steps from where Belle Starr fell. The man that shot her crossed over the fence & went across [field] towards Watsons.[21]

Jackson Rowe told how Belle came to his house

along in the afternoon . . . riding & alone. She staid until nearly night . . . took supper with Barnes . . . said she was going home, left alone. Watson left before she did. She never spoke to him. That night I heard she was killed. Ray England told me. I went along to Alf Whites where she was lying dead on bed. Next morning we went out looking for tracks. . . .

The first I seen of track was 100 yds from where body lay. . . . Track was going towards where woman was & coming from the direction of Watson's field. It was about a seven track. The track went over leaves & it kept us from getting the exact measure. . . . I never went inside Watson's field. Do not know if there was any tracks in field.

Heard Watson calling hogs after he went home that day. It was late in the evening. He called hogs a good while . . . calls them every

morning & evening. Belle had been gone some little bit when I heard
him calling hogs.[22]

Eddie Reed had not seen his mother

in two months. I was staying at Jack Rowes most of the time. Left
Rowes on Sunday evening between three & 4 o'clock. Belle had not
come there yet. I went to ford on river to Andy McAntz . . . it was
swimming & three or four men came down to ford to see me cross.
They were Ridge, McAntz & a man who lives close to ford named
Palmer. It was about half an hour by sun when I got to ford. I had
no arms with me. I got wet in river & went to McAntz to dry my
clothes & staid all night. Went back to Rowes about 9 o'clock next
morning & there Mrs. Barnes told me Belle was killed. I got on my
horse & went to Alf Whites. Belle was lying on bed dead & I got
Jim Cates to show me where she was killed. I found where tracks
had come into field & came up to fence on their toes & stood right
by fence corner on inside of field. She fell about 30 feet from there
& these tracks had got over fence & went up close to her & then
they left there & went right opposite through the woods. Tracks kept
winding around, looked like they were trying to keep on leaves for
almost 200 yds. I then lost track . . . it was about a number seven.[23]

Turner England also received news of the killing Monday
morning:

Fayette Vaughn brought me word . . . I went over there . . . seen
blood in road, seen tracks of man that I thought done shooting . . .
followed these tracks two or three hundred yds. It went through the
bushes kind of southwest then turned pretty near east . . . to southwest of Watson's field. Watson's house was about 150 yards from
where we quit.
Watson and his work hand . . . Ansel Terry . . . came to my house
on Monday morning before I started off . . . came to grind their axes.
They ground their axes. I told him about the killing and he said he
had heard it too away in the night. I told him I was going over & he
had better come along. He came with me as far as Mr. Tates. I left
him there . . . seen him up at White's house when I came back from
tracking. Do not know how long he stayed.[24]

Monday morning before daybreak, Charles Acton rode to
Eufaula, the nearest telegraph station, and wired July at Fort
Smith that his wife had been murdered. "No particulars were

given and nothing to show who did the deed," said an *Elevator* dispatch of February 4. "There was bad blood in . . . Jim Starr's . . . eye when he heard the news, and without delay he saddled his horse, provided himself with a quart of whiskey, struck out on a run for home, saying somebody was going to suffer."

July reached the Bend late Monday night. Shortly after sunup that morning, Belle's body had been wrapped in quilts, placed in Jim Cates's wagon, and hauled by him and his brother, Wiley Cates, across the Canadian to her home where July found her.[25] July knew about Belle's trouble with Watson over the leasing of her land. Eddie Reed told him the killer's tracks led in a round-about way to a point within a hundred yards of Watson's cabin.

Some women in the neighborhood prepared Belle for burial. They washed the body and anointed it with turpentine and oil of cinnamon, dressed Belle in her best riding habit, and placed her in a pine-board coffin lined with black shrouding trimmed in white lace; it had been built by Jim Cates's brother, John I. Cates of Whitefield. Her arms were crossed, "with one of her hands grasping the handle of her favorite revolver."[26]

The funeral was held on Wednesday, February 6. All morning the gravediggers worked with pick and shovel on the rocky clay bench in front of the cedar cabin overlooking Youngers' Bend and the Canadian River Valley. By noon a strange crowd —men and women of the Starr clan, simple Choctaws, Creeks, white sharecroppers, and some of the renegades Belle had befriended—had gathered to pay their last respects. Edgar Watson was there with his wife, "and he seemed to be very nervous."[27] There was no religious ceremony, no minister or prayer, no chanting of Cherokee dirges.[28] Suddenly the pall-bearers, "grim visaged Indians heavily armed," appeared in the doorway bearing the coffin. They carried it to the grave and set it on the ground, then removed the lid and stood back, examining the rows of visitors intently. In single file, whites and Indians passed. Fulfilling an ancient custom, each Cherokee dropped a small piece of corn bread in the casket. After Pearl and Eddie had been allowed a decent interval, the lid was nailed on, the coffin was lowered into the hole, and the gravediggers began shoveling clay and stone over all that was mortal of this sometimes cruel, vengeful, and yet, in many respects, kindly woman.[29]

"Scarcely had the grave been filled when James July . . . turned and approaching Watson," pointed his Winchester at the farmer's belly and shouted: "You murdered my wife!" Mrs. Watson and her husband remained "quite cool," but many of the startled spectators "thought that [Watson] was going to be killed." John Cates was standing nearby, and Watson "took hold of him and pushed Cates between himself and the gun." Cates realized "they were in great danger . . . as a single shot would have been the signal for a desperate fight." He said, "Throw up your hands and don't get us both killed." Watson surrendered and told July that "if he killed him he would kill the wrong man." Watson then "asked not to be left alone with the desperado, and Ben Statham and wife, Jack Rowe and Mrs. Watson" camped at the Starr home overnight. Next morning, "July and Ed Reed took Watson to Fort Smith, Jack Rowe going along" to ensure the prisoner's safety.[30]

Although he had arrested Watson without the formality of a warrant, immediately upon arriving at Fort Smith on February 8, July appeared with his prisoner before U.S. Commissioner Wheeler and made affidavit that "Edgar A. Watson, a white man, did in the Indian Country, within the Choctaw Nation . . . on or about the 3 day of February 1889 feloniously, willfully, premeditatedly and of his malice aforethought kill and murder Belle Starr, against the peace and dignity of the United States, and I pray a writ."[31] Endorsed as federal witnesses were Eddie Reed, Pearl, Milo ("Frog") Hoyt, Ray, Turner and William England, Martha and Alf White, Jackson Rowe, Charles Acton, Benjamin Statham, and Alice and Joseph Tate.

Commissioner Wheeler issued a capias and subpoenas, authorized July to serve them, and "there not being sufficient time to hear and decide upon the charge against [Watson] . . . he is required to give bail in a sufficient sum for his appearance before me on such day as charge can be heard . . . which requisition he has failed to comply with . . . THEREFORE COMMAND" that he be conveyed to the United States jail and there be safely kept until "discharged by due course of law."[32]

J. S. Dunham, publisher of the nearby weekly *Van Buren Press*, obtained from both July and Watson statements which were carried in his edition of Saturday, February 16. July recapped the circumstances surrounding Belle's ambush and added: "I knew enough to satisfy me that Watson was the murderer. We buried Belle at Youngers Bend, and I went after Watson and got him. He showed no fight, or I would have killed him." In jail, Watson said: "I knew very little of Belle Starr, though she for some reason, I know not what, has been prejudiced against me. . . . I have lived near her about a year, and I made a crop in the Choctaw Nation last year. I have never had any trouble with anyone . . . have no idea who killed her . . . I did not . . . had no reason to even feel hard toward her."

Watson employed a prominent Fort Smith attorney, William M. Mellette. The hearing was held before Commissioner James Brizzolara on February 22–23. Assistant District Attorney C. L. Jackson sought to bring Watson before the grand jury on the facts as follow:

(1) Belle Starr had been struck with a load of buckshot and a load of fine shot; three closely spaced buckshot in her back had penetrated her vital organs and caused her death.

(2) Ill feeling existed between defendant and Belle before the killing. July testified: "In November last Deft & Belle had a falling out. . . . As we were coming down [to Fort Smith] Deft said he would rather give $5000.00 than to come down here." Pearl stated that "Deft & mother were not friendly" but did not elaborate. William England thought "it rose about a letter." Turner England "knew of no ill feeling between Deft & Belle, only what they told me themselves. . . . Belle came to me where I was splitting rails & wanted to know why Mr. Tate did not move on her place as he had agreed. I knew why

UNITED STATES OF AMERICA,

WESTERN DISTRICT OF ARKANSAS.

BEFORE JAMES BRIZZOLARA UNITED STATES COMMISSIONER.

UNITED STATES.

versus

Edgar A. Watson } murder.

SEE COMPLAINT AND ENDORSEMENT THEREON FILED HEREWITH.

On this 22d day of February 1889 came the United States of America, the Plaintiff in this cause, by _Jackson_ Esq., U. S. Attorney and the defendant in his own proper person, in custody of the Marshal and by his Attorney _Wm. M. Millette Esq._ when the following testimony was heard and proceedings had to-wit:

Jay England being duly sworn deposes and says: I reside at _Sans Bois county Choctaw Nation_ and know the defendant in this cause _Louis Belle Starr she is dead_ had not seen dead for a month until I seen her dead on the _forties Rolap Gujittle Vaugins_ on the 3d day of February 1889 at after dark came to our house to let me know Belle Starr had been killed & wanted them to go & take care of her: me & _Jack Coe_ went over there this _Vaugins went to let white's family house_ when we got there found Belle Starr dead she was laid out on a bed she was shot on left side

---

Proceedings of February 22-23, 1889, in United States *v.* Edgar A. Watson *for murder of Belle Starr.*

but did not tell her & she said it was that long tongued Watson, tell him that he need not be afraid of the Cherokee officers but he might look out for the Creek officers. When I told him this Deft said they had better look out what they were telling on him."

(3) Watson owned a 12-guage muzzle-loading shotgun. William England had "shot it at target; it throws three shot close together & scattered the other right smart around. Met Deft on Wednesday before Belle was shot. I wanted to borrow some bird shot from Deft & he said he had only one load & refused to let me have any. He said he might need them." July, when he arrested Watson, "wanted to get his gun & he told me his gun was not at home."

(4) Watson left Jackson Rowe's home about an hour before Belle Starr was slain. He was thoroughly familiar with Hoyt Bottom, knew she would have to pass the corner of the Hoyt ranch to reach the ferry on the Canadian, and had ample time to prepare an ambush at the site. The tracks led to a point within one hundred yards of Watson's house. Watson wore a size seven shoe.

Ansel D. Terry, sworn on defendant's behalf, testified:

> I was living at Defts . . . working for him. I had been to Oklahoma [Whitefield] that Sunday . . . got back home about five o'clock . . . Deft was in corn crib getting corn for his hogs. I unsaddled my horse & went to spring for water . . . when I came back heard two shots fired in direction of where Belle was killed. I was sitting on wood pile. Deft was at fence calling his hogs. . . . Heard of Belle being killed about ten o'clock in night. . . . Seen Defts gun on Monday in rack. The day Deft was arrested I took the gun.

Charles Starr examined the weapon and found it "loaded in both barrels with buckshot . . . 14 buckshot in one barrel & ten in the other." Watson denied that he had reloaded the shotgun.

> It was at house that evening in rack . . . never thought about my gun that day. . . . Do not know when Belle left Jack Rowes. I had been home about fifteen or twenty minutes when Terry came . . .

heard two shots when I went out to call my hogs . . . in direction Belle was found. Terry was at wood pile. I was told Belle was mad at me. We never had any difficulty. She never did say a cross word to me. I did not kill Belle Starr . . . know nothing about it.

Mellette succeeded in convincing Commissioner Brizzolara that the evidence was "all circumstantial." Watson was a "quiet, hard-working man whose local reputation was good," he declared, and the parties who trailed Belle's assassin "could not be certain" the footprints they found were his. Assistant District Attorney Jackson pleaded to allow July time to bring in more witnesses, and Commissioner Brizzolara reserved his decision until March 4. July failed to produce further damaging testimony, and Brizzolara ordered the "defendant discharged."[33]

Things might have been different had Pearl told the court of the conversation between Belle and Watson she overheard. Apparently she feared the same fate that had befallen her mother and kept her silence even with brother Eddie and Bill July.

Knowing July's reputation, Watson decided not to remain in Indian Territory. He returned to Hoyt Bottom long enough to pick up his wife and belongings, then left, presumably for Arkansas. No further effort was made by anyone to apprehend the person responsible for Belle's death.

19 The Gem That Sparkles Yet

Much speculation resulted from the government's failure to prove that Watson was Belle's assassin or establish a motive for her murder. Some thought her killer was a younger brother of Jim Reed who, believing Belle had provided the information that resulted in Jim's capture and death in 1874, finally moved into Hoyt Bottom under an assumed name and awaited the opportune moment to blast her from the saddle.[1] Another story was that old Tom Starr killed Belle because she had led his son Sam into outlawry and kept the feud with Frank West boiling. This tale, false on its face, may have originated with Ellis West, who said in a 1937 interview[2] that "three years" after the Whitefield shootout Tom Starr "learned the facts" and remarked to his wife that Belle would "never cause another killing." Ellis said Tom "left his home on the south side of the Canadian . . . lashed some logs together, making a raft and crossed the river about one mile west of Whitefield, proceeding to Belle Starr's place under cover of darkness [and] early Sunday morning, called Belle out of her house and shot her." Tom Starr returned from the Illinois prison early in 1888 in ill health and closed his days quietly at his Briartown home in 1890.

In the fall of 1888, a rancher named Hi Early, who lived near Youngers' Bend, complained to neighbors about Belle's running off some of his cattle and horses. Word reached Belle; a few days later she met him on the trail, sent a rifle bullet whistling past his head, and threatened to kill him if he made any more accusations, whereupon Early publicly offered a seventy-five dollar reward to anyone who would dispose of her. On February 4, the day after her death, Pony Starr of Porum was riding with Early toward Starville when a cowboy in Early's employ, a fellow named Bertholf, stopped them and announced: "I've come for my money." The rancher calmly reached into his saddlebag and "counted out $75.00 in gold coin." To his dying day Pony Starr believed that Bertholf had murdered Belle Starr; he told his story to Emmett Lowery of Briartown, who passed it along to author Ted Byron Hall in 1962.[3]

Hicks names Jim Middleton, brother of John Middleton, as Belle's slayer. While doing research for his book in 1952-53, Hicks interviewed Claude Hamilton, a Porum barber who owned some five hundred acres in Youngers' Bend, including the site of Belle's old home. Hamilton claimed that Dick Starr told him Jim Middleton called Dick to his deathbed at Porum in January, 1938, and admitted shooting Belle off her horse to avenge his brother's death; that John was carrying sixteen thousand dollars from the Creek payroll robbery in his saddlebags, which were empty when officers recovered the horse he was riding; and that Jim always believed Belle had sent someone to "put John out of the way to get his share of the money." In 1953, Dick Starr was dead, so Hicks went to Troy Hunnicutt (formerly of Porum but at the time a smelter worker at Blackwell, Oklahoma), with whom Jim Middleton lived several years. Hunnicutt stated: "[Jim] told me he killed Belle Starr, all right. . . . He always figured she had [John] killed to get $5,000 in his saddlebags." Hicks also talked to Mrs. Florence Watts of Porum, Jim Middleton's stepdaughter. Mrs. Watts told him she was present when her stepfather died, but "not present when he talked to Dick Starr"; that John had "$18,000 from the Creek robbery" when Jim last saw him alive; and that when John's mother went to Fort Smith to identify the body, she saw only the upper portion of it—the face was missing, torn away by a shotgun blast. Hicks believed the Hamilton-Mrs. Watts.-Hunnicutt stories.[4]

The facts surrounding John Middleton's death do not support them, and there is no proof that John Middleton was involved in any Creek payroll escapade. In a letter dated January 16, 1967, Sam Wheat of Kinta, Oklahoma, whose Aunt Mary married Jim Middleton, categorically denied that Jim killed Belle.[5] Jim Middleton stated in an interview the year before his death that his "business transactions with Sam Starr and his wife were always satisfactory . . . during my four years acquaintance with them, until she was killed in 1889, I never saw anything in her life that caused me to think she was a bad woman."[6]

Three weeks after Belle's death, her property at Youngers' Bend was disposed of as follows:

VERBAL WILL OF BELLE STARR

Cherokee Nation)
Canadian District)

Personally appeared before me H. J. Vann, Clerk of Canadian District C. N., M. Kraft and Charles Acton who states on oath that they heard Belle Starr say on several occasions a short time before her death and while in her sound mind, state that if anything should happen or befall her, or that she should die and leave the improvement on which she was then living not disposed of the said improvement would be James Starr's. The improvement is situated on the Canadian River in the Cherokee Nation.

M. Kraft
Charles Acton

Sworn and subscribed to before me this the 25th day of Feby 1889.

H. J. Vann, Clerk
C. D., C. N.[7]

July, alias James Starr, wasn't around to establish his claim to the property. Disgusted with the outcome of the Watson hearing, he jumped bond on his horse-stealing charge, and his sureties offered a one hundred and fifty dollar reward for his capture.

For several months he ran with an outlaw gang on Talala Creek in present Rogers County, then sought refuge in the Chickasaw Nation. On January 23, 1890, Deputy Marshal Heck Thomas hauled him into Fort Smith, badly wounded. He had been shot by Heck's possemen, Bud Trainor and Bob Hutchins, near Ardmore while resisting arrest. On Sunday night, January 26, he died in the prison hospital.[8]

Verbal will of Belle Starr, from Cherokee Records, II, *page 15.*

More than sixty years later, in an article titled "Belle Starr's Avenger" by Elmer Leroy Baker in *Empire Magazine*, Thanksgiving, 1950, edition of the *Denver Post*, Hutchins said he investigated Belle's death and that "Jim July Starr murdered his own wife." Baker recaps the story in his 1969 book *Gunman's Territory:*[9]

Edgar Watson called Hutchins to his jail cell and told the deputy marshal that Belle was killed by his shotgun, but July pulled the trigger; that July came to his house about three o'clock on the afternoon he was supposed to be in Fort Smith and borrowed Watson's double-barreled weapon to kill a wolf that had been getting his chickens. July returned the shotgun that evening; both barrels had been fired. Later, Milo ("Frog") Hoyt rode up to Watson's place with the news that Belle was lying on the road, dead. Watson accompanied him to the scene and found the tracks of sharp-heeled boots, which he "knew for the marks of Jim Starr," and two empty shells in the brush, the percussion caps nicked in a way that he "knew they had been fired from his own gun." Watson allowed that July was trying to frame him. Hutchins repeated Watson's story to Judge Parker, who authorized him "to go to Younger's Bend and look around." Mrs. Watson gave Hutchins the shells her husband "had found at the scene of Belle's murder," and the "marks on the percussion caps were just as Watson had described them." The deputy also talked to Hoyt, who told him July met him on the road that Sunday morning and offered him two hundred dollars to kill Belle. Hoyt declined, and July, spurring his horse savagely, rode away, shouting: "Hell— I'll kill her myself and spend the $200 for whiskey!" Hutchins asked Hoyt why July wanted to kill Belle and Hoyt figured it was because Belle had caught him playing around with "a little Cherokee gal over at Briartown." (Had such been the case, Belle should have played the role of assassin). Hutchins obtained loaded shells from Watson's home, "exactly like the empty ones," and took them to Judge Parker, removed the powder and shot from one, and fired it in the shotgun. "The dent on the cap . . . they found to be a replica of the mark on the shells which had killed Belle." Judge Parker thought Hutchins had "enough proof to . . . convict July" and had Commissioner Brizzolara subpoena the deputy's witnesses. At the hearing, held "the final week of April, 1889," July "appeared surprised at this much opposition on his charge." Hutchins got a postponement to round up more witnesses but soon learned July had "skipped the vicinity." Watson was released. Hutchins soon heard rumors that July intended to kill him. While the deputy was on another assignment in the Chickasaw Nation, he got word that July was heading toward Ardmore. Hutchins and Trainor waited for him in a blackjack thicket and demanded his surrender. July set spurs to his mount and reached for his Colt. Hutchins mortally wounded him with a single shot and killed his horse. July was added to a load of prisoners that Heck Thomas took by rail to Fort Smith. While on the verge of death in the prison hospital, the outlaw asked for Hutchins, saying he had an important confession to make only to the man who had shot him. Hutchins started for Fort Smith, but July died before he arrived. The deputy was confident that July would have told him: "I killed Belle Starr."

Except for the shooting and capture of July, Hutchins's claims are fiction. According to the *Fort Smith Elevator*,[10] July's chief bondsman, Captain J. H. Mershon, withdrew the one hundred and fifty dollar reward for his arrest in mid-January, and July, hiding in the Chickasaw Nation, "had agreed to come in and make a new bond." In fact, he had wired Mershon: "I filled the bond and sent it to you and was fixing to come . . . if I die have Trainor and Hutchins tried for murder. They shot me foul." J. H. Salzer, to whose home the outlaw was taken after being wounded, had telegraphed: "If possible for Jim Starr to be kept here I don't want him moved. He is too badly shot."

At the Fort Smith hospital, July told an *Elevator* reporter the officers "had waylaid him nine miles from Ardmore and fired . . . without warning," that he "did not run until after he was wounded, and they shot his horse three times, killing the animal." When the jailer informed him that the prison doctor had "pronounced his case hopeless," July "said he had something to say to Captain J. H. Mershon, and would talk to no one else." Told that Mershon was in Texas and there would be no opportunity to see him, July "replied that it would not make much difference as what little he had to say to him would not amount to anything. He did not give any more statements. At 11 o'clock Sunday night he died, bravely enduring to the last," and was buried in potter's field.[11]

Nobody in the Eufaula-Briartown-Whitefield area thought July had any part in his wife's death, "but for some time," writes Harman,[12] "some believed that Belle Starr's assassin was none other than her own son, Ed Reed," because of the severe whipping she gave him for mistreating her horse. Several other biographers accept this theory.[13] At Watson's hearing, Eddie Reed furnished a provable account of his whereabouts at the time Belle was slain, and federal authorities gave no credence to the rumor that he had killed his mother. Because of her death, he was granted a continuance in his horse-thievery case until July, 1889.

It developed that Eddie had in his possession several pieces of riding equipment taken when General Lewis' horse was stolen, and the grand jury returned a second indictment on the charge of receiving stolen goods.[14] On July 11, a petit jury returned guilty verdicts on both counts, felonies for which Judge Parker ordered Eddie "imprisoned in the Ohio State Penitentiary . . . at Columbus . . . for the term and period of Five Years [for larceny] . . . that the above term of imprisonment shall commence and date from the expiration of a Two Year's term of imprisonment which [defendant] is this day to undergo upon 2nd count Indictment No. 2689."[15] On August 1, Eddie was delivered to Warden E. G. Coffin at the Ohio institution by Deputy Marshal R. B. Creekmore.[16]

Meanwhile, Pearl had married Will Harrison, Mabel's brother, who came to work at Youngers' Bend after Eddie moved in with the Rowe family in December, 1888. Will was an honest and capable young man of twenty-four, and for a time the couple lived quietly at Tamaha, Choctaw Nation, but their marriage did not last. "Their temperaments clashed, frequent quarrels occurred," and in the spring of 1891, Pearl deserted Will, and he obtained a divorce.[17] After that, Pearl drifted. She entered a brothel in Van Buren, Arkansas, for the purpose, she said, of obtaining money to secure Eddie's release from prison. Within a few months she was financially able to employ attorneys Colonel Benjamin T. DuVal and William M. Cravens. DuVal and Cravens succeeded in getting the ear of the president of the United States, and Eddie was granted a pardon in 1893.[18]

Instead of returning to respectability, Pearl moved her be-

Pearl Starr (right), daughter of Belle Starr, with two unidentified friends.

longings across the river to Fort Smith's Row, or red-light district, and opened a "boarding house." She decorated its front with a large red star draped with a string of pearls and outlined in electric lights. Her "boarders," of course, were pretty girls willing to sell themselves at two dollars to five dollars for a night. This was where Eddie found her when he came home. He was "overwhelmed with sorrow," says Harman, "but Pearl reasoned: 'There are only us two . . . everybody knows the conditions under which we have been placed; a change now would not help matters, and if you cannot bear your sister's disgrace I will provide you with money and you can go far away where I am not known.'"[19] Eddie told her he wished he had stayed in prison.

He returned to the Cherokee Nation, picking up any odd job he could find, but soon was in trouble again. He was arrested and charged before Commissioner Wheeler at Fort Smith with "introducing into the Indian Country on or about the 1st day of March 1894 . . . ten gallons of whiskey . . . against the peace and dignity of the United States."[20] In April the case was dismissed for lack of evidence. It was Eddie's last brush with the law; he felt the oppression of outside forces. As noted by the *Vinita Indian Chieftain* of June 13, "Ed Reed has been variously reported as leader of a new outlaw band . . . he is the son of the late Belle Starr, which gives sensational writers an admirable chance to make a newspaper desperado out of him."

During the fall of 1894 and the winter of 1894–95, several trains and stores were robbed by the infamous Bill Cook gang, which included such lights as Jim French and Crawford Goldsby, alias Cherokee Bill. Guards were hard to come by, and Eddie's prowess with a six-shooter and Winchester was well known; he offered his services and was employed on the Katy Railroad between Wagoner and McAlester. He also was deputized by George J. Crump, the newly appointed U.S. marshal for the Western District of Arkansas. Eddie had no clashes with the Cooks, but after the gang had been decimated, he continued in his capacity as a deputy marshal and was stationed at Wagoner. He married Jennie Cochran, a pretty Cherokee schoolteacher from Claremore, bought a small house on the east side of town, and made (except for his occasional drinking) an excellent officer.

Well known in the town were two part-Cherokee brothers, Zeke and Dick Crittenden, who had lived between Wagoner and Tahlequah for a number of years. Harman describes the Crittendens as "ex-Deputy Marshals . . . well-behaved men when sober, but quarrelsome and dangerous when in their cups."[21] Both had been wounded by Bill and Jim Cook and Cherokee Bill in the 1894 battle at Halfway House when Cherokee Deputy Sequoyah Houston was slain and Jim Cook captured.[22] Early-day Wagoner Postmaster Samuel S. Cobb described them as "outlaws . . . all kinds of depredations were committed by them, from robbing a smokehouse to highjacking, horse stealing and cattle rustling."[23]

On Thursday afternoon, October 25, 1895, the Crittendens came to Wagoner, became drunk and obstreperous, and decided "to paint the town red." While "riding and shooting promiscuously about the streets," they wounded Old Man Burns, proprietor of the principal restaurant, the bullet splitting his scalp. The city marshal made no effort to arrest them, and someone notified Reed. The *Vinita Leader* of October 31 concluded its report:

> When [Reed] attempted to arrest them they resisted and a general shooting match occurred . . . did not last long . . . both of the Crittendens were killed together with one of their horses. Reed was not injured. . . .
>
> Reed passed through Fort Gibson [the same day] on his way to Fort Smith to give himself up to the U.S. authorities. He was alone.

Varied accounts of the affair have been provided by Belle Starr biographers.[24] The facts brought out in the examination before Commissioner Wheeler at Fort Smith in *United States v. James E. Reed* (murder), Case No. —, October 25, 1895, were essentially as summarized by the Vinita press, and Eddie was "exonerated."[25]

The *Vinita Indian Chieftain* of March 19, 1896, reported his next exploit:

> Watt Wafford (col) was arrested last week by Deputy Ed Reed fifteen miles west of Wagoner. Wafford was wanted for cattle stealing and several other depredations committed in the past few years. Some time ago he made his escape from the Cherokee penitentiary

where he was serving a sentence. His career as an outlaw is in all probability about ended. Verily the way of the transgressor is like Arkansas beef — very tough.

Finally, the *Chieftain* of Thursday, December 17, 1896, published this note: "Ed Reed attempted Monday to arrest Joe Gibbs and J. N. Clark at Claremore for selling whiskey and was killed by them. Reed was a hard man and his fate was what might have been expected."[26]

Mooney[27] tells how Eddie's wife traveled forty miles from Wagoner to be at his side when he died. He says Jennie's father, Alec Cochran, had been poisoned some time earlier by bad liquor obtained from the "Gibbs brothers" saloon and gambling room, operated in the rear of their cigar store, and they had tossed him in the city dump so that his death would be attributed to "his drunken stupor and exposure." However, the old Indian lived to tell his son-in-law; Eddie determined to put an end to the Gibbses' illegal activity and was slain when he entered the store "by two shotgun blasts from close range, just as he killed his own mother from ambush seven years before." Mooney then states that on the day Eddie was buried in the Cochran cemetery six miles southeast of Claremore, Pearl Starr confessed to Dr. Jesse, who attended the funeral, that when she found her mother lying in the puddle of mud and blood on the road that Sunday afternoon in 1889 and lifted Belle's head in her arms, Belle whispered in her ear: "Baby you're [sic] brother Eddie shot me, I turned and seen him across the fence 'afore he cracked down on me the second time." Pearl's and Eddie's testimony under oath and the facts developed at Watson's trial refute this claim.

Harman,[28] Barde,[29] Aikman,[30] Cameron Rogers,[31] Sabin,[32] Horan,[33] Drago,[34] and Croy[35] agree that Watson was Belle Starr's killer. In his foreword to Hicks's book, Croy spoofs Hicks's conclusion that Jim Middleton was her murderer and invites the reader to write Hicks and "tell him to jump into the Canadian." Croy also is the first of Belle's biographers to examine Watson's criminal activity in Florida and explode the belief of Harman,[36] Barde[37] and Wellman[38] that, after he left Indian Territory, Watson was sentenced at Van Buren to fifteen years in the Arkansas Penitentiary at Little Rock for horse thievery, escaped, and was killed resisting recapture.

The initial account of Watson's final years is given in a Tampa, Florida, dispatch of October 28, 1910:

Edgar A. Watson, outlaw and slayer of Belle Starr . . . is dead, killed by a sheriff's posse. . . . Watson was a known "bad man" . . . in 1886, while living in North Florida, Watson quarreled with his brother-in-law and after cutting him to pieces, fled to Indian Territory. . . . On February 3, 1889, he shot and killed the "Queen of Outlaws" as she was leaving Rose [Rowe's] for her home. Watson was arrested for this crime and tried and acquitted, for lack of evidence.

The next heard from him was in Arkansas. . . . Watson's career as an outlaw is supposed to have ended there . . . but with his customary elusiveness, he finally found his way back to Florida. In one of the wildest and most out of way places to be found in the United States, Watson took up his abode.

Far out on an island in the Gulf of Mexico, ninety miles from the coast by boat, south of Fort Myers . . . he became involved in trouble with two negroes, and these he shot to death in cold blood. [He] then went to Fort Ogden, in DeSoto county, but his stay there was short. He and Quinn Bass, another outlaw, became involved in a dispute over the spoils of a marauding expedition and Bass was shot through the neck. [Watson then] went to South Florida, and in that section of the state, it is said, he killed no less than six men.

Finally he returned to his old haunts in Columbia county, Florida . . . made an attempt to settle down and become a law-abiding citizen. . . . A well-known business man was shot and killed, and the evidence pointed to Watson. A short time afterwards, a brother of this man, whose name was Toland, was killed in almost the identical spot. . . . Watson was arrested, but a money consideration is reported to have caused proceedings to be dropped. . . .

The last chapter in the life of this man begins with his removal to Chatham Bend, just south of Chokoloskee Bay.

Here he lived with his family . . . who were doing their utmost to live down public disgrace, and here he became implicated in a triple murder. . . . A woman was one of the victims. Another was a planter. The third was a character known as "Dutchy" Reynolds. The woman, known as Miss Ellen Smith, was . . . of unusual stature, masculine in proportions and referred to among the Indians of the Everglades as the "Big Squaw." Watson owed both Miss Smith and Waller, the planter, considerable money. A negro and a man Leslie Cox were brought into a plot to kill the two and "Dutchy."

After the killings the negro confessed and accused Watson of having hired him to assist him. . . . Watson, in the meantime, had gone to the officers at Fort Myers, and during the heavy storms which raged along the Florida coast several days ago, reported the death of the three victims. The discovery was made, he said, while he was on a visit near the place where the bodies were found. He had gone there, he said, to avoid Cox, knowing him to be a dangerous man. The officers listened to his story with unbelieving ears. . . . They suggested that a trip be made to Watson's plantation where it was thought Cox was hiding. Watson agreed to go alone. The next day he returned, bringing Cox's coat. Then the officers told Watson that he must lead them to the plantation in order to effect the capture of Cox. The same stubborn resistance which had manifested itself innumerable times previously manifested itself here. Watson refused to lead, knowing that the capture of Cox alive would mean his own undoing. The officers insisted, and still Watson rebelled. He shot, and this was the signal for more shots from the sheriff and his deputies. Watson had at last been called upon to pay the penalty for his crimes. He fell before the fire of the officers, his body riddled with bullets.

Thirty-seven years later in her book *The Everglades: River of Grass*,[39] Marjory Stoneman Douglas recapped the Chokoloskee Bay events with additional highlights, named members of the posse, and told how they dragged Watson's body into the water, towed it behind a boat down to Rabbit Key, and buried him in "that long oyster and mud bank which at low tide stretches out from the mangroves to a lone twisted mangrove tree at the end." The body subsequently was brought back to the mainland and reburied in a family plot in Fort Myers Cemetery.

Another account of Watson's demise (used by Croy) appears in "Reminiscences of Charles Sherod 'Ted' Smallwood" from *The Story of the Chokoloskee Bay Country*, compiled by Charlton W. Tebeau.[40] Smallwood moved to Chokoloskee Bay in 1891; established himself on Chokoloskee Island in 1896, where he served as postmaster; and wrote down his own experiences and personal knowledge of the area before his death in 1951.

In the light of Edgar A. Watson's many escapades, he almost surely was the man who killed Belle Starr.

As for Pearl, she continued to operate a "girl hotel" on Fort Smith's Row. In 1894 she gave birth to a second child, a girl named Ruth, whose father supposedly was "a society man — prominent in Fort Smith affairs." In 1897, Pearl married a German musician, Arthur Erbach, and gave birth to a son in August, 1898. Three weeks later, Erbach died of "typo-malaria," and the boy died of malaria when he was little more than eleven months old. In November, 1902, Pearl became a mother for the fourth time. This child, a girl, was named Jennette Andrews for the father, Dell Andrews, a well-known horse trader and gambler with whom Pearl lived as a common-law wife. When Jennette reached school age, Pearl placed the two girls in a convent at St. Louis and during the next several years was in and out of jail so often for whiskey and moral violations that finally she was banned from Fort Smith. She lived briefly at Hot Springs and Winslow, Arkansas, then went west. She died of a stroke in the old Savoy Hotel at Douglas, Arizona, on July 6, 1925. Her daughters were sent for; they made the funeral arrangements, and to "keep down as much notoriety as possible," they buried her in the sun-scorched copper town's Calvary Cemetery as Rosa Reed.[41]

Ghouls began work on Belle Starr's grave shortly after her death. A dispatch from Tahlequah to the *Dallas News* on March 20, 1890, reported that "the grave was robbed a few nights ago," supposedly to obtain "her jewelry . . . and a very fine pistol buried with her." The perpetrators were not apprehended. Consequently, Pearl had her mother's resting place walled up with two feet of stone, the wall filled with broken rock, and two large, well-fitted slabs of limestone tilted over the vault in a **V**, like the roof of a house.

During her affluent years on Fort Smith's Row and before Eddie's death, Pearl employed Joseph Dailey, a rural stone-

Belle Starr's grave at Younger's Bend.

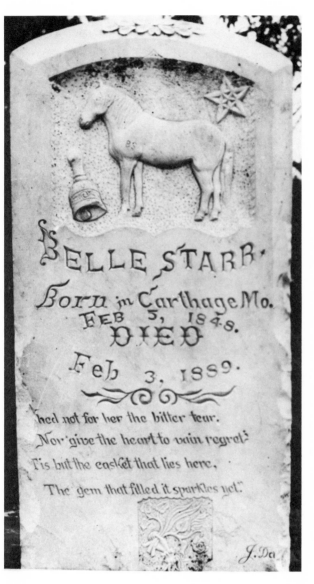

BELLE STARR,

Born in Carthage Mo.
FEB 5, 1848.
DIED
Feb 3, 1889.

Shed not for her the bitter tear.
Nor give the heart to vain regret;
'Tis but the casket that lies here,
The gem that filled it sparkles yet."

J. Da

Belle Starr's white marble gravestone, showing inscription and the work of rural stonecutter

cutter, to engrave a white marble slab which was cemented into the front of the tomb.[42] At its top, chiseled in relief, was the image of Belle's favorite mare, Venus, with a BS brand on the shoulder. Above and to the right was a star, and below, to the left, a bell. At the bottom was a clasped hand filled with flowers. The stone bore this inscription:

BELLE STARR
Born in Carthage Mo.
Feb 5, 1848.
DIED
Feb 3, 1889.

Pearl did not know the place of her mother's birth. However, she could not have supplied a more appropriate poem than the one she had engraved in the tombstone:

"Shed not for her the bitter tear,
Nor give the heart to vain regret;
'Tis but the casket that lies here,
The gem that filled it sparkles yet."

Notes, Comments, and Variants

Chapter 2

1. *Bella Starr, Female Jesse James,* 5.
2. *Hell on the Border,* 558-59.
3. *Lady Wildcats,* 162.
4. *Gallant Ladies,* 118.
5. "My Grandmother, Belle Starr" (Part I).
6. *Belle Starr,* 50-51, 54.
7. *Belle Starr, Bandit Queen,* 3.
8. *Wildcats in Petticoats,* 21.
9. *Desperate Women,* 203.
10. *Last of the Great Outlaws,* 49.
11. *Dynasty of Western Outlaws,* 74.
12. *Outlaws on Horseback,* 90.
13. *Doctor in Belle Starr Country,* 205, 287, 290.
14. *Belle Star in Velvet,* 5.
15. *Bandit Belle,* 8-9.
16. Malcolm G. McGregor, *Biographical Record of Jasper County,* 9-10; Ward L. Schrantz, *Jasper County in the Civil War,* xiv-xvi.
17. Rascoe, *Belle Starr* (54, 56), errs in stating that "not only Preston and Ed Shirley were born, but Myra also" at the present town of Shirley in Washington County before the family filed patent on the land grant in southwest Missouri.
18. *Jasper County, Missouri, Marriage Records* (compiled by Lyda B. Perry, Carthage, and Elizabeth P. Ellsbury, Chillicothe).
19. U.S. Department of Commerce, Bureau of the Census, *Seventh Census of the United States, 1850: Population Schedules, Jasper County, Missouri,* National Archives Microcopy No. 432, Roll 402 (Oklahoma Historical Society).

Drago, *Outlaws on Horseback* (91), claims there were only three children: "Preston, the eldest; Ed (called Bud), the next in line; and Belle, the youngest."

20. U.S. Department of Commerce, Bureau of the Census, *Eighth Census of the United States, 1860: Population Schedules, Jasper County, Missouri,* National Archives Microcopy No. 653, Roll 204 (Oklahoma Historical Society).

Harman, *Hell on the Border* (559), says John Shirley "conducted his hotel for twenty-five years . . . owned, as well, large landed estates and was the possessor of many slaves."

Aikman, *Lady Wildcats* (161), accepts Harman: "John and Eliza Shirley presided over . . . the hospitable little court of good living on the Carthage Main Street for twenty-five years."

Cameron Rogers, *Gallant Ladies* (119), states: "Judge John Shirley, besides conducting a notable hotel, *administered justice* in Carthage for a portion of his *twenty-five* years of residence . . . a man of many acres and *more* slaves."

There is no record that John Shirley ever presided over a court, and his years of residence in Carthage totaled only thirteen.

Rascoe, *Belle Starr* (53), speculates that, while engaged in farming and stock raising, John "at no time owned more than three or four slaves," probably "a stable boy, a yard boy, a hostler and perhaps a cook," but Rascoe (59) names *two* during John's hotel venture: Jordan Gloss, a stable, yard, errand, and general-utility slave, and Leanner Shaw, a maidservant for Mrs. Shirley, both purchased from Archibald McCoy for $611. Rascoe states incorrectly (66) that at the time John Shirley opened his hotel in Carthage, Myra had "at least two brothers, Preston, aged 30, and Ed or 'Bud,' aged 18."

Horan, *Desperate Women* (204), says John Shirley "bought two slaves . . . on the day he opened his hotel-tavern . . . to help with the work."

21. Schrantz, *Jasper County in the Civil War,* 209.

22. Preserved in the Carthage Public Library.

23. Joel T. Livingston, *Jasper County and Its People,* I, 38–39.

24. *Ibid.,* 40–42; Schrantz, *Jasper County in the Civil War,* 24.

25. Croy, *Last of the Great Outlaws* (50), has Myra "sometimes" mounting her horse and dashing "harum-scarum down the street, popping away at nothing, just for the fun of it." Her father thought her "a bit 'wild'" but thought she would "get over it."

26. McGregor, *Biographical Record of Jasper County,* 19; Schrantz, *Jasper County in the Civil War,* 51–52.

27. McGregor, *Biographical Record of Jasper County,* 19.

28. Schrantz, *Jasper County in the Civil War,* 64, 74–75; McGregor, *Biographical Record of Jasper County,* 20.

29. Harman, *Hell on the Border* (559), has Myra's "twin-brother, Ed" becoming a "captain of guerrillas" under Quantrill. Aikman, *Lady Wildcats* (170), calls him "Captain Ed," and Cameron Rogers, *Gallant Ladies* (119), says Myra's brother "Edward" became "a captain." Rascoe, *Belle Starr* (84–85), assumes "Bud" was a nickname for "Edward," finds no "Captain Ed Shirley of Missouri" on either Confederate or Federal enlistment rolls, and concludes that "Edward" was only "a bushwhacker, without rank even among the guerrillas."

Shackleford-Booker, *Belle Starr, Bandit Queen* (5) and *Wildcats in Petticoats* (21), mentions only two Shirley brothers, "the older being Pres—presumably Preston . . . but he was not a soldier. . . . Belle's older brother was known in Carthage as Bud Shirley, but it appears that his name was Edward. There is no evidence Shirley was ever commissioned or enlisted in any army." Horan, *Desperate Woman* (204), thinks "Belle's *elder* brother, *Edward,* joined Lane's bushwhackers . . . another brother, *Prescott,* ran away to Texas." Croy, *Last of the Great Outlaws* (50, 55), says that among John Shirley's sons were "Preston and another, known to the family as 'Bud,'" who "was not a captain . . . but a bushwhacker, and not a very courageous one at that." Scott, *Belle Starr in Velvet* (21), calls him "Buck" Shirley, has him enlisted in the "Missouri Militia . . . soon a captian. . . . He and Quantrill were good friends. Young Eddie, only fifteen years old, was serving under them."

Breihan and Rosamond, *Bandit Belle* (9), who used the federal census records, acknowledge that Edwin was eleven years old in 1860 and younger than Myra but think "Edwin, who was called Bud . . . joined Quantrill's raiders," yet no Shirley is listed in the "Roster of Guerrillas" appended to Breihan's *Quantrill and his Civil War Guerrillas* (166-74).

Drago, *Outlaws on Horseback* (91), is more accurate: "Preston Shirley left Missouri for Texas. He wanted no part of the war [but] his brother Bud got into it, fighting as a Confederate bushwhacker."

30. *Jasper County in the Civil War*, 128-29.

Chapter 3

1. Quoted in Schrantz, *Jasper County in the Civil War*, 128.

2. *Ibid.*, 96-97.

3. *Hell on the Border*, 560-62.

4. Zoe A. Tilghman, *Outlaw Days*, 128-30; Aikman, *Lady Wildcats*, 172-75; Cameron Rogers, *Gallant Ladies*, 120-21; Sabin, *Wild Men of the Wild West*, 318-20; White, *Lead and Likker*, 178; Gish, *American Bandits*, 39-40; Glasscock, *Then Came Oil*, 61-62; Shackleford, *Belle Starr, Bandit Queen*, 5; Scott, *Belle Starr in Velvet*, 21-22.

Rascoe, *Belle Starr* (pp. 90, 93-94), calls it "an exercise in rhetoric" to "depart from the generally accepted date of Belle's birth" and "conform to the assumption" that she and Ed Shirley were twins.

Breihan and Rosamond, *Bandit Belle* (9), note that, although "some writers have taken great pains to discredit this wild ride," the "concerted efforts" of federal authorities to apprehend Myra "meant she was giving them a lot of headaches."

5. *Last of the Great Outlaws*, 51-53.

6. Drago, *Outlaws on Horseback* (91), finds "no reason to believe" either the Harman or Croy versions and labels Myra's race back to Carthage to warn her brother "unadulterated hokum."

7. *Bella Starr, Female Jesse James*, 5.

8. U.S. Department of Commerce, Bureau of Census, *Eighth Census of the United States, 1860: Federal Population Schedules, Vernon County, Missouri*, National Archives Microcopy No. 563, Roll 659.

9. Harman, *Hell on the Border*, 562.

10. Scott, *Belle Starr in Velvet* (30-38), credits Myra Shirley with exploits as far east as Kentucky.

Mooney, *Doctor in Belle Starr Country* (206, 282, 284-85), claims that she was a spy for the Confederacy during the last two years of the war, reporting to Major Jesse Mooney, "Provost Marshall," with a small detachment at Yellville, Arkansas; that she; tipped the major about the armed steamboat *J. R. William* going up the Arkansas loaded with rifles and supplies for Union troops and families at Fort Gibson; that she provided information which enabled the Confederacy to capture the $1,500,000 supply train in the Second Battle of Cabin Creek; and that "on occasion [she] encountered a spy from the Union forces, one Bill [James Butler] Hickok."

White, *Lead and Likker* (179-80), says she used her sex appeal in "getting damn yankees," making dates with commanding officers to locate a Federal detachment, then not keeping the engagement but relaying the information to Quantrill, the Jameses, and Younger brothers; that she almost wrecked the guerrilla organization by "causing most of it to fall in love with her"; and that she could have married any of these big-name, latter-day, dime-novel saints but "demonstrated she was just a country girl . . . by bestowing her undivided affections upon an obscure horsethief named Jim Reed."

11. William Elsey Connelley, *Quantrill and the Border Wars*, 197-98; Albert Castel, *William Clarke Quantrill*, 64.

12. Connelley, *Quantrill and the Border Wars*, 60, 282.

13. *Hell on the Border*, 562.

14. Quoted in Schrantz, *Jasper County in the Civil War*, 129-31.

15. *Jasper County in the Civil War*, 152-55.

16. Quoted in Schrantz, *Jasper County in the Civil War*, 186-88.

17. Rascoe, *Belle Starr* (94-95), persists in killing *Ed* — not Bud — at Sarcoxie in June 1863 and "deeply suspects" that Mrs. Musgrave was "trusting to her memory of literature . . . and not of actual happenings" despite the fact that Mrs. Musgrave refers to young Shirley as Bud and gives Myra's age correctly as sixteen.

Schrantz, *Jasper County in the Civil War* (243-50), provides the most complete roster possible of Jasper County residents who lost their lives during the war and lists "Bud Shirley, a bushwhacker, home Carthage, killed in Sarcoxie by men of Co. C, Seventh Provisional Enrolled Militia, 1864."

Shackleford, *Belle Starr, Bandit Queen* (5), gives "summer of 1864" but calls Bud Shirley "Ed." He credits T. C. Wooten of Carthage, an eyewitness to the killing, with saying, "The members of Company C were all local boys, and the Shirleys knew the name of the trooper who did the shooting."

Breihan and Rosamond, *Bandit Belle* (9), agree on "summer of 1864" and note the name of the slayer "has been lost to the records . . . no one knows whether Bella . . . had her revenge."

Dee Brown, *The Gentle Tamers* (263), is mistaken in stating that "Myra Belle's brother was killed by Yankees while riding with Jim Lane's Red Leg bushwhackers."

Scott, *Belle Starr in Velvet* (23-24), tells a preposterous story of how "Eddie came for a visit . . . when Belle was teaching school at Carthage." The Yankees "got word he was in town," but he and Jesse James escaped through Union lines and "joined Quantrill at Butler, Missouri"; a few days later, in an engagement between Quantrill and Union cavalrymen near Centralia, Eddie was "at the front of the charge" and "shot right between the eyes."

17. Aikman, *Lady Wildcats*, 175-176; Cameron Rogers, *Gallant Ladies*, 121.

18. *Biographical Record of Jasper County*, 20.

Schrantz, *Jasper County and the Civil War* (22-18), quotes several eyewitness accounts of the destruction of Carthage and official reports of military activity that followed.

Chapter 4

1. *Belle Starr*, 96, 99-100.

2. *Desperate Women*, 205.

3. *Last of the Great Outlaws*, 56.

4. *Outlaws on Horseback*, 93.

5. Rascoe, *Belle Starr* (109), and Horan, *Desperate Women* (206), think they moved in with Preston.

6. *Belle Starr*, 150.

7. J. A. Dacus, *Life and Adventures of Frank and Jesse James*, 71; J. W. Buel, *The Border Outlaws*, 116; Jay Donald, *Outlaws of the Border*, 94; Frank Triplett, *Life, Times and Treacherous Death of Jesse James*, 27; Robertus Love, *Rise and Fall of Jesse James*, 60.

8. *Liberty* (Mo.) *Tribune*, February 16, 1866; Breihan, *Younger Brothers*, 65-68, and *The Escapades of Frank and Jesse James*, 45-46.

9. *Belle Starr*, 135-36, 151-52.

Drago, *Road Agents and Train Robbers* (154-55), lists only four — the Jameses, Cole Younger, and Cole's brother Jim — as making the ride to San Antonio.

10. *Belle Starr*, 136-49.

11. *Ibid.*, 115-16.

12. *Ibid.*, 194-95.

13. *Ibid.*, 119.

14. *Ibid.*

15. *Ibid.*, 41-42.

16. *Desperate Women*, 206.

17. *Last of the Great Outlaws*, 56-63.

18. *Dynasty of Western Outlaws*, 130.

19. *Belle Starr and Her Pearl*, 1-10.

20. *Fired in Anger*, 217.

21. *Wild, Wild West*, 84.

22. *Doctor in Belle Starr Country*, 261-63, 280, 283.

23. *Story of Cole Younger*, 72.

24. *Bella Starr, Female Jesse James*, 6.

25. *Ibid.*, 8.

26. *Hell on the Border*, 563-64.

Aikman, *Lady Wildcats* (177-79), thinks a member of the marriage party, John Fisher, "boasted a justice's of peace license."

Cameron Rogers, *Gallant Ladies* (121-24); Sabin, *Wild Men of the Wild West* (320); White, *Lead and Likker* (180); Rascoe, *Belle Starr* (117, 154-57); and Croy, *Last of the Great Outlaws* (86-89), say the mock wedding took place after Cole Younger deserted Belle and child.

Horan, *Desperate Women* (209); Wellman, *Dynasty of Western Outlaws* (131-32); Drago, *Outlaws on Horseback* (95-96); Hicks, *Belle Starr and Her Pearl* (13); Breihan and Rosamond, *Bandit Belle* (10); Mooney, *Doctor in Belle Starr Country* (208, 288); and Scott, *Belle Starr in Velvet* (50), recap Fox and Harman, with their own romantic variations and the year of Pearl's birth ranging from 1867 to 1870.

27. Probate Records, Vernon County, Solomon Reed Administration, Nevada, Missouri. Quoted in Kenneth W. Hobbs, Jr., "Jim Reed, Southwestern Outlaw and Husband of Belle Starr: A Study of the Watt Grayson and San Antonio Stage Robberies," 19.

28. James C. Reed to Mira [sic] M. Shirley, Marriage Records, Collin County, Texas, Vol. 3, p. 49.

29. In the late 1920s, Richard H. Reed compiled a narrative manuscript concerning his early life and that of his family, and in it he recalls the marriage of "brother Jim to Myra Mabelle [sic] Shirley, in Collin County." He tells of his "almost constant" association with Myra in his earliest boyhood and of being present at the birth of their daughter in Missouri. The manuscript is in possession of his son at Ashland, Oregon.

Richard H. Reed's recollection agrees with Cole Younger's autobiographical statement that he saw Belle in 1868 at the home of Reed's mother in Bates County about three months before the birth of her eldest child.

30. *Bella Starr, Female Jesse James,* 6–7.

31. *Ibid.,* 52–55.

32. *Belle Starr,* 279.

33. *Belle Starr and Her Pearl,* 13.

34. Outlaws on Horseback, 94.

35. *Doctor in Belle Starr Country,* 207.

36. In an obituary, "Belle Starr's Mother," January 7, 1894.

37. U.S. Department of Commerce, Bureau of Census, *Ninth Census of the United States, 1870: Federal Population Schedules, Dallas County, Texas,* National Archives Microcopy No. 593, Roll 1581.

38. Grace Steele Woodward, *The Cherokees,* 229–30.

39. Edward Everett Dale and Gaston Litton, *Cherokee Cavaliers,* 38.

Chapter 5

1. Grant Foreman, *Five Civilized Tribes,* 296; Morris L. Wardell, *Political History of the Cherokee Nation,* 8.

2. H. F. and E. S. O'Beirne, *The Indian Territory,* 93; Foreman, *Five Civilized Tribes,* 296–97; Wardell, *Political History of the Cherokee Nation,* 8; Marion L. Starkey, *The Cherokee Nation,* 167, 309–10.

3. Wardell, *Political History of the Cherokee Nation,* 13–14; Woodward, *The Cherokees,* 223–24.

4. Wardell, *Political History of the Cherokee Nation,* 14.

5. Foreman, *Five Civilized Tribes,* 292–93; Wardell, *Political History of the Cherokee Nation,* 16–17; Ralph Henry Gabriel, *Elias Boudinot,* 176–77.

6. Foreman, *Five Civilized Tribes,* 324–25; Wardell, *Political History of the Cherokee Nation,* 53; Starkey, *The Cherokee Nation,* 316.

7. Wardell, *Political History of the Cherokee Nation,* 62.

8. Foreman, *Five Civilized Tribes,* 327.

9. "Reminiscences of Mr. R. P. Vann, East of Webbers Falls, Oklahoma, September 28, 1932" (as told to Grant Foreman), *Chronicles of Oklahoma,* Vol. XI, No. 11 (June, 1933), 843.

10. Foreman, *Five Civilized Tribes*, 328.

11. *Ibid.*, 343-44.

12. *Ibid.*, 338; Wardell, *Political History of the Cherokee Nation*, 64.

13. Foreman, *Five Civilized Tribes*, 338; Helen Starr and O. E. Hill, *Footprints in the Indian Nation*, 5-6.

14. Wardell, *Political History of the Cherokee Nation*, 54.

15. Carolyn Thomas Foreman, "The Balentines, Father and Son, in the Indian Territory," *Chronicles of Oklahoma*, Vol. XXXIV, No. 4 (Winter, 1956-57), 427.

16. Foreman, *Five Civilized Tribes*, 348-49; Wardell, *Political History of the Cherokee Nation*, 72-73.

17. Wardell, *Political History of the Cherokee Nation*, 73.

18. O'Beirnes, *The Indian Territory*, 92.

19. Antislavery Cherokees who wore crossed pins on their shirts to let others know they favored the Union.

20. Ted Byron Hall, *Oklahoma, Indian Territory* (19), indicates the bend in the South Canadian was given the Younger name after the Liberty, Missouri, bank robbery in 1866.

John M. Oskison, Indian Territory native and Oklahoma novelist, who at different times served as exchange writer and editor of the *New York Evening Post* and later was associate editor of *Collier's Weekly*, traveled extensively through the West at the turn of the century, collecting material on train bandits. He interviewed survivors and witnesses of the early James-Younger gang robberies, which he describes in "To 'Youngers' Bend'" (*Frank Leslie's Popular Monthly*, Vol. XVI, No. 2 [June, 1903]), and tells of the outlaws' flight to one of their choice hideouts: Tom Starr's ranch. "So deeply was this border chief impressed by the daring of these visitors," writes Oskison, "that he gave to his retreat the name of 'Youngers' Bend.'"

21. *Belle Starr*, 166.

22. Carolyn Foreman, "The Balentines," 426.

Chapter 6

1. *Hell on the Border*, 564.

2. Aikman, *Lady Wildcats* (180-81), and Cameron Rogers, *Gallant Ladies* (124-25), accept Harman but give the year as 1870. Aikman has a murder warrant issued for Reed in Indian Territory. Rogers is uncertain of "how and where he met and warred with the Shannons" but says he picked up Myra and Pearl "on the run," reaching California just ahead of an "Arkansas sheriff."

3. "My Grandmother, Belle Starr" (Part I).

4. *Belle Starr*, 157, 162, 165.

5. Shackleford-Booker, *Belle Starr, Bandit Queen* (7) and *Wildcats in Petticoats* (22); Horan, *Desperate Women* (210); Wellman, *Dynasty of Western Outlaws* (134); Hicks, *Belle Starr and Her Pearl* (20-21); and Breihan and Rosamond, *Bandit Belle* (10), generally follow the Harman-"Flossie"-Rascoe versions. There are a couple of startling digressions:

Croy, *Last of the Great Outlaws* (90), states that Reed, after "he got into a neighborhood feud and killed two men," headed for Texas. Soon a reward of one thousand dollars was offered for him. Reed found Belle and her child living near Scyene. Having lost Cole Younger, Belle listened to "his pleasant words and Carthage memories"; they were married on horseback and galloped away to California.

Drago, *Outlaws on Horseback* (97-98), locates the feud in Vernon County, Missouri, and labels "a mystery" the reason three Shannon brothers "felt it incumbent on them to slay John Fischer, the outlaw who played preacher." Jim received word of his brother's death shortly after returning to Texas "with his share of the Grayson loot [this robbery did not occur until November, 1873]." Although Belle was "seven months pregnant," Jim "knew what his duty was as head of the Reed clan." He took her to Tom Starr's, the "occasion that Belle became acquainted with Sam Starr, old Tom's stalwart son." After she "had rested a day or two," they proceeded to Rich Hill. Jim found the Shannons, "with some help from Fischer," and killed two of them.

6. *United States* v. *John Fisher* et al., Case No. −, U.S. District Court, Western District of Arkansas.

7. *Ibid.*

8. *Belle Starr in Velvet*, 54.

9. *Belle Starr*, 165-66.

10. *Belle Starr and Her Pearl*, 22-23.

11. Dacus, *Life and Adventures of Frank and Jesse James*, 93-96; Donald, *Outlaws of the Border*, 126-34; Triplett, *Life, Times and Treacherous Death of Jesse James*, 47-49; Love, *Rise and Fall of Jesse James*, 90-92; Breihan, *The Escapades of Frank and Jesse James*, 69-70.

12. *Story of Cole Younger*, 58.

13. *Ibid.*, 67.

14. May 15, 1874.

15. *Story of Cole Younger*, 67-68.

16. *Bella Starr, Female Jesse James*, 13-15.

17. *Lady Wildcats*, 185-86.

18. Augustus C. Appler, editor of the *Osceola* (Missouri) *Weekly Democrat*, in his 1875 *Guerrillas of the West* (181-83), has John Younger striding into the sheriff's office in Dallas, "walking straight up" to Nichols, drawing his revolver, and shooting the sheriff in the chest.

19. Mooney, *Doctor in Belle Starr Country* (288), claims Eddie's "full, correct name" was "James Edward Reed, Jr." and that Jim Reed actually was "James Edward Reed, Sr."

The 1866 administration records of Solomon Reed's estate filed in Nevada, Missouri, give "James C."

20. "My Grandmother, Belle Starr" (Part I).

21. *Hell on the Border*, 565-66.

Chapter 7

1. *Story of Cole Younger*, 72.

2. *Belle Starr*, 167.

3. *Bella Starr, Female Jesse James*, 9–10.

4. *Lady Wildcats*, 182–85.

5. *Belle Starr*, 154.

6. Shackleford, *Belle Starr, Bandit Queen* (8); Wellman, *Dynasty of Western Outlaws* (135–36); Hicks, *Belle Starr and Her Pearl* (24); and Scott, *Belle Starr in Velvet* (77), follow Aikman and Rascoe.

7. *Hell on the Border*, 565–67.

8. August 10, 1874.

9. *Bella Starr, Female Jesse James*, 17–19.

10. *Hell on the Border*, 567–68.

11. Aikman, *Lady Wildcats* (182); Sutton, *Hands Up!* (230–31); Sabin, *Wild Men of the Wild West* (321); White, *Lead and Likker* (183–84); and Breihan and Rosamond, *Bandit Belle* (11), follow Harman. Aikman interpolates: "Belle was innocently asleep at the ranch near Dallas." Rascoe, *Belle Starr* (172), says four persons were present and the fourth member "may well have been Belle." John William Rogers, *Lusty Texans of Dallas* (151), credits Myra and Jim Reed with engineering the robbery, "supposed to be Belle's first actual participation in such a crime." Horan, *Desperate Women* (211), writes: "Belle took part . . . dressed as a man." Croy, *Last of the Great Outlaws* (91), says one of the four robbers "was smaller than the other three—Belle in men's clothes." Wellman, *Dynasty of Western Outlaws* (136), names Reed, Evans, and W. D. Wilder and thinks "Belle's diary claim that she was present is probably true." Hicks, *Belle Starr and Her Pearl* (25), says four men entered Grayson's home and one of them "was a woman dressed in men's clothes." Scott, *Belle Starr in Velvet* (78–79), says the party consisted of Jim Reed, Blue Duck, Belle, and Sam Starr, "with Tom Starr planning the raid and afterwards splitting the loot five ways." Drago, *Outlaws on Horseback* (97), rejects "the story that Belle took part" but accepts Reed, Evans, and Wilder as the culprits.

12. Letters filed with transcript of *United States* v. *William D. Wilder*, Case No. —, U.S. District Court, Western District of Arkansas.

13. *United States* v. *William D. Wilder*, Case No. —.

14. *Ibid.*

15. *Ibid.*

16. *Ibid.*

Chapter 8

1. *Bella Starr, Female Jesse James*, 19.

2. "My Grandmother, Belle Starr" (Part I).

3. *Belle Starr*, 19–21, 23.

4. Here, for its titillating worth, is the Fox tale (19–23):

Bella arrived in Paris early in the afternoon. She had on her person $7,000, over $1,000 being in gold coin. Dressed in cowboy attire she walked about town to a clothing house, where she purchased a suit of black clothes, and appeared a few minutes later looking like a smart young lawyer. She had taken the precaution of cutting her hair close and otherwise completing her disguise.

Our heroine rode into Bonham . . . that evening, in a heavy rain. She saw that the night would continue wet and determined to remain over at the Rigg's House. As she entered the outer office was full of men, talking, as if for wager, over the Grayson robbery, the news of which had just reached town. Everybody had something to say, or some question to ask about the Bandit Queen. Among those present Bella recognized Judge Thurman, of Dallas, who she had met in social circles on several occasions. Some of the hotel guests were very severe in their denunciations of Bella, until the host recommended them to keep their sentiments to themselves.

"Gentlemen," said he, "you'll please excuse me, but I don't want to get burned out some night or other. . . . You don't know but right here among us, there is one or more of the gang, and as for Bella, she can assume any disguise with such success that not one of you could recognize her."

Upon hearing this the big judge laughed long and heartily.

"I'd know Myra," said he, "if those fiery eyes of hers were set in the head of a cabbage. Yes, she's a wild one, but she cannot fool me, ha! ha! ha!"

The conversation continued for an hour, and many improbably and unlikely stories of rapine and bloodshed were accredited to the Bandit Queen. A hack drove up to the door and five or six men jumped out and asked for accommodation for the night. The proprietor told them that the beds were full, but that if the boarders would agree to "double up" he could give them a "shake down" of some kind. Turning to Judge Thurman he said:

"Judge, would you object to sharing your bed with the gentleman in the corner?"

"Not in the least," was the answer. "I guess I can hold my own share of the coverlet with any man."

The same question was put to Bella who, though pale with fear for the consequence, agreed to "double up" with the fat criminal lawyer. Two of the parties who arrived in the hack were officers on their way to the territory in search of Jim Read. . . . Our heroine stepped out in the open air for several minutes before retiring . . . first thought of saddling her horse and striking out immediately, but such an act would have set the officers on her trail . . . suspecting her identity. The next thought was to conceal the rubber belts which were laden with gold coin and almost prevented her moving.

Slipping into the stable where her horse was hitched, she threw aside some of his bedding, and beneath it laid her little burden of $7,000.

[Next] thing for her to do, as soon as she had extricated herself from the present difficulty, would be to notify Read at Jefferson, Marshall, Paris, or any other place whither he would be likely to visit within the next few weeks. With [this] uppermost in her mind, Bella entered the room occupied by the judge. Asleep? No, he was not asleep, but in a most sociable mood, ready to talk upon any subject, especially Myra, or as he called her, "his own dear Myra."

The judge was a bachelor, and remarkable for his attentions to the gentler sex, a reputation which he appeared proud of to the day of his death.

"But," said he, as she timidly crept in beside him, "it's all gammon about Myra being equal to men in craft and courage. As for me, I consider myself superior to any woman living. Just think of her going round in man's clothes and fooling people! Why, it's all utter bosh. I'll bet that right now she's waltzing with some Dallas chap. There, there's where the woman excels. I tell you, young man, she's got animation enough to light a dark room with her presence."

Bella listened patiently, answering no or yes whenever it was necessary to speak, till at last the judge sank to sleep and filled the apartment with the horrors of his snoring. . . .

She never closed her eyes. She lay all night thinking of the danger which threatened her husband. At the first break of dawn she was up and in the stable attending to her horse. Now, thought she, replacing the rubber belts around her waist, I'll make old Thurman sick, even at the risk of my capture. After partaking of a hurried breakfast,

Bella saddled her horse and hitched him to the gate in front of the house . . . ascended the stairway to the judge's room and awoke him.

"Judge," said she, "Mrs. Read, of whom you were speaking last night, is down stairs waiting to see you. Get up at once. She hasn't a moment to spare."

"Dear me," said he, "I wonder what in the mischief she wants at this hour of the morning?" saying which he crawled from beneath the blankets and proceeded to dress.

"My friend," said he, as Bella was leaving the room, "you must be mistaken. I can't believe such a thing until I see for myself."

Our heroine was on the porch awaiting Thurman, who descended with a cautious step, till he reached the door. Looking out and seeing nothing of "his own dear Myra," as he had called her . . . he broke out with the following remarks:

"Young man, it ill becomes you to play practical jokes on your elders. I was particularly anxious for sleep this morning, and you—"

"Wait a moment, judge," said she. "Just step as far as the gate and you'll see the Bandit Queen."

Bella opened the gate, and laying one hand on the withers of her horse, vaulted into the saddle.

"Where? Where is she?" asked the judge.

"Look right into my face—look well. I am Bella Read, and you—well, you are a consummate old fool. Your own self-conceit will damn you without the devil's help. . . . Go home and tell your friends that you have had the honor and glory of sleeping with the Bandit Queen." With these words Bella put spurs to her horse and struck westward like a blue streak.

"Flossie" refers to the fictional Thurman as "Judge Blank" and concludes her version:

She sent a boy into the hotel to ask Judge Blank to come out, that Myra Reed wanted to see him. Imagine his astonishment when the "young man" that had been his bed-fellow came toward him, saying, "Tell the folks that you have had the honor of meeting Myra Reed." And striking him with her riding whip, she mounted her horse and rode off like a streak.

5. *Belle Starr,* 177–78.

6. *Belle Starr and Her Pearl,* 26–27.

7. *Belle Starr in Velvet,* 80.

8. Hicks, *Belle Starr and Her Pearl* (28), includes a dime-novel yarn about a local doctor who indignantly remarked that it was inconceivable that a woman could bluff so many men. The word reached Belle. One day she encountered him riding down a Scyene street, drew her .45s, and told him to dismount. The astonished doctor complied. "Now," said Belle, "walk around to the rear of your horse." Again the doctor obeyed, and Belle said, "Lift your horse's tail. . . . Now, you son-of-a-bitch, *kiss it!*" The doctor did as ordered.

Another tale, originating with "Flossie," in "My Grandmother, Belle Starr" (Part I), is that Jim Reed was arrested and jailed at a little town near Dallas:

The next day [Myra] went to see him and slipped him a spool of black thread. She slipped around to the window of James' cell and found a note hanging from the thread. The note told her what to do.

Next morning Myra went to the jail wearing a black dress of the type any old lady would be likely to affect and a heavy black veil. As she went by, she stopped and chatted with the jailer. Myra had a nice visit with Jim and the jailer let out the neat little old lady. Some time passed before it was discovered that the "man" sitting in James Reed's cell was Myra Reed!

She argued, smiling blandly, "I am Jim Reed's wife and I want out. I am guilty of no crime." The jailer said, "Don't you know there is a reward on Jim's head?"

Myra declared she knew nothing about it. And continued, "I'd just as lieve be here as out. It will give Jim a little rest. . . . I only did my duty."

Years afterward she would convulse the crowd telling how she had dressed Jimmie up in her clothes. She always insisted that the jailer was convinced with her argument that a "woman should cleave to her husband."

9. *Dallas Daily Commercial,* February 20 and June 9, 1874.

10. February 14 and 23, 1874.

11. August 10, 1874; also *Austin Daily Democratic Statesman,* April 9, 1874.

12. *Dallas Daily Commercial,* April 10, 1874.

13. The Fox opus (10-11) has "Bella herself and Read" planning and executing the holdup. They were experiencing considerable resistance from a couple of the passengers when "a quiet looking, clerical gentleman, advanced in years, spoke up: 'Brethren, better yield our goods than provoke loss of life,'" and handed Bella his watch and a heavy purse. "Feeling an interest in the elderly gentleman, [she] inquired his name. He said he was Bishop Gregg of San Antonio. Without any deliberation the purse and watch were restored. It was too mean to deprive the old preacher of the riches which falls to his share in the fierce race for wealth."

Rascoe, *Belle Starr* (160, 180), properly pooh-poohs the story but states: "Bishop Gregg's purse and watch . . . were not returned" and points to the description of Nelson, alias Jack Rogers, as "strangely indicative of Cole Younger."

Horan, *Desperate Women* (212), writes: "Reed, Jesse James, and Cole Younger held up the San Antonio-Austin stage." Breihan, *Younger Brothers* (119), accepts the Bishop Gregg fiction and claims "reliable sources" have "pinned down" the robbers as "Jesse and Frank James, Arthur McCoy, Jim Greenwood, and Jim Read." Croy, *Last of the Great Outlaws* (91), mentions only "three men—one noticeably shorter than the others." Hicks, *Belle Starr and Her Pearl* (30), says the party consisted of "Cole Younger . . . using the name Jack Rogers . . . Reed and Carter." Scott, *Belle Starr in Velvet* (81), lists "Reed, Blue Duck, and John Middleton, a cousin of Jim's." Drago, *Outlaws on Horseback* (99-100, 102), concludes that the robbery was "definitely" the work of "Jim Reed and two members of his gang" but includes Bishop Gregg as "one of the passengers . . . relieved of his watch and other valuables."

14. Also *Dallas Daily Commercial,* April 20, 1874.

15. April 11, 1874.

16. April 9, 1874.

17. *Waco Daily Examiner,* April 14, 1874.

18. *Austin Daily Democratic Statesman,* April 17, 1874.

19. *Belle Starr,* 160-61.

20. *Outlaws on Horseback,* 100-101.

21. Hicks, *Belle Starr and Her Pearl* (30), infers much from the horse-trading episode in which Woolfork paid Reed "twenty-five dollars to boot in cash for

his wife"; Reed called Woolfork's bluff and pocketed a twenty-dollar gold piece and a five-dollar gold piece the man took from his wallet, telling him, "You got yourself a woman," and they even traded saddles, which was not part of the deal; Dickens and his wife "shook with merriment" at the joke; Cole Younger looked up from his Bible "long enough to grin"; Belle, "blushing with shame and amazement" suddenly leaped upon her own horse and galloped off with Woolfork, filling the air with her "loud laughter."

22. Several reliable sources contain information on the McCommas family from 1844 to 1877. These are listed and quoted by Kenneth W. Hobbs, Jr., in his carefully compiled 1975 thesis "Jim Reed, Southwestern Outlaw and Husband of Belle Starr: A Study of the Watt Grayson and San Antonio Stage Robberies," 50–53.

23. July 25, 1874.

24. August 10, 1874.

25. April 21, 1874.

Chapter 9

1. *Austin Daily Democratic Statesman,* April 22, 1874.

2. Rascoe, *Belle Starr* (182–85), interprets the statement to mean Purnell accompanied Wilder "to the lair of the bandit chief to question . . . Belle as to the whereabouts of her husband" and is convinced that Wilder was "in reality John T. Morris, a former member of Reed's outlaw gang" whom the marshal "let out of a rap" on a promise to "bring Reed in dead or alive" and share the reward.

Drago, *Outlaws on Horseback* (103), assents, saying "the real W. D. Wilder had long since been apprehended and sent to prison for his part in the Watt Grayson robbery" and Morris was to receive "one-third of the total $4,500 [$7,000] reward posted" for the San Antonio stage bandits.

Later developments show the fallacy of these deductions.

3. *United States* v. *Jim Reed* et al., Case No. 142, U.S. District Court, Western District of Texas, Austin.

4. *Ibid.*

5. *United States* v. *Calvin Carter* et al., Case No. −, U.S. District Court, Western District of Arkansas, Fort Smith.

6. *Ibid.*

7. *Dallas Daily Commercial,* August 10, 1874.

8. August 10, 1874.

9. Wide-ranging and varied accounts of Reed's death by Belle Starr biographers began with the Fox opus (17, 23–24) claim that Morris was a member of the Reed gang before the Grayson robbery:

Read . . . drifted to Paris, Texas, where he once more met John Morris. Morris was financially embarrassed, having lost his last cent, including his horse, at a poker table a few nights previously. Read, in the fullness of his large, liberal heart, opened his purse and handed him $500. Remaining several days in Paris, they rose . . . one morning and rode about five miles down Bois D'arc Creek, where they stopped for breakfast at the house of one of Morris's friends [whom Morris] offered part of the reward set upon Read's head if he would assist in the assassination.

Harman, *Hell on the Border* (568–70), dates the killing "in the summer of 1875" when

Jim Reed made his last trip home to wife and children . . . by stealth and was met by Belle in a strip of timber and conducted to their home after night fall. On leaving again, after a few happy but nervous days, he was accompanied by John Morris who, attracted by the offered reward, sought to encompass Reed's death.

Harman locates the killing at a farmhouse "near McKinney, in Collin county," amends the Fox story in colorful detail, then says:

It was necessary for the assassin in order to secure the reward . . . to furnish proof of [Reed's] death, and as the murdered man was a stranger in that portion of the country . . . there were none to identify the body. The weather was sultry, making an early burial imperative, and word was sent to Belle informing her of her husband's death, the supposition being that she would weep, as would ordinary wives, over the remains. . . . But Belle was far from "ordinary." When she received word to come and take charge of her husband's dead body her eyes took on a hard look and she said, "They've killed him for the reward but they will never get it," and rode to the house where the body lay. As she entered the room where a number of men, Morris among them, were gathered about the corpse, one of their number removed the covering, exposing the features, while the others silently fell back expecting to witness a heartrending scene of weeping. They also expected to make oath to what they saw, and thus assist the murderer to obtain the reward. Belle walked to the body, gave a glance at the face of her loved one and without the least sign of emotion, but with a scornful curve of the lips, quietly remarked:

"I am sorry, gentlemen, that you have made such a mistake and killed the wrong man; very sorry, indeed. John Morris, you will have to kill Jim Reed if you desire to secure the reward offered for Jim Reed's body."

This was a turn in affairs on which [Morris] had not counted. Belle rode calmly away, suffering the anguish she would not indicate, and her husband's body was buried in the potter's field.

Aikman, *Lady Wildcats* (187–88); Cameron Rogers, *Gallant Ladies* (321); White, *Lead and Likker* (184); "Flossie," "My Grandmother, Belle Starr" (Part I); Shackleford-Booker, *Belle Starr, Bandit Queen* (9–10) and *Wildcats in Petticoats* (22), accept the Harman version, including incorrect year, date, and location, and repeat the story of Belle's refusing to identify the body. Walter Biscup made much of this tale in his 1927 two-part feature, "Dashing Belle Starr Was Called 'Lily of the Cimarron,'" for *The American Indian* (Vol. 1, No. 4, January, 1927, 5; Vol. 1, No. 5, February, 1927, 6, 14), reprinted in the *Tulsa World* of March 17, 1929. It became the subject of a long poem, "Belle Starr," by Stanley Vestal in his book of ballads, *Fandango* (1927). George Milburn's "Honey Boy" story, published in *Collier's Weekly* in 1934, is another variant.

A. W. Neville, *Red River Valley, Then and Now* (49), says Belle's denial that the body was that of her husband was told to him by "several persons who lived in Paris at the time." Rascoe, *Belle Starr* (25), questions the story but credits its origin to Fox. Croy, *Last of the Great Outlaws* (93); Hicks, *Belle Starr and Her Pearl* (33); Drago, *Outlaws on Horseback* (103); and Breihan and Rosamond, *Bandit Belle* (11), conclude that Belle never saw the body.

Scott, *Belle Starr in Velvet* (82–83), maintains that Pearl, who was "old enough to remember her father's death," told how "mother explained over and over" to her and little Eddie "why she did not want them to say it was father, when they were shown the body," and Pearl "laughed and said, 'That's not my daddy!'"

10. *Denison Daily News*, August 19, 1874.

11. *Ibid.*, August 22, 1874.

12. *United States* v. *Jim Reed* et al., Case No. 142.

13. Fox's writer (25–26) says "Bella avenged the death of her husband" and retrieved the reward money. Neville, *Red River Valley* (49), notes that some thought Morris bought a small ranch west of Fort Worth, went out one morning to feed his horses, and was "shot and killed by an unknown person."

On the contrary, John T. Morris lived on to die at age eighty in 1924.

14. *United States* v. *Jim Reed* et al., Case No. 142.

15. *Ibid.*

16. Ledger No. 122, p. 576 (in Federal Archives and Records Center, Fort Worth, Texas).

17. House of Representatives records, Watt Grayson claim file, Exhibit E (quoted by Hobbs, "Jim Reed, Southwestern Outlaw and Husband of Belle Starr: A Study of the Watt Grayson and San Antonio Stage Robberies," 75–76).

18. Sworn affidavit before G. W. Ingalls, U.S. Indian Agent for the Union Agency, Muskogee, I.T., in House of Representatives records, Watt Grayson claim file, Exhibit E (quoted by Hobbs, 74–75).

19. *United States* v. *William D. Wilder*, Case No. —.

20. October 6, 1874; also *Dallas Daily Herald*, October 10, 1874.

21. *United States* v. *William D. Wilder*, Case No. —; *Fort Smith New Era*, October 14, 1874.

22. King to U.S. Indian Agent Ingalls.

23. *Fort Smith New Era*, October 14, 1874.

24. *United States* v. *William D. Wilder*, Case No. —.

25. *Ibid.*

26. *Ibid.*

27. *Fort Smith New Era*, June 30 and September 8, 1875.

28. None of Belle Starr's biographers mention Marion (J. M.) Dickens, alias Burns.

29. House of Representatives records, Watt Grayson claim file, Exhibit G (quoted by Hobbs, 88–89).

30. *Ibid.*, Exhibit H.

31. The following law appears in *The Statutes at Large of the United States*, 50th Congress, 1st session, Vol. XXV, 53:

For reimbursement to the estate of Walter (or Watt) Grayson for stolen money under sections twenty-one hundred and fifty-four and twenty-one hundred and fifty-five, Revised Statutes, as certified to Congress in House Executive Document Number Nineteen, Fiftieth Congress, first session, thirty-two thousand dollars.

Chapter 10

1. *Hell on the Border*, 570–72.

2. Rascoe, *Belle Starr* (188), and Hicks, *Belle Starr and Her Pearl* (3), think Preston Shirley was "Shug."

3. *Hell on the Border*, 572–75.

4. Sabin, *Wild Men of the Wild West* (323–24); White, *Lead and Likker* (185–91); "Flossie," "My Grandmother, Belle Starr" (Part I); Wellman, *Dynasty of Western Outlaws* (143–44); Hicks, *Belle Starr and Her Pearl* (35–38); Scott, *Belle Starr in Velvet* (93–167); Elman, *Fired in Anger* (218–19), who identifies a pistol Belle allegedly carried in Dallas; Breihan and Rosamond, *Bandit Belle* (12); and Mooney, *Doctor in Belle Starr Country* (209).

Aikman, *Lady Wildcats* (191–97), says Belle returned to Dallas and her livery-stable business, consorting with "bands of horse-stealing outlaws" and sharing in their proceeds as a "fence" and "tipster," finally participating in the raids herself; that the philanthropic Patterson's "Freudian generosity" cost him twenty-five hundred dollars, which Belle used to pay her children's board and schooling "for two years in advance"; that she bound and gagged the amorous banker before riding off with thirty thousand dollars; and that the "emotional turnkey," upon returning from his elopement, insisted that his role "was not that of a lover, but of escort, cook, horse-wrangler, wood-fetcher and water-carrier, at the point of his own pistol." For the next two years, Belle, "out in the wilds for good," rode the ranges of northwest Texas and the Oklahoma and Texas panhandles with Jim French, Blue Duck, and Jack Spaniard, their gangs swelling in numbers to "nearly fifty" as they picked up mavericks and rustled cattle from trail drivers en route to Kansas shipping points, stole horses from the Indians, held up cow-town banks, and did a little stagecoach agentry on the side, meanwhile maintaining "at least an hospitable acquaintance" with what remained of the Younger and Sam Bass gangs of train robbers. Belle dominated them all by the "force of her will" and "proud, increasingly harsh personality." When Blue Duck lost two thousand dollars borrowed from the outfit's "temporarily flush treasury" in a dishonest poker game at Fort Dodge, Belle "strolled into the gambling house . . . with a gun in each hand . . . and raided the pot for $7,000."

Sutton, *Hands Up!* (230–33), characteristically claims to have witnessed the Fort Dodge raid and explains that it was possible for Belle to get away with such a feat in a roomful of armed gamblers, gunmen, and killers, because they "wuz all jest so plum flabbergasted."

Cameron Rogers, *Gallant Ladies* (127–35), has the widowed Belle in Dallas operating a "racing stable" and a large "house of hospitality." She "burnt down a grocery store" and so "incensed the bench" with her "attitude of disdain" that she would have found the going rough had not Patterson "paid the large fine imposed." The wealthy stockman also offered her the remains of his fortune, but Belle refused, throwing herself "without reserve into a career of reckless and unscrupulous diversion." After the bank robbery "in which $30,000 were stolen and the reputation of a solid citizen badly damaged," Belle beguiled her jailer into eloping with her, returning him shortly to his family with a card sewed in his coat which bore the words, "Found to be unsatisfactory on using." Within a year Belle became the "sensation of the Southwest . . . the particular pride of newspaper editors with a flair for the smashing scarehead and clamorous headline" on how she robbed various citizens, shot town marshals, and fought and won pitched battles with the Rangers. Among her "spurred and booted squires" were the "notorious if personable ruffians" Jack Spaniard, Jim French, and Blue Duck, and she departed from the Fort Dodge gambling house in a hail of bullets, "not one of which . . . achieved their mark." Belle "shone darkly" in Nebraska from 1878 to 1880, where she was "frequently confounded with her who is mentioned in the 17th chapter of Revelation," and by the time she married Sam Starr in the Cherokee Nation, she was "a figure far more considerable in the popular imagination of the West than Benedict Arnold or Ulysses S. Grant."

Rascoe, *Belle Starr* (189-93, 197-200), labels the Patterson story "one of the most fantastic yarns in the annals of Belle Starr whoppers," calls the elopement of her turnkey "fanciful" and the Fort Dodge raid "incredible but piquant" but he bows to popular belief that Belle became the directing mind for various bands of outlaws and "kept men under subjection by her imperious will, scathing tongue, superior intelligence and her sex appeal."

Horan, *Desperate Women* (212-14, 217), says Belle sent "thick rolls of greenbacks" to Cole Younger's lawyers in her "untiring efforts" to get him a parole (the James-Younger gang was blasted apart in the attempted bank robbery at Northfield, Minnesota, on September 7, 1876, less than a month after Myra's letter to F. M. Reed at Metz, Missouri) and thinks Belle's raid on the Fort Dodge gambling house "makes a grand scene even if the serious historians of the *Queen of the Cowtowns* forget to mention it."

Croy, *Last of the Great Outlaws* (93, 133-36), clings to the Belle–Cole Younger relationship; in a Dallas gambling hall where Belle is a faro dealer, Jesse James tells her what happened at Northfield. Croy also is "inclined to believe" the Fort Dodge escapade.

5. Drago, *Outlaws on Horseback* (105), sums it up nicely. He is convinced that writers preceding him, unable to discover anything about Belle during this period, "dragged out such tales . . . only to gloss over the four-year gap."

6. *Bella Starr, Female Jesse James*, 26–28, 45.

7. *Belle Starr*, 218.

8. *Belle Starr, Bandit Queen*, 12–13.

9. "My Grandmother, Belle Starr" (Part I).

10. See note 29, Chapter 4.

11. Vol. I, 328–29.

12. Indian Archives Division, Oklahoma Historical Society.

13. Croy, *Last of the Great Outlaws* (139), quoted this document in 1956. Wellman, *Dynasty of Western Outlaws* (144), evidently overlooked it, for he says Belle married Starr "by the sketchy Cherokee custom . . . simply moving in and living with him."

Wellman (144); Rascoe, *Belle Starr* (203–204); and Hicks, *Belle Starr and Her Pearl* (44), repeat the oft-told tale that when Belle proposed to marry Sam and take up permanent residence at the Bend, an elderly chief of the tribe advised Tom Starr to "kill her as you would a snake . . . she is wicked and poisonous and will bring ruin to your boys." But old Tom "perhaps seeing the devil in Belle himself . . . admired his son's choice." Besides, he "could not harm a woman."

Chapter 11

1. Section 2, Township 9, Range 19 in present Muskogee County.

2. Aikman, *Lady Wildcats,* 199; Cameron Rogers, *Gallant Ladies,* 135.

3. Fox's writer (48) claims "summer of 1882" after Jesse "heard at Nevada [Missouri]" that Belle could be found in the Cherokee Nation. "She agreed Jesse was to assume the name of Ford . . . and as such introduced him to her husband."

Harman, *Hell on the Border* (578), says it was "not long after Belle had become comfortably located in her nook in the mountains . . . Sam Starr was away from home . . . the two men had never met . . . Starr came home before the other left, and not liking her husband to know of her acquaintance with the outlaw, she gave a fictitious name" and the Indian did not learn the identity of their visitor until several months later.

"Flossie," in "Belle Starr's Granddaughter" (Part II), states: "James Reed had grown up close to the James boys"; they had been "on the scout [in the war] together"; when Jesse asked Belle to hide him "for just a little while, she could not turn him down."

Horan, *Desperate Women* (214-15), writes: "Only once [during Jesse's stay] was Sam suspicious"; when one of the Starrs came riding up to the ranch, Jesse leaped to the window "with the grace of a cat," Colt in hand, blue eyes "as cold as frozen seas" and blinking furiously.

Mooney, *Doctor in Belle Starr Country* (215), embroiders the incident: Jesse whipped *two* Colts out of their holsters, his eyes "cold as ice," but calmed down after Belle assured him the rider "is just one of Sam's brothers"; still, Sam was not informed of the fast-drawing man's identity or that Belle "took some of Jesse's hard cash for his keep and protection"; Belle was "one of few Jesse could trust . . . they both rode together in an outlaw gang after the Civil War."

4. Rascoe, *Belle Starr* (211-12), thinks Jesse "lit out" for Youngers' Bend after the Blue Cut robbery; that his relations with Belle were "cool and meretricious . . . for he had no way of knowing Belle had married Starr" and Belle "demanded a heavy price" for the protection the Bend offered. Rascoe errs in his "Chronology and Necrology" (285): "1880 – Belle visited by Jesse James and Younger boys at Younger's Bend after her marriage the same year to Sam Starr." The Youngers had been in prison nearly four years.

5. Harman, *Hell on the Border* (580), writes: "At times Belle . . . would lay aside her scouting suit . . . and, packing her trunks with raiment suitable to civilization, hie away to the popular Eastern watering places, there to spend money lavishly and mingle freely with the wealth and culture of the nation." During these periods the scouting depredations "would seem to largely cease" but would be resumed upon her return, and people would remark: "Belle

Starr is back again," although "much of this was imaginary and the woman was not really half as black as she was painted."

Rascoe, *Belle Starr* (16), mentions corresponding with many people claiming to have authentic and exclusive information from persons who had known Belle Starr or from the lips of a grandfather or grandmother. He acknowledges that "in nearly every instance" the stories turned out to be "garbled versions" of anecdotes invented by the Fox writer and that the grandfather or grandmother was "not lacking in creative imagination." However, later in his book (195-96) he accepts Belle as a "fix" who had the money and intelligence to arrange *nolle prosequis*, paroles, releases, pardons, verdicts, and suspended or light sentences for any member of her gang caught by the law; that most of her ruffianly crew looked upon her as a magician because she could read and write, an accomplishment that "must have seemed like witchcraft to Jim French, Jack Spaniard and Sam Starr."

Croy, *Last of the Great Outlaws* (140-141), refers to Youngers' Bend as "Robbers' Roost" where more outlaws hid out than any other place in the United States; Belle was their "brains" or "guiding spirit"; her "moral fiber had weakened . . . since she had parted with Cole"; she rode, robbed and plundered with them, and she and Sam "soon became the most prosperous couple in the section."

Drago, *Outlaws on Horseback* (141-42), *Notorious Ladies of the Frontier* (173), and *Road Agents and Train Robbers* (228), doesn't believe Belle and her cohorts could have stolen enough horses and cattle to provide the money to engage high-priced lawyers, post bail, and win commutations, but he thinks Belle deserves the distinction of being "Queen of the Outlaws" because she consorted with the worst thieves and bandits in the country, sheltered them, planned and advised them on their forays, shared in the proceeds, and took "at least four, each in his time, as her lovers."

6. La-Vere Shoenfelt Anderson, "A Hill Perpetuates Belle Starr's Memory," *Tulsa World*, August 20, 1933, and "Site of Belle Starr's Lookout Tower on Bald Hill Still Mecca for Tourists," *Tulsa World*, February 3, 1936.

7. Mooney, *Doctor in Belle Starr Country*, 284-85.

8. Henry L. Peck, *The Proud Heritage*, 150-51.

9. Mrs. J. D. Benedict, "Belle Starr, the Bandit Queen," *Twin Territories*, Vol. II, No. 9 (October, 1900), 198; Nolen Bulloch, "Tourists Take Robbers' Trail," *Tulsa Tribune*, June 26, 1851; Richard J. Reed, "Steal Away to Robbers Cave," *Oklahoma's Orbit*, May 15, 1966; Pat Crow, "Vacationers Follow Outlaws' Footsteps," *Tulsa World*, May 25, 1969; Clyde E. Wooldridge, *Wilburton: I. T. and OK, 1890-1970*, 221-23.

Chapter 12

1. Harman, *Hell on the Border* (580-81), writes:

In the autumn of 1882, Belle and Sam met with their first real trouble. . . . Pearl was the possessor of a beautiful young black stallion; it became a source of no little annoyance to their neighbors . . . and finally the animal was shot, supposedly by one Andrew Crane, a white man, who had a ranche in the vicinity. Soon after, Belle with

Sam and Pearl, was on a visit to the home of John West who lived some seven miles away, back from the river on the open prairie, his ranche adjoining that of Crane. . . . The Wests and the Starrs were on a very friendly footing and frequent visitors, Mrs. West being of a refined and lovable disposition and a favorite of Belle's. During the day in question, as West, his wife and little boy, with their guests, were sitting in the shade of a tree, a fine young horse was seen feeding on Crane's ranche nearby, and West remarked to Sam:

"You ought to go and take that colt to pay for the one Crane killed."

An ex-deputy United States marshal, named Childs, who was standing near, was preparing to leave the country and he soon after caught the horse spoken of by West and rode it away. A few days later, when Crane began searching for his property, West took fright and fearing, in his terror of the Federal Court at Fort Smith, that he might be accused of horse-stealing, he went before a United States commissioner and swore to a complaint charging Belle Starr and Sam Starr with the larceny of the horse. He also attempted to make his little boy swear to having seen them take the horse but received the answer:

"Pa, you know they didn't; you know Childs rode him off."

Sam Starr had never suffered the ignominy of arrest, and when he and Belle learned of the nature of the warrant, never doubting they could establish their innocence, they gave themselves up.

"Flossie," in "Belle Starr's Granddaughter" (Part II), follows Harman.

Harrington, *Hanging Judge* (91–95), notes: "Childs, a border drifter," helped the Starrs in their horse thievery and lived with Belle "in the early weeks of 1882" while Sam was laid up at his father's house with the measles; Sam "expected she would run off with Childs . . . or kill Sam . . . that was the kind of slut she was," and Sam "took the precaution of stealing Childs' pistol."

Drago, *Outlaws on Horseback* (108–109), says the Wests were John Ross adherents—"they hated the Starrs and the Starrs hated them"; John West was a member of the Indian police, and when Frank saw Sam and Belle "crossing his head-right . . . with two blooded horses belonging to . . . Crane," he and brother John made "a sworn statement . . . before the U.S. marshal at Fort Smith."

Scott, *Belle Starr in Velvet* (211–12), claims Belle and Sam made a trip to Kansas where they "bought . . . several head of horses"; a few days after they returned to Youngers' Bend, "Deputy Marshals were at the ranch with a warrant . . . charging them with horse stealing."

2. In 1897, Barnes was President William McKinley's choice for fourth territorial governor of Oklahoma.

3. Mrs. Fannie Blythe Marks to James Carselowey, September 9, 1937. *Indian-Pioneer History*, Foreman Collection, Vol. 16, 78–82.

4. Croy, *Last of the Great Outlaws* (142–44), uses Mrs. Marks's story, adding some detail of his own. Elias Rector, the only surviving deputy of the two hundred who rode for Judge Parker and past ninety when Croy interviewed him at Fort Smith for material in *He Hanged Them High* (92–93), indicated he accompanied Deputy Marshal Marks on this expedition. Rector verifies Mrs. Marks's story, except the deputies "secreted themselves in the barn" and when they seized Belle they "found a forty-five strapped around her waist, under her skirt" and inside her blouse only one derringer.

5. Rascoe, *Belle Starr* (215), calls it a "frontier sensation"; reports on the progress of the trial "went out over the telegraph wires," and the metropolitan journals, seizing upon Belle as copy, "promptly labeled her 'The Queen of the Bandits,' 'The Petticoat Terror of the Plains' and 'The Lady Desperado.'"

Croy, *He Hanged Them High* (156-57) and *Last of the Great Outlaws* (144); Horan, *Desperate Women* (218); and Drago, *Outlaws on Horseback* (109), follow Rascoe.

6. *United States* v. *Sam and Belle Starr,* Case No. 2370.

7. *Hell on the Border,* 582-84.

8. "Belle Starr's Granddaughter" (Part II).

9. Rascoe, *Belle Starr* (218), puzzles that Belle should write "sentenced to nine months" when her sentence was "for one year." Belle and Sam had been advised by the court that both could be released in nine months for good behavior.

Croy, *Last of the Great Outlaws* (146) and "Sources," Chapter 13 (230), is "unable to identify Aunt Ellen, Marion or Mamma Mc."; doubts that Belle would "place-date a letter 'Pandemonium,'" or that she "could spell it" or "knew what it meant"; quibbles about grammatical structure and spelling *wont* for *won't* (a word used only twice and in both instances spelled correctly); and concludes the letter was "invented by Harman."

Drago, *Outlaws on Horseback* (111-13), calls *Hell on the Border* "a dull, trashy book" with long passages "lifted bodily from the National Police Gazette" and containing other material "as shadowy as [Belle's] letter." He follows Croy in "place-dating it Pandemonium—a word . . . not in Belle's vocabulary"; thinks that Aunt Ellen, Marion and Mamma Mc, who "have never been identified," were "added verisimilitude"; and concludes that the letter, "almost in its entirety," is a Harman hoax.

10. Shackleford, *Belle Starr, Bandit Queen,* 17.

11. Mittimus, *United States* v. *Sam and Belle Starr,* Case No. 2370.

Chapter 13

1. White, *Lead and Likker,* 193.

2. Aikman, *Lady Wildcats,* 202.

3. "Belle Starr's Granddaughter" (Part II).

4. *Hell on the Border,* 584-85.

5. *Bella Starr, Female Jesse James,* 50.

6. "Flossie," "Belle Starr's Granddaughter" (Part II).

7. *Ibid.*

8. *Hell on the Border,* 575.

9. Aikman, *Lady Wildcats,* 196; Horan, *Desperate Women,* 217-18; Hicks, *Belle Starr and Her Pearl,* 50.

10. Biscup, "Lily of the Cimarron," *The American Indian,* Vol. 1, No. 5 (February, 1927).

11. Hicks, *Belle Starr and Her Pearl,* 49.

12. "Territorial History," *Haskell News,* June 20, 1926.

13. *Vinita Indian Chieftain,* June 20, 1895.

14. Wellman, *Dynasty of Western Outlaws*, 145.

15. Hicks, *Belle Starr and Her Pearl*, 56-57, 92.

16. *Muskogee Indian Journal*, March 1, 1883.

17. Rascoe, *Belle Starr*, 69; Horan, *Desperate Women*, 201.

18. Stoney Hardcastle, "Belle Starr's Piano," *True West*, Vol. 24, No. 5 (May-June, 1977), 22-23, 42-45.

19. Hicks, *Belle Starr and Her Pearl*, 48.

20. *Doctor in Belle Starr Country*, 227.

21. Harman, *Hell on the Border*, 585.

22. *Belle Starr and Her Pearl*, 50, 61.

23. James Middleton to James S. Buchanan, May 10, 1937. *Indian-Pioneer History*, Foreman Collection, Vol. 7, 203-205. Oklahoma Historical Society.

Chapter 14

1. *Muskogee Indian Journal*, May 28, 1885.

2. Neville, *Red River Valley*, 57.

3. *Muskogee Indian Journal*, May 28, 1885; Harman, *Hell on the Border*, 585-86.

4. Neville, *Red River Valley*, 57-58.

5. *Muskogee Indian Journal*, May 28, 1885; Harman, *Hell on the Border*, 586.

6. Harman, *Hell on the Border*, 586.

John West was commissioned Indian policeman in 1884 and rose to the rank of captain. He served as city marshal of Muskogee from 1889 to 1892, during which time he carried deputy's commissions under U.S. Marshal Jacob Yoes at Fort Smith, Arkansas, and U.S. Marshal Thomas B. Needles of the first "white man's court" in Indian Territory, established in 1889 at Muskogee. In 1894 and 1895, West was sheriff of the Canadian District, Cherokee Nation.

7. Interview, Ellis West to O. C. Davidson, June 18, 1937. *Indian-Pioneer History*, Foreman Collection, Vol. 49, 219. Oklahoma Historical Society.

8. *Bella Starr, Female Jesse James*, 55-57:

[Belle and her gang] camped in a stretch of timber, close to Wewoka [where] Brown had a fine house, and kept a large stock of the best goods in his store. They fixed upon a certain night for the accomplishment of their scheme, and expected smooth sailing; but in this they were sadly disappointed. John Brown . . . no sooner observed strangers in the vicinity than he "smelled a rat," and . . . detailed a small band of Seminoles to remain around . . . his business house until such time as the strangers had left the neighborhood. After being disappointed for three successive nights, one of the men, who played spy for the bandits on that occasion, returning to camp stating . . . it was not possible to make a successful break at the present time. Sam Starr . . . and the rest of the gang . . . agreed it would be better to postpone the robbery . . . but Bella grew wroth at the suggestion.

"Remain in camp," said she, next morning after breakfast; "I shall return in an hour."

Disguised as an old wrinkled grandmother . . . the Bandit Queen rode towards Wewoka, and dismounted in the woods close to town. Tottering as far as Brown's store, she purchased a package of candy, a pipe and some tobacco, and soon afterwards [was] seen sitting on the porch in front of the treasurer's private house. The [Brown] children were playing on the lawn. They stopped occasionally to gaze at the queer old woman, as she puffed away at her cob pipe. At length she persuaded them to approach, giving each a few candies. The little girl soon began to lose her shyness, but the boy, who was two years older, was more distant.

"Come," said Bella to the girl, "and I'll take you to your papa's store and buy you a doll." She lifted the child in her arms, but instead of going toward the store, struck out for her horse . . . hitched in the woods close by. Two minutes and she was off at full speed with the crying child sitting in front of her. Five minutes and she was in the bandits' camp.

"Get up, boys, and make ready," said she. "Here's Brown's little daughter . . . he and the Seminole bodyguard [soon] will be out in search for the child. We must get into the thicket back of his house, and make the break during his absence."

Meanwhile the little boy, seeing that his sister failed to return, repeated the story to John Brown . . . there was general confusion in the village, and before half an hour everybody was away in pursuit of the kidnaped girl. The house was abandoned to the mistress, and the store left in charge of one clerk. Riding up to the door of the private residence, Starr and his gang dismounted . . . the safe was burst open, and a large sum of money secured. The child was then handed back to its mother, and the Bandit Queen led her men in triumph from the spot.

Ibid., 57–59:

The capture of the Seminole treasury had proven such a success that Bella determined on trying her hand once more, this time upon the Creeks. Old Sam Brown, of Weataka [*sic*], was custodian of the public funds, and she determined to ease him of every cent of the Muskogee National Treasury. . . . [Belle and Sam] camped in the brush of a small branch, within four hundred yards of the town. . . . Bella left her husband [and] rode to the store, hitching her horse in front of the establishment. After exchanging courtesies with Sam Brown, she told him that she had come to make affidavit against certain parties, and to turn State's evidence in a very important case. She was about to reform and lead a new life. The old Creek appeared to credit her assertions, and escorting her to his desk, gave her the use of pen and paper. . . . The large safe was directly behind her, and what she really wanted was to get the combination. . . . Whenever a large payment was made Brown or his chief clerk worked the combination . . . and Bella turned and looked across the shoulder of the cashier on each occasion, putting down the letters on her tablet. She stayed in the office all evening, and feigned to be busy writing a confession of her sins and offences. . . . At nine o'clock, Brown closed up for the night. . . . As [they were] leaving the store, our heroine heard Brown whisper to a young Indian whom she had seen behind the counter:

"James, you must sleep in the store to-night; and mind don't be later than 11 o'clock."

"Now," thought Bella to herself, "I must carry the fort before 10:30."

She walked out into the darkness, and after having made certain no human eyes were set upon her actions, she raised the window that opened to the department . . . in which the safe was deposited. Entering cautiously, she lighted a kerosene lamp . . . screening the dull glimmer from the window, went to work at the combination, and soon threw the heavy door aside. . . . She seized papers, documents, cash, and everything that represented money, and tying them securely in an old coffee sack, extinguished the light, and closing the window after her, hurried to the camp, where she found Sam Starr awaiting her return. They did not stop to count their gain, but . . . put out for Younger Bend. Bella thought she had a big haul . . . but as it so happened there was not over $1,200 in the treasury.

9. Rascoe, *Belle Starr* (224), claims the Creek treasury was robbed by Sam Starr and "one Felix Griffin"; they had been "recognized, warrants were out

for their arrest," and so many U.S. marshals, accompanied by deputies and Indian police, rode up Belle Starr Canyon searching for Sam that he "hid out with some kin above Webbers Falls." Croy, *Last of the Great Outlaws* (146); Wellman, *Dynasty of Western Outlaws* (146); and Drago, *Outlaws on Horseback* (147), follow Rascoe. The Indian police were hunting Sam, says Drago, but an "additional post office job" put the marshals on his trail.

During this period no warrants had been issued for Sam Starr. Neither was he wanted nor being hunted by the Indian police or U.S. marshals.

Hicks, *Belle Starr and Her Pearl* (62–63), gives this version of the Seminole robbery: In "the early part of 1885" a Seminole payroll amounting to thousands of dollars arrived by train at Eufaula, was taken by stage, "with several armed horsemen riding guard," to Sasakwa, and was turned over to Governor Brown. At that moment, Belle Starr appeared "from nowhere." While everyone was entranced by her magnificent horsemanship, she suddenly leaned from her saddle, "plucked up an Indian child," and dashed away, with the Indians in hot pursuit. She soon dropped the child along the road, and when the braves returned with the little girl, they learned that "Sam Starr, John Middleton, and Grant Cook had suddenly appeared, guns in their hands, and made off with the payroll."

John F. Brown had served in official capacities for the Seminole tribe since the Washington Conference of 1866 and became principal chief of the Seminole Nation in 1885. Wewoka was the national capital. Brown developed considerable business interests—mainly merchandizing and cotton ginning—at Wewoka and Sasakwa, farther south on the Canadian. He also was in charge of the national treasury, but if it was ever robbed, history does not record it.

S. R. Lewis, well-known Tulsa attorney and authority on the Five Civilized Tribes, stated in a September 24, 1937, interview for *Indian-Pioneer History* (Vol. 19, 219) that

Captain Sam Brown, Euchee chief, was treasurer of the Creek Nation. He lived at Wealaka, near where Leonard is today. He kept the money belonging to the Creeks in a safe in his store. About noon one day [spring of 1886] . . . two men hitched their horses in front of the store. One was a white man, the other a mixed blood. They walked in and covered him and demanded the money . . . about $6,000. They made a good get-away. Captain Brown called on the Euchees to rally and they trailed the robbers past Muskogee to a place near where Warner is today, and then lost them. Suspicion was attached to Sam and Belle Starr . . . but evidence was lacking.

10. *Muskogee Indian Journal*, August 23, 1884; *Atoka Indian Champion*, August 23, 1884.

11. *Bella Starr, Female Jesse James*, 50.

12. *Belle Starr*, 223–24.

13. Horan, *Desperate Women* (220), claims that Sam Starr "vanished" from the Bend shortly after Christmas and a "round of wild parties," at which "whiskey flowed freely," and watched Belle and Middleton "whispering together"; that during his absence "romance bloomed," and when the "dashing young" Middleton suggested to Belle that they leave the Bend for "more fertile fields," Belle "eagerly agreed to go."

Wellman, *Dynasty of Western Outlaws* (146-47), leans with Rascoe. Sam Starr "rarely came home," Belle grew "increasingly discontented . . . taking into her bed whatever handy outlaw most appealed to her," but Middleton "ousted" them all and for "six months" was the favorite of this "bandit queen [whose] appetite for new bedmates seemed exceeded only by that other celebrated 'royal' nymphomaniac, Catherine the Great of Russia."

Hicks, *Belle Starr and Her Pearl* (62), has Middleton spending a "wonderful Christmas" at the Bend; Belle played the piano and "sang Christmas songs, with Pearl joining in"; by the time the "warm breeze of spring came up the Canadian river valley," Belle and her "new protege" were in love, and although Sam came home "at fleeting intervals," he seemed to "approve of John Middleton . . . as Belle did."

Drago, *Outlaws on Horseback* (147), says that because of Sam's annoying habit of returning home when least expected, Belle agreed to accompany Middleton to his mother's home in Arkansas "to escape these interruptions."

14. Harman, *Hell on the Border*, 586.

15. *Muskogee Indian Journal*, May 28, 1885.

16. Harman, *Hell on the Border*, 587.

17. *Ibid.*

18. Harman, *Hell on the Border* (587), gives the date as May 3. Rascoe, *Belle Starr* (224), says May 5 and that Frank Cook was "a fugitive from justice"; that Middleton "rode ahead on a saddle horse, from the pommel of which hung Belle's pistol and in his side holsters were two of his own"; and "Belle took his *Winchester* in the wagon with her."

19. Harman, *Hell on the Border*, 587.

Emery, *Court of the Damned* (98), thinks Pearl "became angry" because of Middleton's "affectionate attention to her mother" (despite Sam Starr's presence), and Hicks, *Belle Starr and Her Pearl* (67), says the rift between Pearl and Middleton occurred "the night before the expedition started."

20. *United States* v. *Belle Starr*, Case No. 1180, U.S. District Court, Western District of Arkansas; *Muskogee Indian Journal*, May 28, 1885.

21. Wellman, *Dynasty of Western Outlaws* (148), claims Sam Starr rode off with Middleton, "still protesting friendship [and] asserting that he also had to avoid possible recognition in Fort Smith."

Sam was not a wanted man and had no reason to avoid officers.

22. *United States* v. *Belle Starr*, Case No. 1180; *Muskogee Indian Journal*, May 28, 1885.

23. *Fort Smith Elevator*, May 15, 1885; *Muskogee Indian Journal*, May 28, 1885; Harman, *Hell on the Border*, 588-89.

24. Harman, *Hell on the Border*, 588-89.

25. *Hell on the Border*, 589.

26. According to Fox's writer (51-52),

Bella immediately set out for the place where Middleton's body was interred. Having arrived there, she summoned the neighbors to assist her to raise the body, after which she moved it . . . beneath an overhanging shade tree, and there reburied it with every symptom of sorrow and respect.

"When the flowers bloom," said she to a little Choctaw girl—"gather them and place them on the grave, and I will give you fifty dollars every year for this service." Saying which she commenced by paying the first installment in the shape of a ten dollar bill.

Rascoe, *Belle Starr* (228), and Hicks, *Belle Starr and Her Pearl* (66), accept this fiction.

27. Fox's writer (52) claims that Frank Cook was "captured for a robbery at Briartown"; Harman, *Hell on the Border* (589), says "West served a warrant on young Cook, charging a misdemeanor"; Rascoe, *Belle Starr* (228), and Hicks, *Belle Starr and Her Pearl* (66), state that Cook was taken to Fort Smith and received a penitentiary sentence on a larceny charge.

28. Rascoe, *Belle Starr* (228-29), wonders whether Belle explained the matter to Sam or thought an explanation necessary. He suggests that "John Middleton's face and half of his head were not eaten away by buzzards," but Sam Starr, aware of the elopement and inscrutable Indian that he was, "blew the face away with a shotgun, having trailed Middleton silently."

Horan, *Desperate Women* (220), has Belle "glibly telling Sam . . . that she had gone off to visit relatives."

Emery, *Court of the Damned* (97), says "it was thought" that Sam Starr tracked down his wife's secret lover, "blasting away his face . . . at close range" with a shotgun.

Wellman, *Dynasty of Western Outlaws* (148); Hicks, *Belle Starr and Her Pearl* (67); Drago, *Outlaws on Horseback* (148); Elman, *Fired in Anger* (221); and Mooney, *Doctor in Belle Starr Country* (289), follow Horan and Rascoe.

Chapter 15

1. *United States* v. *Sam Starr* (robbery), Case No. —, June 15, 1885, and *United States* v. *Sam'l Brown* et al. (rob the mail), Case No. —, Feb. 13, 1886, U.S. Commissioner's Court, Western District of Arkansas, Muskogee, I.T.

2. *United States* v. *Sam Starr, Felix Griffin and Richard Hays*, Case No. 59, Nov. 9, 1885, U.S. Commissioner's Court, Western District of Arkansas, Fort Smith.

3. *Fort Smith Elevator*, January 1, 1886.

4. *Ibid.*, January 12, 1886.

5. *Ibid.*, April 16, 1886.

6. Yarn spinners down the years speculate that Griffin had offered Belle fifty dollars to sleep with Pearl. Belle accepted the money, then leveled her six-shooter at the miscreant's head and said: "Now, you son-of-a-bitch, get in bed and sleep with my baby—but if you so much as lay a hand on her, I'll blow your brains out." Griffin crawled in beside Pearl, but he kept to the edge of the bed in mortal fear that the girl might roll against him in her sleep. Belle sat in a chair nearby, six-shooter on her lap. Griffin got no sleep, but he lived through the night. His complaint to Sam about the crude joke Belle had played on him resulted in the duel.

Hicks, *Belle Starr and Her Pearl* (68), repeats the tale but thinks the outlaw "may well have been Middleton."

John Middleton had been dead more than a year.

7. *Fort Smith Elevator*, April 16, 1886.

8. Rector was a ninety-year-old former deputy marshal Homer Croy interviewed for material in *He Hanged Them High* (91–92). Rector's story is repeated by Horan, *Desperate Women* (216–17); Hicks, *Belle Starr and Her Pearl* (57–58); and Scott, *Belle Starr in Velvet* (238–39).

9. *United States* v. *Belle Starr*, Case No. 1180; *Fort Smith Elevator*, January 22, 1886; *Vinita Indian Chieftain*, January 28, 1886.

10. *United States* v. *Belle Starr*, Case No. 1180; *Fort Smith Elevator*, February 12, 1886.

11. *United States* v. *Samuel Starr* et al., Case No. 1213, U.S. District Court, Western District of Arkansas, Fort Smith.

12. *Fort Smith Elevator*, March 12, 1886.

13. *Ibid.*

14. Frederick S. Barde, "The Story of Belle Starr," *Sturm's Oklahoma Magazine*, Vol. XI, No. 1 (September, 1910), 20; "Says Belle Starr's Ghost Still Rides," *St. Louis Republic*, August 21, 1910.

15. *United States* v. *Belle Starr* et al., Case No. —, U.S. Commissioner's Court, Fort Smith.

16. *Hell on the Border*, 591–92. Harman dates Belle's arrest incorrectly "in midsummer, 1886."

17. *Muskogee Indian Journal*, April 15, 1886; *Fort Smith Elevator*, April 16, 1886.

18. April 16, 1886; see also *Vinita Indian Chieftain*, April 22, 1886.

19. *Muskogee Indian Journal*, April 22, 1886.

20. *Ibid.*, June 3, 1886; Ltrs. John F. Weaver to Frederick Barde, July 20 and 25, 1910.

21. *Muskogee Indian Journal*, June 3, 1886.

22. *United States* v. *Blue Duck and William Christie*, Case No. 1089, U.S. District Court, Western District of Arkansas; *Fort Smith Elevator*, January 22, 1886; *Vinita Indian Chieftain*, February 4 and 18, 1886; *Muskogee Indian Journal*, April 8, and May 6, 1886.

23. Harman, *Hell on the Border* (260–61, 575), claims that Blue Duck was "remembered in his tribulations . . . by his dashing friend, Belle Starr [who] employed able counsel . . . and spent many hundred dollars to save his rascally neck . . . his sentence being finally commuted to life imprisonment and after a year he was pardoned."

This Harman fiction has been accepted and romanticized by most subsequent biographers.

Sutton, *Hands Up!* (234): "Belle came to [Blue Duck's] rescue . . . hired the best lawyers in the country and had his death sentence commuted. . . . After he had spent one year in prison she had him pardoned."

Sabin, *Wild Men of the Wild West* (326): "Belle Starr's money carried his case on until his sentence was commuted . . . after a year he was pardoned."

Rascoe, *Belle Starr* (223): "J. Warren Reed, the criminal lawyer [was] retained" by Belle "to bring about the commutation of 'Blue Duck's' death sentence" and his pardon within a year.

Croy, *Last of the Great Outlaws* (137–38): "Belle raised money, got Lawyer

J. Warren Reed . . . (and finally got the president of the United States to commute Blue Duck's sentence. . . . Belle took up with her murderous admirer when she was low in her mind about Cole."

Wellman, *Dynasty of Western Outlaws* (150): "Belle employed counsel for Blue Duck, his sentence was commuted"; pardoned after a year, he returned "to her arms [and] was killed in July 1886 by an unknown party . . . in all probability . . . the jealous and murderous Sam Starr."

Drago, *Red River Valley, Mainstream of Frontier History* (271): Belle "hired J. Warren Reed to defend [Blue Duck], but her presence antagonised the jury and Blue Duck was convicted." Drago admits that Belle's having Duck's sentence changed to life imprisonment "is absurd." However, in *Outlaws on Horseback* (146-47), he follows Rascoe and Wellman; conjectures that Belle footed the bill with "profits derived from selling stolen horses . . . arranging defense . . . supplying perjured witnesses, manufacturing alibis" for the vicious, ignorant outlaws who frequented Youngers' Bend; and concludes (149) that "her romance with Blue Duck ended temporarily when he was put away for life . . . she got him back [but] he was killed a few months later . . . very likely" by Sam Starr.

Hicks, *Belle Starr and Her Pearl* (92): "Belle came to Fort Smith with [Blue Duck] and put down the cold cash for the best lawyers she could find. . . . When [her cash] was depleted, she hocked one of her precious six-guns to raise more."

Elman, *Fired in Anger* (220): "Shortly after [Blue Duck's] release, the renegade was supposedly ambushed and killed in the Indian Territory. Belle . . . may have been his killer."

Breihan and Rosamond, *Bandit Belle* (13): "Bella engaged the services of the famous J. Warren Reed . . . raised enough money to take [Blue Duck's] case out of Judge Parker's hands . . . and [had] Blue Duck's sentence commuted to life imprisonment." After Duck's pardon, "he became involved in a fatal disagreement in a Kansas gambling palace and ended up in the local cemetery."

On the contrary, in 1886, lawyer Reed was practicing law with a cousin, former Judge Ira H. Reed, at San Andrea, California. From 1879, when he was admitted to the bar, Reed had practiced in his native West Virginia and southeastern Ohio. In 1887-88 he toured Mexico, the United States, and Canada and returned to West Virginia to resume practice there. In 1889 he came to Fort Smith to defend a noted case and, attracted by the magnitude of court business, settled down to permanent practice. He was never Belle's attorney.

Blue Duck was in the Fort Smith jail awaiting commutation in July, 1886, when Wellman alleges he was killed by Sam Starr. Wellman also errs in stating that the photograph of Blue Duck and Belle was "probably taken after their reunion."

When Blue Duck was pardoned in 1895, Sam Starr had been dead nearly nine years and Belle had been dead more than six years. Blue Duck died of consumption in 1895 and is buried in the Catoosa cemetery.

24. Mittimus, *United States* v. *Blue Duck and William Christie*, Case No. 1089; *Fort Smith Elevator*, March 29, 1895.

25. *Fort Smith Elevator*, May 28, 1886.

26. Some magazine-article writers credit the *Dallas News* story to a reporter named Larkin Lareau, claiming that Belle stalked him in the street, screaming, "You God-damned dirty double-crosser, I'm going to kill you!" and reached for her Colt. Lareau knocked the weapon from her hand, the crowd laughed, and Belle walked away, shaken and sobbing.

The incident is not mentioned by the Fort Smith press.

27. *United States* v. *Belle Starr* et al., Case No. —.

Chapter 16

1. *Muskogee Indian Journal*, June 24, 1886.

2. *Ibid.*, July 1, 1886.

3. *Vinita Indian Chieftain*, July 8, 1886.

4. *United States* v. *Jack Spaniard and Frank Palmer*, Case No. —, U.S. District Court, Western District of Arkansas, Fort Smith.

5. *Ibid.*

6. *United States* v. *Samuel Starr*, et al. Case No. 1213.

7. *Vinita Indian Chieftain*, May 5, 1887.

8. "Recipes Used by Belle Starr Still Popular," *Daily Oklahoman*, June 5, 1938; Louise Riotte, "Outlaw Candy," *Grain Producers News*, Vol. 28, No. 6 (June, 1977), 26–28.

9. *United States* v. *Belle Starr*, Case No. 1180.

10. *Hell on the Border*, 593.

11. *Vinita Indian Chieftain*, October 7, 1886.

12. "Reminiscences of Mr. R. P. Vann, East of Webbers Falls, Oklahoma, September 28, 1932," *Chronicles of Oklahoma*, Vol. XI, No. 2 (June, 1933), 842.

13. According to Fox's writer (58), Sam Starr "was riding along the road towards Eufaula [when] some Indian officers . . . five or six in number . . . rushed upon him from the thicket. . . . He gave them an interesting chase, and would have escaped, had not his horse fallen dead beneath him. Sam fell, pierced with three bullets, but none of the wounds were dangerous." Carried to a neighboring house, he "lay four days under his wounds." Three guards watched him. He got hold of one of the guard's guns, "disarmed the other two," jumped on one of their best horses, and was back with his wife at the Bend "in two hours' time."

Rascoe, *Belle Starr* (235–36), accepts R. P. Vann's version.

Horan, *Desperate Women* (222), says Sam was "shot by the Indian police after robbing the treasury of the Creek Nation"; they "held Sam overnight in a farmhouse but a mob of his followers freed him."

Emery, *Court of the Damned* (102), has Sam "surprised . . . riding down a mountain trail . . . by four deputy marshals"; his horse was "shot from under him . . . in the fall [he] was injured and captured." That night, while the marshals were engaged in a game of cards, Sam "jumped from his pallet, grabbed a rifle and made his escape."

Scott, *Belle Starr in Velvet* (221), claims a posse of officers attacked Sam and some of his boys while they were visiting a whiskey supplier at a dance. Sam was wounded in the head, his horse shot from under him; another man was wounded and several were captured. The posse left "four of their number" to guard Sam and the wounded man; the others returned to camp with their prisoners. Sam "slipped up on the guards . . . appropriated a rifle . . . and made good his escape."

Breihan and Rosamond, *Bandit Belle* (15), think Sam "regained consciousness in the sheriff's office where he was taken after the shooting, seized a guard's gun and escaped."

14. *United States* v. *Samuel Starr* et al., Case No. 1213.

15. *Ibid.*

16. *Fort Smith Elevator*, October 15, 1886.

17. September 17, 1886.

18. September 23, 1886.

19. *Vinita Indian Chieftain*, October 21, 1886.

20. *Hell on the Border*, 593–94.

21. Aikman, *Lady Wildcats* (205), repeats only the Powe incident, dating it "in 1887." Cameron Rogers, *Gallant Ladies* (139–40); Sabin, *Wild Men of the Wild West* (325–26); and Allsopp, *Folklore of Romantic Arkansas* (328–29), use Harman's story without mentioning Powe.

Rascoe, *Belle Starr* (220–21), thinks the Wild West exhibition occurred "in October, 1884"; that "contemporary newspaper accounts . . . tell of the part Judge Parker played," but not Belle. He discards the "play-acting of stern Judge Parker" since the press would have made "a great deal" of the event and Belle was "too shrewd a woman" to have considered killing Clayton "in the presence of a thousand witnesses."

Croy, *He Hanged Them High* (158–60), sets the event in October, 1886, but has Belle just arriving in Fort Smith, "having finished her course in caning chairs" at Detroit.

Horan, *Desperate Women* (220), says the Fort Smith Wild West Show occurred in "the fall of 1884."

Emery, *Court of the Damned* (101), thinks Parker was "invited" to ride in the stagecoach but "judiciously declined."

Wellman, *Dynasty of Western Outlaws* (149), notes Rascoe's "doubt that Belle was the lady holdup artist" but is "inclined to think [Harman's story] may be true."

Hicks, *Belle Starr and Her Pearl* (55–56), favors Croy, dating the event "October, 1884," after Belle's and Sam's "nine months educational tour at the House of Correction, Detroit."

Scott, *Belle Starr in Velvet* (226–30), says "October of 1886." His allegation that afterward Belle, disguised as a young man, slept with District Attorney Clayton in a roadside tavern near Fort Smith is reminiscent of the Judge Thurman tale in the Fox opus.

Drago, *Outlaws on Horseback* (149), labels the entire affair "fantastic"; he believes the holdup occurred but "Belle took no part in it . . . Fort Smith newspapers do not mention her name."

22. *United States* v. *Samuel Starr* et al., Case No. 1213.

23. *Ibid.*; *Fort Smith Elevator*, November 19, 1886.

24. *United States* v. *Thomas Starr*, Case No. —, February 27, 1885; *United States* v. *Thomas Starr*, Case No. —, December 15, 1885; and *United States* v. *Tom Starr*, Case No. —, November 2, 1886, U.S. Commissioner's Court, Fayetteville, Arkansas.

25. Indictment and Mittimus, *United States* v. *Thomas Starr*, Case No. 1670, U.S. District Court, Western District of Arkansas.

26. December 22, 1886.

27. Versions of this double killing vary with almost every Belle Starr biographer.

28. Hall, *Oklahoma, Indian Territory*, 24.

29. *Ibid.*

30. Rascoe, *Belle Starr* (238); Croy, *Last of the Great Outlaws* (147); Emery, *Court of the Damned* (104); and Drago, *Outlaws on Horseback* (154), have the bodies of Sam Starr and Frank West hauled away in the "same wagon" that night.

Chapter 17

1. Wellman, *Dynasty of Western Outlaws* (152), says Belle "relieved her unhappiness" by taking in Spaniard; when his arrest and conviction for murdering Deputy Irwin "removed him as a mate," she "dallied" with Jim French as a lover "for a short time."

Drago, *Outlaws on Horseback* (154-55), accepts: Jack Spaniard dropped by the Bend; Belle "took him to her bed" but the marshals soon came for him; Belle and "Lawyer Reed" did their best to save him from the gallows but lost the battle; "to relieve her loneliness" Belle took up with Jim French but French proved worthless both physically and mentally and she "soon sent him packing."

2. *Fort Smith Elevator*, March 30, 1888.

3. *United States* v. *Jack Spaniard and Frank Palmer*, Case No. —; *Fort Smith Elevator*, April 19, July 26, August 9, and August 16, 1889.

4. "Story of Belle Starr," 24.

5. Rascoe, *Belle Starr* (239); Horan, *Desperate Women* (223-24); Croy, *Last of the Great Outlaws* (148); Emery, *Court of the Damned* (104); Hicks, *Belle Starr and Her Pearl* (84); Drago, *Outlaws on Horseback* (155) and *Notorious Ladies of the Frontier* (173); Mooney, *Doctor in Belle Starr Country* (216).

6. *Hell on the Border*, 595-97.

7. *Ibid.*, 598-601.

8. Aikman, *Lady Wildcats* (203-204); Shackleford-Booker, *Belle Starr, Bandit Queen* (20-21) and *Wildcats in Petticoats* (24); Emery, *Court of the Damned* (104); Wellman, *Dynasty of Western Outlaws* (151); Drago, *Outlaws on Horseback* (72-74) and *Notorious Ladies of the Frontier* (174).

Mooney, *Doctor in Belle Starr Country* (259), claims Pearl gave birth to her child "in August."

9. "Belle Starr's Granddaughter" (Part II).

10. *United States* v. *Bill July* alias *Jim Starr*, Case No. 103, August 30, 1887, U.S. Commissioner's Court, Western District of Arkansas, Fort Smith.

11. *Ibid.*

12. *Muskogee Indian Journal*, July 28, 1887.

13. *United States* v. *Bill July* alias *Jim Starr*, Case No. 103.

14. Some journalists have claimed that, bored with the routine of the Starr ranch, Belle would ride to Fort Smith and stay for days at a time, making a spectacle of herself by strutting down the streets armed with two revolvers and boasting of her exploits with bloodthirsty outlaws. From this she gravitated to the whorehouses. Too old now to ply her trade, she would pound the keys of the pianos for her supper, booze, and bed or rip out wild tales of robbery and murder interspersed with vile profanity that would have curled the hair on the most lurid dime-novelist. Because she bragged about being a bandit queen, the prostitutes and their pimps called her Queenie. They greeted her fabrications with raucous laughter, winked at each other knowingly, and made sport of her, but she was too tired to care. And these journalists were probably too tired to search for facts.

15. "Story of Belle Starr," 19-20.

16. Harman, *Hell on the Border*, 601-602.

17. *United States* v. *Ed Reed* (larceny), Case No. −, July 21, 1888, U.S. Commissioner's Court, Western District of Arkansas, Fort Smith.

18. *Ibid.*

19. *Hell on the Border*, 602.

20. Rascoe, *Belle Starr* (239-40), does not mention Eddie's being wounded or Belle's letter. He thinks Pearl returned to the Bend in 1887 after the birth of her daughter at Siloam Springs, leaving the child with Arkansas relatives; Eddie had begun his career "in the footsteps of his father and mother" and had been sentenced "July 12, 1888," to "seven years" in the federal prison at Columbus, Ohio, but was released after serving only a few months.

Shackleford, *Belle Starr, Bandit Queen* (21), dates Eddie's gunshot wound and Pearl's return to Youngers' Bend "the Autumn of 1887."

Croy, *Last of the Great Outlaws* (149), and Emery, *Court of the Damned* (105), follow Rascoe, but Eddie was sent off to Columbus "on July 14, 1888," for "horse stealing"; Belle got a lawyer, and "in four months" Eddie was paroled.

Wellman, *Dynasty of Western Outlaws* (152), makes Eddie "a bootlegger at fourteen . . . a horse thief soon after" and doesn't mention his gunshot wound or prison sentence; Pearl simply "abandoned her child to an aunt in Wichita and returned to her mother."

Hicks, *Belle Starr and Her Pearl* (90-91), sends Eddie to Columbus "on July 12, 1888," for "seven years" for "grand larceny"; he is paroled within a few months; "in October . . . [he] got himself shot up"; Belle then tricked Pearl as John Shirley had tricked her "when she was off with Cole Younger"—Ed was "in no danger of dying."

Drago, *Outlaws on Horseback* (155), decides that Eddie was sentenced "July 12, 1888 . . . to seven years in the Ohio State Penitentiary for horse stealing" and in *Notorious Ladies of the Frontier* (174–75) alleges he "got shot during a fracas . . . with some whiskey peddlers," was in "no danger of dying," but Pearl was "taken in by [her mother's] hoax."

21. *Fort Smith Elevator*, August 10, 1888.

22. *Ibid*.

23. *United States* v. *Ed Reed*, Case No. —, October 13 and 25, 1888, U.S. Commissioner's Court, Western District of Arkansas, Fort Smith. *United States* v. *Ed Reed* (indictment for larceny), Case No. 3015, U.S. District Court, Western District of Arkansas, Fort Smith.

24. *United States* v. *Ed Reed*, Case No. 3015.

25. *Vinita Indian Chieftain*, October 4, 1888.

26. "Belle Starr's Granddaughter" (Part II).

27. Hall, *Oklahoma, Indian Territory*, 13–15, 37–39.

28. *Ibid.*, 22.

29. *Hell on the Border*, 605–606.

30. R. P. Vann, "Reminiscences" (842), dates the incident more than two years earlier by indicating the animal was Belle's mare Venus, shot from under Sam Starr on September 16, 1886.

Rascoe, *Belle Starr* (248–49), follows Harman, adding that there were "incestuous relations" between mother and son and Belle's whipping Eddie for using her horse "is only an apocryphal allusion to her dark sins." All of which Drago, *Outlaws on Horseback* (159), properly labels "unadulterated nonsense . . . far more sensational than anything that ever appeared in the *National Police Gazette*."

Hicks, *Belle Starr and Her Pearl* (94–95), and Mooney, *Doctor in Belle Starr Country* (239–40), embroider the Harman story with much gory detail and violent conversation that was never recorded. Mooney states that Eddie rode thirteen miles "that same night" to Dr. Jesse Mooney's house at Tamaha, had his cuts and lacerations sutured and bandaged, and rode away under cover of darkness three nights later, vowing to the doctor that he would "kill the old sow!"

31. Hall, *Oklahoma, Indian Territory*, 26.

Chapter 18

1. Charles J. Kappler, *Indian Affairs: Laws and Treaties*, II, 712.

2. *Constitution and Laws of the Choctaw Nation, 1869*, 483/87.

3. Hall, *Oklahoma, Indian Territory*, 25.

4. *Constitution and Laws of the Choctaw Nation* (compiled 1894), 237/42.

5. *Vinita Indian Chieftain*, June 24, 1884; Hall, *Oklahoma, Indian Territory*, 25, 331–32.

6. *Laws of the Choctaw Nation, 1886 to 1890*, 12.

7. Hall, *Oklahoma, Indian Territory*, 25.

8. *United States* v. *Edgar A. Watson*, Case No. —, February 22–23, 1889, U.S. Commissioner's Court, Western District of Arkansas, Fort Smith.

9. Harman, *Hell on the Border*, 603.

10. Barde, "Story of Belle Starr," 24-25.

11. Hall, *Oklahoma, Indian Territory*, 26, 492.

12. *United States* v. *Edgar A. Watson*, Case No. –.

13. Transcript of testimony, 5-6.

14. *Ibid.*, 9-10.

15. *Ibid.*, 10.

16. *Ibid.*, 16-17.

17. *Ibid.*, 18-19.

18. *Ibid.*, 17.

19. *Ibid.*, 22.

20. *Ibid.*, 10-11.

21. *Ibid.*, 2-4.

22. *Ibid.*, 12-13.

23. *Ibid.*, 13-15.

24. *Ibid.*, 6-8.

25. Hall, *Oklahoma, Indian Territory*, 514.

Mooney, *Doctor in Belle Starr Country* (228-29, 283), states that Belle "lived for over an hour" after being shot; that Dr. Jesse happened to be at Briartown, visiting with Uncle Isaac Mooney, and Pearl sent a messenger to bring him post haste to her bedside at "the Starr home," where Milo Hoyt had "brought Belle in his wagon." Dr. Jesse "pushed his horse relentlessly over the six miles . . . to Belle's home," but Belle died "about fifteen minutes before [he] arrived." At that time the sobbing Pearl told the doctor her mother "whispered in my ear" the name of her assassin, and "someday, I'll tell you, Jesse."

The testimony in *United States* v. *Edgar A. Watson* does not support the story, nor is Dr. Jesse Mooney's presence mentioned. Belle had been dead nearly fourteen hours when her body was removed to the Bend.

26. *The Tahlequah Telephone*, March 1, 1889; Hall, *Oklahoma, Indian Territory*, 27, 514.

Rascoe, *Belle Starr* (242), says Belle was clad in "a black silk dress with a white waist and frilled collar" and laid in "a *square* coffin" built by a Briartown carpenter "with one of [her] crossed hands clasping her favorite six-shooter."

Croy, *Last of the Great Outlaws* (153), has "her arms crossed . . . bouquet of flowers in one hand, Cole's six-shooter in the other."

Hicks, *Belle Starr and Her Pearl* (97), thinks she also was "adorned with her favorite jewelry. . . . In one of her hands they placed a six-shooter . . . which Cole Younger had given her."

Mooney, *Doctor in Belle Starr Country* (230), states that Dr. Jesse "placed white bandages on her neck and left side of her face . . . to hide the shotgun wounds," then "bent the stiff fingers of Belle's left hand around one of her pearl handled pistols at her waist . . . the same pistol . . . Cole Younger gave her before Pearl was born." Mooney (232, 281) also insists that Uncle Isaac Mooney "made the pine-board coffin . . . void of any cloth or decorative attachments . . . only a bedroom pillow was placed under Belle's head."

27. *United States* v. *Edgar Watson*, Case No. —, testimony of James (July) Starr, 18.

28. In a *Daily Oklahoman* article of April 23, 1939, Joseph Burckhalter, a Holy Roller evangelist who came to Indian Territory from Texas and did special work for the Fort Smith court in curbing white-slave traffic and handling juvenile offenders, claimed he "preached Belle Starr's funeral." However, Starr family members denied it and declared he would not have been allowed to speak if he had been present.

29. *The Tahlequah Telephone*, March 1, 1889.

Mooney, *Doctor in Belle Starr Country* (239, 281), denies that Eddie Reed was at his mother's funeral; "he was wanted by the law at the time . . . there were warrants for his arrest by the Deputy Marshalls [sic] from Judge Parker's Court, and Eddie was on the Scout."

On the contrary, Eddie had been free on his own recognizance since November, 1888, on a single larceny charge set for trial in March, 1889.

30. *Vinita Indian Chieftain*, February 14, 1889, and June 20, 1895; *The Tahlequah Telephone*, March 1, 1889.

Hall, *Oklahoma Indian Territory* (27), says "Charley Afton [sic] suddenly drew his gun and levelled down on Edgar A. Watson." However, July testified (*United States* v. *Edgar A. Watson*, 18): "After I buried [Belle] I arrested Deft. I suspected him."

31. *United States* v. *Edgar A. Watson*, Case No. —.

32. *Ibid.*

33. *Ibid.; Fort Smith Elevator*, February 22, 1889; *Vinita Indian Chieftain*, March 7, 1889.

Chapter 19

1. Hall, *Oklahoma, Indian Territory*, 29.

2. *Indian-Pioneer History*, Vol. 49, 223–24.

3. *Oklahoma, Indian Territory*, 29.

4. *Belle Starr and Her Pearl*, 109–12.

5. Hall, *Oklahoma, Indian Territory*, 644.

6. *Indian-Pioneer History*, Vol. 7, 205.

7. *Cherokee Records*, II, 15.

8. *Fort Smith Elevator*, January 24 and 31, 1890; *Vinita Indian Chieftain*, January 30, 1890.

9. Pages 123–37.

10. January 24, 1890.

11. *Fort Smith Elevator*, January 31, 1890.

12. *Hell on the Border*, 605.

13. Rascoe, *Belle Starr* (14), considers this "a more credible motive" than the one attributed to Watson.

Shackleford-Booker, *Belle Starr, Bandit Queen* (24) and *Wildcats in Petticoats* (22), claims "the Reeds always contended Pearl was responsible . . . if Ed had done the killing it was Pearl who 'put him up to it' . . . after Belle went an' ruined her life that-a-way."

Horan, *Desperate Women* (225), and Peter Lyon, *Wild, Wild West* (89), think Eddie murdered Belle.

Emery, *Court of the Damned* (108–109), mentions the "unmerciful whipping . . . another angle" to the case that "reflected on the son."

Wellman, *Dynasty of Western Outlaws* (154), "surmises" that Belle would not have ridden past Watson "standing in full view of the corner of the field . . . armed with a gun . . . who she considered an enemy," but had the man been Eddie, she would have "spoken and gone on"; that she would have named her assailant if it had been Watson, but not if the murderer had been her son.

Another story about how Eddie "shot Belle in the back with a .45 calibre pistol" was published in the Checotah, Oklahoma, *McIntosh County Democrat* on April 9, 1964. In it, William Henry (Harrison) Draper, a former Checotah resident then 85 years old and living near Muskogee, asserted that "I Saw Belle Starr Murdered." It is full of untruths and error but has been used extensively by magazine writers.

14. Indictment for receiving stolen goods, *United States* v. *Ed Reed*, Case No. 2689, U.S. District Court, Western District of Arkansas, Fort Smith.

15. *United States* v. *Ed Reed*, Case No. 3015 and Case No. 2689; *Vinita Indian Chieftain*, July 18, 1889.

16. Mittimus, *United States* v. *Ed Reed*, Case No. 3015 and Case No. 2689.

17. *Fort Smith Elevator*, April 3, 1891; Harman, *Hell on the Border*, 606.

18. Scott, *Belle Starr in Velvet* (252–53), errs in saying Eddie was "given a stiff sentence by Judge Parker [for] shooting up a saloon" and Pearl later went to the judge, who was "her friend," and "arranged for his pardon."

Mooney, *Doctor in Belle Starr Country* (263), has Dr. Jesse remembering when Eddie "was sentenced to seven years in prison twice for bootlegging" by Judge Parker, and "both times he was pardoned."

19. *Hell on the Border*, 607.

20. *United States* v. *Ed Reed*, Case No. –, March 24, 1894, U.S. Commissioner's Court, Western District of Arkansas, Fort Smith.

21. *Hell on the Border*, 608–609.

22. Glenn Shirley, *Law West of Fort Smith*, 113.

23. L. W. Wilson, "A History of Wagoner, Oklahoma, From S. S. Cobb." *Chronicles of Oklahoma*, Vol. 50, No. 4 (Winter, 1972), 491.

24. Harman, *Hell on the Border*, 609–10; Harris, *This Is Three Forks Country*, 53; Hicks, *Belle Starr and Her Pearl*, 121; Mooney, *Doctor in Belle Starr Country*, 249, 268–69.

25. Testimony of witnesses to the Crittenden killings is as follows:

JAMES A. HARRIS being duly sworn, deposes and says: I reside at Wagoner, I. T. and know defendant in this cause. About 4 o'clock in the afternoon I heard shots from my store. I went out on sidewalk & saw Zeke and Dick Crittenden. Zeke had a pistol in each hand, and Dick with one pistol in his hand, both apparently shooting at random and people were running up and down the street. I went back into the store and in a few minutes saw from the window a crowd and from the shots I heard fired I supposed that some of them had been killed. I walked down to the crowd & saw Zeke Crittenden lying dead on the sidewalk and was told that Ed Reed had killed him, then walked to the back end of Burns residence and saw Ed Reed standing on the walk with Winchester in hand. Saw Dick Crittenden on horseback, pistol in hand, running towards where Zeke was killed. Saw Dick get off his horse with pistol in hand and again mount, reel as to shoot down the street, when Ed Reed called to Dick saying something that I did not understand. At that point Reed shot the horse through the shoulder, then shot Dick Crittenden through the body and after falling from his horse he raised to his knees with his pistol pointed towards Reed, when Reed shot again, the ball taking effect in his left side. Dick died about 12 o'clock last night.

J. J. TURNHAM being duly sworn says: About 4 o'clock in afternoon, the Crittendens were shooting up the town, and Zeke came by my store with a pistol in each hand. I went out and asked him to let me have his guns, he said, "I won't do it." Reed came out into the street and said "Zeke Crittenden, throw up those guns." Zeke replied "The hell you say," and threw one of his pistols down on Reed and shot at him. Ed then shot him down, and Zeke said to me as he sank "He has killed me." Some 10 or 15 minutes after, Dick came galloping up the street. I said to him "Zeke is dead, what shall I do with him." He replied "Put him in a rosewood box and bury him. Where is Ed Reed?" I said I did not know. . . . About that time he turned his horse around and commenced shooting, his horse was first shot down, I then saw Dick fall and after falling he fired 3 shots in different directions. After he fell I went to him.

26. Harman, *Hell on the Border* (610), says that "one day in November" Eddie "begun to feel too much his own importance, or because of too free use of whiskey, and becoming reckless . . . drove two men, the proprietors, from a saloon; they returned and killed him."

Hicks, *Bell Starr and Her Pearl* (121), accepts Harman's date, assumes the incident occurred "in the town of Wagoner," and claims Reed was drunk, boisterous, and shooting his six-shooter when two saloonkeepers whom he had chased from their places of business returned and killed him.

27. *Doctor in Belle Starr Country*, 252–55.

28. *Hell on the Border*, 605.

29. "Story of Belle Starr," 25.

30. *Lady Wildcats*, 206.

31. *Gallant Ladies*, 142.

32. *Wild Men of the Wild West*, 327.

33. *Desperate Women*, 225.

34. *Road Agents and Train Robbers*, 230.

35. *Last of the Great Outlaws*, 157.

36. *Hell on the Border*, 605.

37. "Story of Belle Starr," 25.

38. *Dynasty of Western Outlaws*, 153.

39. Pages 319–21.

40. Pages 77–81.

41. This phase of Pearl's life is covered very well in Hicks's *Belle Starr and Her Pearl* (122–67), which is the chief value of his book.

42. *Vinita Indian Chieftain*, June 30, 1895; Barde, "Story of Belle Starr," 25.

Bibliography

Manuscripts and Documents

Cherokee Records (marriage records, bills of sale, court records, permits to noncitizens). Vol. 1-B. Indian Archives Division, Oklahoma Historical Society, Oklahoma City.

———. Vol. II. Indian Archives Division, Oklahoma Historical Society, Oklahoma City.

Constitution and Laws of the Choctaw Nation, 1869. Wm. P. Lyon & Son, Printers and Publishers, New York.

Constitution and Laws of the Choctaw Nation. John F. Worley, Printer and Publisher, Dallas, 1894.

Kappler, Charles J., comp. and ed. *Indian Affairs: Laws and Treaties.* 2 vols. Washington, Government Printing Office, 1903.

Laws of the Choctaw Nation, Made and Enacted By the General Council, From 1886 to 1890, Inclusive. Indian Citizen Print, Atoka, I.T., 1891.

S. R. Lewis to Effie S. Jackson, September 24, 1937. *Indian-Pioneer History,* Foreman Collection, Vol. 19. Oklahoma Historical Society, Oklahoma City.

Mrs. Fannie Blythe Marks to James Carselowey, September 9, 1937. *Indian-Pioneer History,* Foreman Collection, Vol. 16. Oklahoma Historical Society, Oklahoma City.

Marriage Records, Collin County, McKinney, Texas. Vol. 3, p. 49.

Marriage Records, Jasper County, Missouri. Compiled by Lyda B. Perry, Carthage, and Elizabeth P. Ellsbury, Chillicothe, Mo., 1962.

James Middleton to James S. Buchanan, May 10, 1937. *Indian-Pioneer History,* Foreman Collection, Vol. 7. Oklahoma Historical Society, Oklahoma City.

Probate Records, Vernon County, Nevada, Missouri. Box 14, Packet 5.

Statutes at Large of the United States, 50th Congress, 1st session, Vol. XXV.

U.S. Department of Commerce, Bureau of the Census, *Seventh Census of the United States, 1850: Population Schedules, Jasper County, Missouri.* National Archives Microcopy no. 432, Roll 402 (Oklahoma Historical Society).

U.S. Department of Commerce, Bureau of the Census, *Eighth Census of the United States, 1860: Population Schedules, Jasper County, Missouri.* National Archives Microcopy No. 653, Roll 204.

U.S. Department of Commerce, Bureau of the Census, *Eighth Census of the United States, 1860: Federal Population Schedules, Vernon County, Missouri.* National Archives Microcopy No. 563, Roll 659.

U.S. Department of Commerce, Bureau of the Census, *Ninth Census of the United States, 1870: Federal Population Schedules, Dallas County, Texas.* National Archives Microcopy No. 593, Roll 1581.

U.S. District Court, Austin, Texas. Ledger No. 122.

United States v. *Sam'l Brown* et al. (rob the mail), Case No. —, February 13, 1886, U.S. Commissioner's Court, Western District of Arkansas, Muskogee, I.T.

United States v. *Calvin Carter* et al., Case No. —, U.S. District Court, Western District of Arkansas, Fort Smith.

United States v. *Blue Duck and William Christie,* Case No. 1089, U.S. District Court, Western District of Arkansas, Fort Smith.

United States v. *John Fisher* et al., Case No. —, U.S. District Court, Western District of Arkansas, Fort Smith.

United States v. *Bill July* alias *Jim Starr,* Case No. 103, August 30, 1887, U.S. Commissioner's Court, Western District of Arkansas, Fort Smith.

United States v. *Ed Reed* (larceny), Case No. —, July 21, 1888, U.S. Commissioner's Court, Western District of Arkansas, Fort Smith.

United States v. *Ed Reed,* Case No. —, October 13 and 25, 1888, U.S. Commissioner's Court, Western District of Arkansas, Fort Smith.

United States v. *Ed Reed,* Case No. —, March 24, 1894, U.S. Commissioner's Court, Western District of Arkansas, Fort Smith.

United States v. *Ed Reed* (indictment for larceny), Case No. 3015, U.S. District Court, Western District of Arkansas, Fort Smith.

United States v. *Ed Reed* (indictment for receiving stolen goods), Case No. 2689, U.S. District Court, Western District of Arkansas, Fort Smith.

United States v. *James E. Reed* (murder), Case No. —, October 25, 1895, U.S. Commissioner's Court, Western District of Arkansas, Fort Smith.

United States v. *Jim Reed* et al., Case No. 142, U.S. District Court, Western District of Texas, Austin.

United States v. *Jack Spaniard and Frank Palmer,* Case No. —, U.S. District Court, Western District of Arkansas, Fort Smith.

United States v. *Belle Starr,* Case No. 1180, U.S. District Court, Western District of Arkansas, Fort Smith.

United States v. *Belle Starr* et al., Case No. —, U.S. Commissioner's Court, Western District of Arkansas, Fort Smith.

United States v. *Sam and Belle Starr,* Case No. 2370, U.S. District Court, Western District of Arkansas, Fort Smith.

United States v. *Sam Starr* (robbery), Case No. —, June 15, 1885, U.S. Commissioner's Court, Western District of Arkansas, Muskogee, I.T.

United States v. *Sam Starr, Felix Griffin and Richard Hays,* Case No. 59, November 9, 1885, U.S. Commissioner's Court, Western District of Arkansas, Fort Smith.

United States v. *Samuel Starr* et al., Case No. 1213, U.S. District Court, Western District of Arkansas, Fort Smith.

United States v. *Thomas Starr,* Case No. —, February 27, 1885, U.S. Commissioner's Court, Western District of Arkansas, Fayetteville.

United States v. *Thomas Starr,* Case No. —, December 15, 1885, U.S. Commissioner's Court, Western District of Arkansas, Fayetteville.

United States v. *Thomas Starr,* Case No. 1670, U.S. District Court, Western District of Arkansas, Fort Smith.

United States v. *Tom Starr,* Case No. —, November 2, 1886, U.S. Commissioner's Court, Western District of Arkansas, Fayetteville.

United States v. *Edgar A. Watson,* Case No. —, February 22-23, 1889, U.S. Commissioner's Court, Western District of Arkansas, Fort Smith.

United States v. *William D. Wilder,* Case No. —, U.S. District Court, Western District of Arkansas, Fort Smith.

Ellis West to O. C. Davidson, June 18, 1937. *Indian-Pioneer History,* Foreman Collection, Vol. 49. Oklahoma Historical Society, Oklahoma City.

Thesis

Hobbs, Kenneth W., Jr. "Jim Reed, Southwestern Outlaw and Husband of Belle Starr: A Study of the Watt Grayson and San Antonio Stage Robberies." Master's thesis, Texas Christian University, Fort Worth, 1975.

Newspapers and Tabloids

Atoka Indian Champion, August, 1884.
Austin Daily Democratic Statesman, April, 1874.
Carthage (Mo.) *News,* January, 1953.
Carthage (Mo.) *Southwest News,* March 29, 1961.
Dallas Daily Commercial, February, April, June–August, 1874.

Dallas Daily Herald, April–May, 1874; October, 1874.

Dallas Morning News, June, 1886; February, 1889; March, 1890; January, 1894; April–May, 1933.

Dallas Weekly Herald, September, 1867; February, 1871.

Denison Daily News, May, 1874; August, 1874; October, 1874.

Fort Smith Daily Times, July, 1886.

Fort Smith New Era, November, 1873; October, 1874; June, September, 1875; February, 1883.

Fort Smith Weekly Elevator, January–May, September–December, 1886; March, August, 1888; February, April, July–August, 1889; January, 1890; April, 1891.

Fort Smith Weekly Herald, June, 1869; November, 1873.

Haskell (Okla.) *News,* June, 1926.

Joplin (Mo.) *News,* August, 1876.

Kansas City Star, August, 1910.

Liberty (Mo.) *Tribune,* February, 1866.

Little Rock Daily Arkansas Gazette, November, 1873; September, 1886.

Muskogee Daily Phoenix, January, 1898.

Muskogee Indian Journal, March, 1883; August, 1884; May, 1885; April–July, December, 1886; July, 1887.

National Police Gazette, Vols. 53–57, September 29, 1888–March 14, 1891. Richard K. Fox, Editor and Proprietor, Franklin Square Publishing, Printing and Engraving House, New York.

New York Times, February, 1889.

St. Louis Republic, August, 1910.

Tahlequah Cherokee Advocate, November, 1873; July, 1874.

The Tahlequah Telephone, March, 1889.

Van Buren (Ark.) *Press,* February, 1889.

Vinita Indian Chieftain, July, 1884; January–February, April, July, September–October, 1886; May, 1887; October, 1888; February, July, 1889; January, 1890; June, 1894; June, 1895; March, December, 1896.

Vinita Leader, October, 1895.

Waco Daily Examiner, April, 1874.

Books and Pamphlets

Aikman, Duncan. *Calamity Jane and the Lady Wildcats.* New York: Henry Holt and Company, 1927.

Allsopp, Fred W. *Folklore of Romantic Arkansas.* 2 vols. Grolier Society, 1931.

Anderson, Charles D., comp. and ed. *Outlaws of the West.* Los Angeles:

Mankind Publishing Company, 1973.

Appler, Augustus C. *The Guerrillas of the West; or, The Life, Character and Daring Exploits of the Younger Brothers.* St. Louis: John T. Appler, Publisher and Proprietor, 1875.

Baker, Elmer LeRoy. *Gunman's Territory.* San Antonio, Texas: Naylor Company, 1969.

Bartholomew, Ed. *The Biographical Album of Western Gunfighters.* Houston: Frontier Press of Texas, 1958.

————. *Some Western Gunfighters.* Toyahvale, Texas: Frontier Book Company, n.d.

Bearss, Ed, and Arrell M. Gibson. *Fort Smith: Little Gibraltar on the Arkansas.* Norman: University of Oklahoma Press, 1969.

Beebe, Lucius, and Charles Clegg. *The American West: The Pictorial Epic of A Continent.* New York: E. P. Dutton & Co., 1955.

Bella Starr, The Bandit Queen, or The Female Jesse James. A Full and Authentic History of the Dashing Female Highwayman, with Copious Extracts from Her Journal. Handsomely and Profusely Illustrated. New York: Richard K. Fox, Publishers, 1889.

Beverly, Bob. *Hobo of the Rangeland.* Lovington, N.M.: privately printed, *circa* 1941.

Booker, Anton S. *Wildcats in Petticoats: A Garland of Female Desperadoes — Lizzie Merton, Zoe Wilkins, Flora Quick Mundis, Bonnie Parker, Katie Bender and Belle Starr.* Girard, Kans.: Haldeman-Julius Publications, 1945.

Botkin, B. A., ed. *A Treasury of Western Folklore.* New York: Crown Publishers, 1951.

Breihan, Carl W. *The Complete and Authentic Life of Jesse James.* New York: Frederick Fell, 1953.

————. *The Escapades of Frank and Jesse James.* New York: Frederick Fell, 1974.

————. *Great Gunfighters of the West.* San Antonio, Texas: Naylor Company, 1962.

————. *Quantrill and his Civil War Guerrillas.* Denver: Sage Books, 1959.

————. *Younger Brothers.* San Antonio, Texas: Naylor Company, 1961.

————, and Charles A. Rosamond. *The Bandit Belle.* Seattle: Hangman Press, Superior Publishing Company, 1970.

Brown, Dee. *The Gentle Tamers: Women of the Old Wild West.* New York: G. P. Putnam's Sons, 1958.

Buel, J. W. *The Border Outlaws.* St. Louis: Sun Publishing Company, 1882.

Castel, Albert. *William Clarke Quantrill: His Life and Times.* New

York: Frederick Fell, 1962.

Chrisman, Harry E. *Fifty Years on the Owl Hoot Trail: Jim Herron, the First Sheriff of No Man's Land, Oklahoma Territory.* Chicago: Sage Books, 1969.

Clairmonte, Glenn. *Calamity Jane Was Her Name.* Denver: Sage Books, 1959.

Connelley, William Elsey. *Quantrill and the Border Wars.* Cedar Rapids, Iowa: Torch Press, 1910.

Crawford, Thomas Edgar. *The West of the Texas Kid, 1881–1910.* Norman: University of Oklahoma Press, 1962.

Croy, Homer. *He Hanged Them High: An authentic account of the fanatical judge who hanged eighty-eight men.* New York: Duell, Sloan and Pearce, 1952. Boston: Little, Brown and Company, 1952.

———. *Last of the Great Outlaws: The Story of Cole Younger.* New York: Duell, Sloan and Pearce, 1956.

Dacus, J. A. *Life and Adventures of Frank and Jesse James, the Noted Western Outlaws.* San Francisco, Indianapolis, and Chicago: N. D. Thompson and Company, 1880.

Dale, Edward Everett, and Gaston Litton. *Cherokee Cavaliers.* Norman: University of Oklahoma Press, 1941.

Dale, Henry. *Adventures and Exploits of the Younger Brothers, Missouri's Most Daring Outlaws, and Companions of the James Boys.* Secret Service Series No. 35. New York: Street & Smith, 1890.

Dalton, Captain Kit. *Under the Black Flag.* Memphis, Tenn.: Lockard Publishing Company, 1914.

Donald, Jay. *Outlaws of the Border.* Cincinnati: Forsee and McMakin, 1882.

Douglas, Marjory Stoneman. *The Everglades: River of Grass.* New York and Toronto: Rinehart and Company, 1947.

Drago, Harry Sinclair. *Notorious Ladies of the Frontier.* New York: Dodd, Mead & Company, 1969.

———. *Outlaws on Horseback: The History of the Organized Bands of Bank and Train Robbers Who Terrorized the Prairie Towns of Missouri, Kansas, Indian Territory, and Oklahoma for Half a Century.* New York: Dodd, Mead & Company, 1964.

———. *Red River Valley: The Mainstream of Frontier History From the Louisiana Bayous to the Texas Panhandle.* New York: Clarkson N. Potter, 1962.

———. *Road Agents and Train Robbers: Half a Century of Western Banditry.* New York: Dodd, Mead & Company, 1973.

Eaton, Frank. *Pistol Pete, Veteran of the Old West.* Boston: Little, Brown and Company, 1952.

Elman, Robert. *Badmen of the West.* New York: A Ridge Press/Pound

Book, 1974.

———. *Fired in Anger: The Personal Handguns of American Heroes and Villains.* Garden City, N.Y.: Doubleday & Company, 1968.

Emery, J. Gladstone. *Court of the Damned: Being a Factual Story of the Court of Judge Isaac C. Parker and the Life and Times of the Indian Territory and Old Fort Smith.* New York: Comet Press Books, 1959.

Farber, James. *Those Texans.* San Antonio, Texas: Naylor Company, 1945.

Foreman, Grant. *The Five Civilized Tribes.* Norman: University of Oklahoma Press, 1934.

Gabriel, Ralph Henry. *Elias Boudinot, Cherokee, and His America.* Norman: University of Oklahoma Press, 1941.

Gaddy, Jerry J., compiler. *Dust to Dust: Obituaries of the Gunfighters.* San Rafael, Calif.: Presidio Press, 1977. Fort Collins, Colo.: Old Army Press, 1977.

Gard, Wayne. *Frontier Justice.* Norman: University of Oklahoma Press, 1949.

Gardner, Raymond Hatfield (Arizona Bill). *The Old Wild West: Adventures of Arizona Bill.* San Antonio, Texas: Naylor Company, 1944.

Gideon, D.C. *Indian Territory, Descriptive, Biographical and Genealogical, Including the Landed Estates, County Seats etc., with a General History of the Territory.* New York and Chicago: Lewis Publishing Company, 1901.

Gish, Anthony. *American Bandits: A Biographical History of the Nation's Outlaws — From the Days of the James Boys, the Youngers, the Jennings, the Dalton Gang and Billy the Kid, Down to Modern Bandits of Our Own Day, Including Dillinger, "Pretty Boy" Floyd, and Others.* Girard, Kans.: Haldeman-Julius Publications, 1938.

Glasscock, C. B. *Then Came Oil: The Story of the Last Frontier.* Indianapolis and New York: Bobbs-Merrill Company, 1938.

Gordon, Mike. *I Arrested Pearl Starr and other stories of Adventure as a Policeman in Fort Smith, Arkansas for 40 years.* N.p., n.d.

The Gunfighters. New York: Time-Life Books, 1974.

Hagan, William T. *Indian Police and Judges: Experiments in Acculturation and Control.* New Haven and London: Yale University Press, 1966.

Hall, Frank O., and Lindsey H. Whitten. *Jesse James Rides Again.* Lawton, Okla.: LaHoma Publishing Company, 1948.

Hall, Ted Byron. *Oklahoma, Indian Territory.* Fort Worth, Texas: American Reference Publishers, 1971.

Harman, Samuel W. *Belle Starr, the Female Desperado.* Reprint of

Chapter XXXII from (Harman's) *Hell on the Border*. Houston: Frontier Press of Texas, 1954.

———. *Hell on the Border: He Hanged Eighty-Eight Men*. Fort Smith, Ark.: Phoenix Publishing Company, 1898.

Harrington, Fred Harvey. *Hanging Judge*. Caldwell, Idaho: Caxton Printers, 1951.

Harris, Phil. *This Is Three Forks Country*. Muskogee, Okla.: Hoffman Printing Company, 1965.

Harrison, Fred. *Hell Holes and Hangings*. Clarendon, Texas: Clarendon Press, 1968.

Henderson, Jeff S., ed. *100 Years in Montague County, Texas*. Saint Jo., Texas: Ipta Printers, *circa* 1958.

Hendricks, George David. *The Bad Man of the West*. San Antonio, Texas: Naylor Company, 1941.

Hicks, Edwin P. *Belle Starr and Her Pearl*. Little Rock, Ark.: Pioneer Press, 1963.

Holloway, Carroll C. *Texas Gun Lore*. San Antonio, Texas: 1951.

Horan, James D. *Desperate Women*. New York: G. P. Putnam's Sons, 1952.

———, and Paul Sann. *Pictorial History of the Wild West: A True Account of the Bad Men, Desperadoes, Rustlers and Outlaws of the Old West—and the Men Who Fought Them to Establish Law and Order*. New York: Crown Publishers, 1954.

House, Boyce. *Cowtown Columnist*. San Antonio, Texas: Naylor Company, 1946.

Howe, Charles Willis. *Timberleg of the Diamond Tail and Other Frontier Anecdotes*. San Antonio, Texas: Naylor Company, 1949.

Hunter, J. Marvin, and Noah H. Rose. *The Album of Gunfighters*. Bandera, Texas: privately printed, 1951.

Hutto, Nelson A. *The Dallas Story, From Buckskins to Top Hat*. Dallas: William S. Henson, 1953.

James, Jesse Lee, III. *Jesse James and the Lost Cause*. New York: Pageant Press, 1961.

Kane, Larry, comp. *100 Years Ago with the Law and the Outlaw*. N.p., n.d.

Kelley, Thomas P. *Jesse James*. Toronto, London, and New York: Export Publishing Enterprises, 1950.

Kingston, Charles. *Remarkable Rogues: The Careers of Some Notable Criminals of Europe and America*. London: John Lane, Bodley Head, 1921. New York: John Lane Company, 1921.

Larkin, Lew. *Missouri Heritage*. Columbia, Mo.: American Press, 1968.

Lavender, David. *The American Heritage History of the Great West*.

New York: American Heritage Publishing Co., 1965.

Lindquist, Allan Sigvard. *Jesse Sweeten, Texas Lawman.* San Antonio, Texas: Naylor Company, 1961.

Livingston, Joel T. *A History of Jasper County, Missouri, and Its People.* 2 vols. Chicago, New York, and San Francisco: Lewis Publishing Company, 1912.

Logue, Roscoe. *Tumbleweeds and Barb Wire Fences.* Amarillo, Texas: Russell Stationery Company, 1936.

Lombroso, Cesar, and Guglielmo Ferrero. *The Female Offender.* New York: D. Appleton and Company, 1903.

Love, Robertus. *The Rise and Fall of Jesse James.* New York and London: G. P. Putnam's Sons, 1926.

Lyon, Peter. *The Wild, Wild West.* New York: Funk and Wagnalls, 1969.

McGregor, Malcolm G. *The Biographical Record of Jasper County, Missouri.* Chicago: Lewis Historical Company, 1901.

McKennon, C. H. *Iron Men: A Saga of the Deputy United States Marshals Who Rode the Indian Territory.* Garden City, N.Y.: Doubleday & Company, 1967.

Maddox, Web. *Black Sheep.* Quanah, Texas: Nortex Press, 1975.

Mapes, Ruth B. *Old Fort Smith, Cultural Center on the Southwestern Frontier.* Little Rock, Ark.: Pioneer Press, 1965.

Masterson, V. V. *The Katy Railroad and the Last Frontier.* Norman: University of Oklahoma Press, 1952.

Miller, Ronald Dean. *Shady Ladies of the West.* Los Angeles: Westernlore Press, 1964.

Monaghan, Jay, ed. *The Book of the American West.* New York: Julian Messner, 1963.

Mooney, Colonel Charles W. *Doctor in Belle Starr Country.* Oklahoma City: Century Press, 1975.

Morrison, William Brown. *Military Posts and Camps in Oklahoma.* Oklahoma City: Harlow Publishing Corporation, 1936.

Munsell, Marion Ebenezer. *Flying Sparks, as told by a Pullman conductor.* Kansas City: Tiernan-Dart Printing Company, 1914.

Neville, A. W. *The Red River Valley, Then and Now: Stories of People and Events In the Red River Valley During the First Hundred Years of Its Settlement.* Paris, Texas: North Texas Publishing Company, 1948.

Newsom, J. A. *The Life and Practice of the Wild and Modern Indian: The Early Days of Oklahoma, Some Thrilling Experiences.* Oklahoma City: Harlow Publishing Company, 1923.

O'Beirne, H. F., and E. S. O'Beirne. *The Indian Territory: Its Chiefs,*

Legislators and Leading Men. St. Louis: C. B. Woodward Company, 1892.

Oklahoma, Past and Present: Brief Sketches of Men and Events in Oklahoma History—from Coronado to the Present. N.p.: Frontier Publishing Company, 1907.

The Only True History of the Life of Frank James, Written by Himself. Pine Bluff, Ark.: Norton Printing Company, 1926.

Parkhill, Forbes. *The Wildest of the West.* New York: Henry Holt and Company, 1951.

Peck, Henry L. *The Proud Heritage of LeFlore County.* Van Buren, Ark.: Press Argus, 1963.

Perry, George Sessions, ed. *Roundup Time: A Collection of Southwestern Writing.* New York and London: Whittlesey House, 1943.

Plenn, J. H. *Saddle in the Sky: The Lone Star State.* Indianapolis and New York: Bobbs-Merrill Company, 1940.

Randolph, Vance. *Who Blowed Up the Church House? and Other Ozark Folk Tales.* New York: Columbia University Press, 1952.

Rascoe, Burton. *Belle Starr, "The Bandit Queen."* New York: Random House, 1941.

Ray, Grace Ernestine. *Wily Women of the West.* San Antonio, Texas: Naylor Company, 1972.

Rayburn, Otto Ernest. *Ozark Country.* New York: Duell, Sloan and Pearce, 1941.

Rogers, Cameron. *Gallant Ladies.* New York: Harcourt, Brace and Company, 1928.

Rogers, John William. *The Lusty Texans of Dallas.* New York: E. P. Dutton and Company, 1951.

Sabin, Edwin L. *Wild Men of the Wild West.* New York: Thomas Y. Crowell Company, 1929.

Santerre, George H. *Dallas' First Hundred Years, 1856–1956.* Dallas: Book Craft, 1956.

Schrantz, Ward L. comp. *Jasper County, Missouri in the Civil War.* Carthage, Mo.: Carthage, Press, 1923.

Scott, Kenneth D. (as told by Jennette S. Scott). *Belle Starr in Velvet.* Tahlequah, Okla.: Pan Press, 1963.

Shackleford, William Yancey. *Belle Starr, The Bandit Queen: The Career of the Most Colorful Outlaw the Indian Territory Ever Knew.* Girard, Kans.: Haldeman-Julius Publications, 1943.

Shirley, Glenn. *Henry Starr, Last of the Real Badmen.* New York: David McKay Company, 1965.

———. *Law West of Fort Smith: A History of Frontier Justice in the Indian Territory, 1834–1896.* New York: Henry Holt and Company, 1957.

Shoemaker, Floyd C., ed. *Missouri, Day by Day.* 2 vols. Jefferson City, Mo.: State Historical Society of Missouri, 1941.

Sonnichsen, C. L. *Cowboys and Cattle Kings: Life on the Range Today.* Norman: University of Oklahoma Press, 1950.

Starkey, Marion L. *The Cherokee Nation.* New York: Alfred A. Knopf, 1946.

Starr, Helen, and O. E. Hill. *Footprints in the Indian Nation.* Muskogee, Okla.: Hoffman Printing Company, 1974.

The Story of Cole Younger, By Himself: Being an Autobiography of the Missouri Guerrilla Captain and Outlaw, his capture and prison life, and the only authentic account of the Northfield raid ever published. Chicago: Press of the Henneberry Company, 1903.

Sutton, Fred E. (as written down by A. B. MacDonald). *Hands Up! Stories of the Six-Gun Fighters of the Old Wild West.* Indianapolis: Bobbs-Merrill Company, 1927.

Tebeau, Charlton W., comp. *The Story of the Chokoloskee Bay Country.* Copeland Studies in Florida History. Miami, Fla.: University of Miami Press, 1955.

Thorp, N. Howard (Jack). *Pardner of the Wind: Story of the Southwestern Cowboy.* Caldwell, Idaho: Caxton Printers, 1945.

Tilghman, Zoe A. *Outlaw Days: A True History of Early-Day Oklahoma Characters.* Oklahoma City: Harlow Publishing Company, 1926.

Triplett, Frank. *The Life, Times and Treacherous Death of Jesse James.* Chicago, St. Louis, and Atlanta: J. H. Chambers and Company, 1882.

Varigny, Charles Victor Crosnier de. *La Femme aux Etats-Unis.* Paris: Armand Colin & Cie, Editeurs, 1893 (reprinted as *The Women of the United States;* New York: Dodd, Mead, 1895).

Walker, Henry J. *Jesse James, the Outlaw.* Des Moines, Iowa: Wallace-Homestead Company, 1961.

Wardell, Morris L. *A Political History of the Cherokee Nation, 1838–1907.* Norman: University of Oklahoma Press, 1938.

Webb, Walter Prescott, and H. Bailey Carroll, eds. *The Handbook of Texas.* 2 vols. Austin: Texas State Historical Association, 1952.

Wellman, Paul I. *A Dynasty of Western Outlaws.* Garden City, N.Y.: Doubleday & Company, 1961.

White, Owen P. *Lead and Likker.* New York: Minton, Balch and Company, 1932.

Williams, Brad, and Choral Pepper. *The Mysterious West.* Cleveland and New York: World Publishing Company, 1967.

Woodward, Grace Steele. *The Cherokees.* Norman: University of Oklahoma Press, 1963.

Wooldridge, Clyde E. *Wilburton: I. T. and OK, 1890–1970.* Wilburton, Okla.: privately printed, 1976.

Younger, Scout (Bison Bill). *True Facts of the Lives of America's Most Notorious Outlaws.* N.p., n.d.

Articles

Adrean, Tony. "The Life of Belle Starr, From Civil War Spy to Bandit Queen and Death." *Muskogee Times-Democrat,* April 21, 1921.

Anderson, La-Vere Shoenfelt. "A Hill Perpetuates Belle Starr's Memory." *Tulsa World,* August 20, 1933.

———. "Site of Belle Starr's Lookout Tower on Bald Hill Still Mecca for Tourists." *Tulsa World,* February 3, 1936.

Barde, Frederick S. "How Belle Starr Died." *Kansas City Star,* August 14, 1910.

———. "Says Belle Starr's Ghost Still Rides." *St. Louis Republic,* August 21, 1910.

———. "The Story of Belle Starr." *Sturm's Oklahoma Magazine,* Vol. 11, No. 1, September, 1910.

Benedict, Mrs. J. D. "Belle Starr, The Bandit Queen." *Twin Territories,* Vol. 2, No. 9, October, 1900.

Biscup, Walter. "Dashing Belle Starr Was Called 'Lily of the Cimarron.'" 2 parts. *The American Indian,* Vol. 1, No. 4, January, 1927, and Vol. 1, No. 5, February, 1927.

Blanton, Kelsey. "The Killer of Belle Starr." *All-Florida Magazine, Pensacola News-Journal,* July 17, 1960.

Boder, Bartlett. "Belle Starr—and Her Times." *Museum Graphic,* Vol. V, No. 2, Spring, 1953.

Boswell, Charles. "Belle of the Six Gun." *True Western Adventures,* Vol. 4, No. 21, August, 1961.

Breihan, Carl W. "Bad Bella Starr." *Western Action,* Vol. 22, No. 5, March, 1959.

———. "Belle Starr—Oklahoma Whirlwind." *The West,* Vol. 6, No. 4, March, 1967.

Breshears, Claudia. "The Outlaw Was A Lady." *Big West,* Vol. 1, No. 1, August, 1967.

Brown, Florence V. "The Legend of Belle Starr, Courtesan." *Great West,* Vol. 1, No. 10, April, 1967.

Bulloch, Nolen. "Tourists Take Robbers' Trail." *Tulsa Tribune,* June 26, 1951.

Burkholder, Edwin V. "Belle Starr—Petticoat Desperado." *Argosy,* Vol. 343, No. 2, August, 1956.

Chrisman, J. Eugene. "America's Most Incredible Nymph." *Glance,* Vol. 3, No. 6, August, 1960.

Claunch, Zula. "Memories of Belle Starr." *Looking Back,* Vol. 3, No. 3, Fall, 1975.

Crow, Pat. "Vacationers Follow Outlaws' Footsteps." *Tulsa World,* May 25, 1969.

Denton, Cyclone (as told to Ramon F. Adams). "I Danced With Belle Starr." *True West,* Vol. 17, No. 6, July–August, 1970.

"Flossie." "The Story of My Grandmother, Belle Star" (Part I). *Dallas Morning News,* April 30, 1933.

———. "The Story of Flossie, Belle Starr's Granddaughter" (Part II). *Dallas Morning News,* May 7, 1933.

Flynn, Claire. "The Children of Belle Starr." *True Frontier,* No. 43, August, 1975.

Foreman, Carolyn Thomas. "The Balentines, Father and Son, in the Indian Territory." *Chronicles of Oklahoma,* Vol. 34, No. 4, Winter, 1956–57.

Gilstrap, Harry. "The Gem That Sparkles Yet." *Southwest Heritage,* Vol. 1, No. 4, Fall, 1967.

Hardcastle, Stoney. "Belle Starr's Piano." *True West,* Vol. 24, No. 5, May–June, 1977.

"Hellcats in Skirts." *Great West,* Vol. 3, No. 4, September, 1969.

"He Preached Sermon For Belle Starr." *Daily Oklahoman,* April 23, 1939.

Hicks, Edwin P. "Who Killed Belle Starr?" *Exposé for Men,* Vol. 3, No. 1, June, 1959.

Holding, Vera. "Belle Starr: Queen Bandit." *True Frontier,* Vol. 1, No. 12, November, 1969.

Kelly, Bill. "Pearl Younger and the Falling Starrs." *Real West,* No. 148, Vol. 19, November, 1976.

Lester, D. C. "Belle Starr, Oklahoma's Woman Outlaw: She Died as She Had Lived 'With Her Boots On.'" *Daily Oklahoman,* August 21, 1921.

Mason, John. "Belle Starr, Sister of Sin." *Real West,* Vol. 2, No. 6, February, 1959.

Mooney, Charles W. "Belle Starr As Her Doctor Knew Her." *True Frontier,* No. 32, April, 1973.

———. "Belle Starr's Killer Revealed." *True West,* Vol. 16, No. 3, January–February, 1969.

———. "The Secret Belle Starr Took to Her Grave." *The West,* Vol. 11, No. 6, November, 1969.

Mote, Wayne D. "The Wildest Woman of the West." *Man's Exploits,* Vol. 1, No. 4, January, 1958.

Mumey, Nolie. "Belle of the Ozarks." *Frontier Times*, Vol. 29, No. 8, May, 1952.

Oskison, John M. "To 'Youngers' Bend.'" *Frank Leslie's Popular Monthly*, Vol. 16, No. 2, June, 1903.

Paddock, Mary. "Queen of the Outlaws Lived, Loved and Died Beyond the Law." *Daily Oklahoman*, August 23, 1959.

Park, Robert A. "Colorful Belle Starr: Immortal Hoyden's Life Full of Twists, Turns." *Muskogee Daily Phoenix*, November 17, 1940.

Qualey, J. S. "The Legend of Belle Starr." *Famous Outlaws of the West*, Americana Library Book No. 2, Fall, 1964.

"Recipes Used By Belle Starr Still Popular." *Daily Oklahoman*, June 5, 1938.

Reed, Richard J. "Steal Away to Robbers Cave." *Oklahoma's Orbit*, May 15, 1966.

"Reminiscences of Mr. R. P. Vann, East of Webbers Falls, Oklahoma, September 28, 1932" (as told to Grant Foreman). *Chronicles of Oklahoma*, Vol. 11, No. 11, June, 1933.

Repp, Ed Earl. "Belle Starr Saved My Life." *Real West*, Vol. 13, No. 79, February, 1970.

———. "Gun-Toting Female Killer." *Pioneer West*, Vol. 5, No. 2, April, 1971.

Riotte, Louise. "Outlaw Candy." *Grain Producers News*, Vol. 28, No. 6, June, 1977.

Robinson, Ruth. "Belle Starr Dramatized." *Oklahoma News*, April 25, 1937.

Semple, William F. "Isaac C. Parker, Judge of the United States Court." *The Journal* (Oklahoma Bar Association), Vol. 22, No. 30, August 25, 1951.

Shirley, Glenn. "Outlaw Queen." *Old West*, Vol. 1, No. 3, Spring, 1965.

Stansbery, Lon R. "Early Oklahoma Outlaws Contributed by Many States." *Tulsa World*, February 7, 1937.

Sutton, Fred E. "Belle Starr, Queen of Outlaws." *The 101 Magazine*, Vol. 2, No. 4, June, 1926.

Synar, Joe, and Richard Venator. "Lonely Memorial in Hills Marks Grave of Woman Outlaw, Belle Starr." *Muskogee Daily Phoenix*, January 5, 1936.

Towns, Leroy. "Was Belle Starr Killed By Mistake?" *True West*, Vol. 18, No. 4, March–April, 1971.

"Weapons of Belle Starr, Famous Woman Outlaw, Part of K. C. Man's Relic Collection." *Kansas City Journal-Post*, June 13, 1926.

"Weather-Beaten Hut Still Stands, Amid Chat Piles, Monument to Outlaw Days." *Daily Oklahoman*, August 11, 1918.

Wilson, L. W. "A History of Wagoner, Oklahoma, From S. S. Cobb." *Chronicles of Oklahoma*, Vol. 50, No. 4 (Winter, 1972).

Poetry

"A Two-Gun Woman." Date and origin unknown.
"Belle Starr." In *Fandango* by Stanley Vestal. Houghton Mifflin Company, Boston and New York, 1927.
"Belle Starr, Queen of the Desperadoes." Date and origin unknown.
"Belle Starr Rides Again." In *A Collection of Cash Stevens' Poems, Including Beel Meezon*. *Shawnee American*, Shawnee, Okla., 1948.
"Immortalized in Rhyme." In *Bella Starr, The Bandit Queen, or The Female Jesse James*. Richard K. Fox, Publishers, New York, 1889.
"The Last Ride of the Bandit Queen." Written by George Riley Hall for the *Muskogee Daily Phoenix*, January 13, 1898.

Plays

Cheat and Swing: A legend based on the life of Belle Starr. Written and directed by John Woodworth. University Playhouse, Holmberg Hall, University of Oklahoma, Norman, April 22–23, 1938. Restaged by Town and Gown, Theatre in the Round, Stillwater, Oklahoma, November 9–11, 1953.
Missouri Legend. With Elizabeth Ginty as Aunt Belle. Broadway Theatre, New York City, 1939–40.

Motion Pictures

Badman's Territory (Isabel Jewell as Belle Starr with Lawrence Tierney as Jesse James and Tom Tyler as Frank James). RKO Radio Pictures, 1946.
Belle Starr. (Gene Tierney as Belle and Randolph Scott as Sam Starr). 20th Century–Fox Film Corporation, 1941.
Belle Starr. (Elizabeth Montgomery as Belle Starr, co-starring Cliff Potts as Cole Younger and Michael Cavanaugh as Jesse James). CBS-TV premiere, 1980.
Belle Starr's Daughter. (Ruth Roman with George Montgomery and Rod Cameron). 20th Century–Fox Film Corporation, 1948.
Court-Martial. (Betty Compson as Belle Starr, co-starring Jack Holt). Columbia Pictures, 1928.
The Long Riders. (Pamela Reed as Belle Starr, co-starring James Keach as Jesse James, Stacy Keach as Frank James, and David Carradine as Cole Younger). United Artists, 1980.

Montana Belle. (Jane Russell as Belle Starr, co-starring George Brent). RKO Radio Pictures, 1952.

Son of Belle Starr. (Keith Larsen with Dona Drake and Peggy Castle). Allied Artists, 1953.

Novels

Appell, George C. *Belle's Castle.* New York: Macmillan Company, 1959.

Hardcastle, Stoney. *The Legend of Belle Starr.* New York: Carlyle Books, 1979.

Morgan, Speer. *Belle Starr.* Boston and Toronto: Little, Brown and Company, 1979.

Shirley, Glenn. *Outlaw Queen.* Derby, Conn.: Monarch Books, 1960.

Index